" The history of a man's own life is, to himself, the most interesting history in the world. Every man is an original and solitary character. None can either understand or feel the book of his own life like himself. The lives of other men are to him dry and vapid when set beside his own."
—Cecil's Remains.

" In old age alone we are masters of a treasure of which we cannot be deprived, the only treasure we can call our own. The pleasures of memory, and the retrospect of the varied images which in an active life have floated before the mind, compensate, and more than compensate, for the alternate pleasures and cares of active life."
—Sir Archibald Alison.

PREFACE

THE following pages—the autobiography of a man whose books have been sold by hundreds of thousands in his own country, and translated into every language of Europe, and into most of those of Asia and America—require no apology other than that which the author himself has seen fit to set down in the opening paragraphs of his work. The life, as conceived and chronicled by himself, of an author whose thoughts have arrested and held the attention of more than a generation of readers, cannot fail to be of interest, even when, as in the present case, there is nothing eventful, apart from the writing of his books, to be recorded.

Dr Smiles' first book was published in 1836, and he continued to write till nearly the close of the century. The period of his literary labours, therefore, is almost exactly coincident with the reign of the late Queen Victoria, the age pre-eminently of mechanical invention. Dr Smiles' achievement is that by common consent he is recognised as the authorised and pious chronicler of the men who founded the industrial greatness of England.

His works, therefore, have a historical value peculiarly their own. They are a storehouse of facts, gathered not so much from books as from intercourse with the living actors in the events which he

chronicles, and from inquiry made on the scene of
their labours. He has thus rescued from oblivion
many incidents in the lives of the great Engineers
which would have been irretrievably lost, but for his
pious and enthusiastic care.

Nor is the monument which he has raised to their
memory a mere collection of dry-as-dust facts.
Leaving the technical details to the text-books, and
to the records of scientific societies, he has introduced
his heroes to a wider public, and made them live again
in his pages. His was a new departure in biography.
He saw that the everyday work of applied science had
its romance. He grasped the fact that the million
had become readers, and required to be amused as
well as instructed. This, from the literary point of
view, is his great merit, and entitles him to be enrolled
in the honourable company of story-tellers. Apart
from the historical value of his biographies, they are
told in a manner so vivacious and dramatic that they
have proved themselves irresistibly attractive to young
and old in all countries of the world. Both in regard
to the interest of the theme commemorated, and the
literary skill with which it is presented, the *Life of
George Stephenson* has made good its right to rank as
an English classic. In that volume and in the *Lives
of the Engineers*, the didactic element is less pro-
nounced than in other of his works, and, for this
reason perhaps, they will be for some readers more
completely enjoyable.

At the same time the great popularity of the more
professedly didactic books, such as *Self-Help*, *Thrift*,
Duty, is in itself a noteworthy and characteristic
episode in the second half of the nineteenth century.
In more than one passage in the following pages,
and also in the preface prefixed to the later editions of

Self-Help, Dr Smiles has noticed the remarks of those who charge him with an excessive adulation of mere success. Such criticism seems to recoil on those who level it at Dr Smiles. The whole point of his philosophy is that good work can be done, character and independence built up, and happiness preserved, amid humble surroundings, and notwithstanding the absence of worldly success. A materialistic view of life must rather be imputed to those who are contemptuous of the merely spiritual triumphs ascribed by him to the virtues of patience and thrift, because they have based their hopes of progress on organic changes with which Dr Smiles rightly or wrongly has shown no sort of sympathy. His apology is perhaps unnecessary, but the reader's attention is directed to a passage in this autobiography which seems, by anticipation, to vindicate even more amply than the later apology of the preface to *Self-Help*, the high-minded liberality of his attitude. On page 131 of this volume the autobiographer has incorporated a long quotation from *The Education of the Working Classes*, the lecture delivered in 1845, which grew in time by expansion and addition into his volume on *Self-Help*. The passage quoted contains a plain and dignified statement of the advantages of education to the poorer class. The man who entered on his exposition of the Arts of Thriving in this admirable spirit must be acquitted by every impartial critic of harbouring an unworthy and sordid reverence for mere worldly success. If any further vindication were necessary, it is to be found in his own use of his talent for biography. He might, as he tells us, have been biographer in general, and have set up a factory of biography on a large scale. This prospect, lucrative as it must have been, he deliberately declined, and preferred to follow his own bent. His work displays everywhere the excessive and genuine pleasure which he took in rescuing forgotten worthies from oblivion, and in recording the obscure labours of humble enthusiasts who had found happiness and independence in the pursuit of some by-path of knowledge.

Though a Scotsman by birth, Dr Smiles took apparently little interest in metaphysics. He is interested in the man, his friend Samuel Brown (Alchemist Brown as he was called by his contemporaries), but very little in his speculations; and the same intensely practical turn of mind controls his whole outlook into life. Accordingly, we find nowhere any deliberate appreciation of modern socialism and its teaching. Robert Owen and his "spinning jenny of a universe" (see p. 106) seem too far removed from practical life to merit more than a passing notice. He conceived from the first that the fundamental bases of society were permanent, and his happy optimism was content with the situation. In the quotation which he cites from his early lecture, and to which reference has already been made, he says, "My object in citing these instances," and we may here interpolate that this remained to the end the key-note of all his work, "has been merely to show that adverse circumstances —even the barrenest poverty—cannot repress the human intellect and character, if it be determined to rise; that man can triumph over circumstances, and subject them to his will; that knowledge is no exclusive heritage of the rich and the leisured classes, but may be attained by all; or at all events, that no difficulties of situation, however great, can furnish any reason for despair" (p. 132).

Dr Smiles was, of course, an ardent opponent of privilege, and therefore of protective duties on corn, but he had obviously no sympathy with the modern attempt to create privilege for the classes to whom Democracy has now given power. When Free Trade had been won, a national system of education established, and when the franchise had been settled on a liberal basis, his interest in politics seems to have ceased. A career, if not of worldly success, at least of self-respect and independence, was now open to honest industry, and the policy of laying burdens on one class for the benefit of another class seemed to him unnecessary, even if he did not regard it as unjust.

Though Dr Smiles has, for these reasons, ignored the socialists, they have not ignored him. His cheerful optimism, and the spirited attempts he makes to justify it, are things abhorrent to them. To them he is typical of the plain man, the bourgeois who assumes that the constitution of society cannot be materially altered. He encourages us to make the best of it, and shows that the best of it is not so very bad, and his genial and kindly exposition of the success that attends the practice of the ordinary arts of thriving is very distasteful to those who believe in the necessity of revolutionary and organic change. This is not the place to argue out the issue, but no appreciation of Dr Smiles and his work would be complete without a reference to the fact that he is very properly regarded as a representative of that sound middle class common sense which has created for the English of all classes a very solid fabric of comfort and contentment. The socialist recognises that it is this measure of material prosperity, and the common sense that has created it, and still continues to defend it as tolerable, which bar the way to any practical acceptance of his doctrine. Hence the bitter and scornful reference to the

"Gospel according to Smiles," which is so familiar a commonplace in the socialist's invective against the existing order of things.

This divergence of view reaches its limit theoretically, when a leading socialist solemnly appears before a Royal Commission, and records his opinion that thrift is a crime, and that to encourage poor men to practise it is merely to incite them to new privations. Happily, even those members of the poorer class who might describe themselves as socialists, unconsciously incline in practice to the view of Dr Smiles rather than to that of their own teacher. The man who thinks at all of his own future and of social conditions generally, will be found, through his Friendly Society, his Co-operative Store, or his Savings Bank, to be paying some homage to those arts of thriving of which Dr Smiles will always be regarded as a foremost panegyrist. It is this involuntary adherence to a line of conduct which identifies them and their interests with the established economic order which makes any thorough application of socialist ideas an improbable and remote contingency. It is this impenetrable common sense—stupidity perhaps the socialist will call it—that has barred and probably will bar the way to attempts at revolutionary change, such as the socialist desires.

So much it seems necessary to set down, in order to show the representative character of Dr Smiles' work. For the rest, we doubt if any but the most austere exponents of new ideals will be able to resist the cheerful optimism of Dr Smiles' narrative.

It is a satisfaction to learn from these pages, that as he wrote for others, so he found it for himself. His life was one of great contentment and of continuous industry, and in his case at all events, wisdom was justified in her children. The following narrative, written at different times, the later portion in extreme old age, and with failing powers, has, with some omissions, been printed as the author left it. A few verbal and grammatical corrections, such as an author would naturally have made for himself, have been introduced, but the sense has nowhere been altered.

The autobiography is a popular author's last message to readers, who have been pleased and encouraged by his work. It will be a satisfaction to those who have praised his books, to learn how appreciative he was of their sympathy. The simplicity of his character, and his enjoyment of the world's good-will, as revealed in these pages, will, it is hoped, increase their grateful remembrance of an instructor at once so kindly and so entertaining.

T. M.

CONTENTS

THE AUTOBIOGRAPHY OF
SAMUEL SMILES

CHAPTER I

BOYHOOD AND EDUCATION

I HAVE begun and finished many books, but I never began a manuscript with more trepidation than I now do the following narrative. I would not have dreamt of writing out these memoirs but for the repeated counsels of William Rolston Haigh of Huddersfield, an old friend, whom I had known intimately at Leeds, at Bradford, and at Huddersfield, of which town he was a magistrate, and where I frequently enjoyed his hospitality.

Mr Haigh was a very intelligent man, and a great reader, especially of biography. Many years since, he asked me, "Have you written out your Autobiography yet?"

"Oh, no!" I answered, "there is no probability of that ever being done. I am too busy, besides, with other things that I wish to finish. I have been interviewed, it is true, like most other book writers, artists, and men of notoriety. But my life has been comparatively uneventful; there is really nothing in it."

1

"Nothing in it?" responded my Mentor. "Why, your books are extensively read in this country and America. They have been translated into nearly every language in Europe. They appear in many of the Indian languages, and even in Siamese and Japanese. I am quite sure that your readers would like to know much more about yourself than has yet been published by your interviewers."

"That may be," I said, "but I do not think there are any passages in my life likely to be interesting to the public. My books, such as they are, must speak for themselves, without any biographic introduction."

"Well!" he observed finally, "think of my advice: I am persuaded that a history of yourself would be more interesting than any of your books."

This conversation occurred in 1879. I doubted my friend's counsel; but he returned to the subject again and again. He even took the trouble to tell me how I should write my Autobiography. He gave me the heads of it, extending to four pages. He copied out for me John Bartram's advice to his friend Benjamin Franklin as to the preparation of his biography.

On Anthony Trollope's autobiography making its appearance, Mr Haigh wrote to my wife, "Tell your husband to go and do likewise." My answer was, Benjamin Franklin was a celebrated philosopher, and Anthony Trollope was a distinguished novelist. Thousands will read about them, while few will read about me. They had a history, while I have none—at least, none of any consequence. Nevertheless, I will proceed at my leisure to write out some passages relating to my past life, and leave them for the entertainment of my children and grandchildren, or,

should my sons desire, for the perusal of the general
public.

I was born at Haddington on the 23rd of
December 1812. The house in which I first saw the
light, stood at the head of the High Street, and commanded a view of the Mail Coach, the Union, the
Stage Coaches, and the Friday Market.*

About the beginning of the century, when
Napoleon was at the height of his power, the town
formed the centre of a camp. Some hundred and thirty
thousand of the best troops of France were assembled
at Boulogne—with artillery, horses, and transports—
flat-bottomed boats—and threatened the invasion of
England. It proved to be but a feint, but this
country was prepared. Some thought that the Bay
of Aberlady might be the point of landing for the
foreign troops, and barracks were erected all round
Haddington, for the accommodation of infantry,
cavalry, and artillery. Other barracks were erected
at Belhaven, near Dunbar. Beacons were erected
along the coast, to give timely notice of the approach
and landing of the French. Regiments of militia
were marched into the barracks in constant succession ; for the purpose of enabling the regular troops to
keep up their forces by enlistment.

Napoleon, however, broke up "the army of
England," as it was called, and proceeded to invade
Austria, Prussia, and Russia. The continental war
went on for several years. Wellington was now in
the Peninsula with his victorious army ; and at the
time when I was born, at the end of 1812, Napoleon

* The house has since been pulled down and replaced by a Banking Office.

was returning to France with the wreck of his army, baffled by the snows of Russia. Still the militia continued to occupy the barracks around our little town, while the regulars drummed them up constantly for recruits.

Then came the battle of Leipzig, the retreat of Napoleon upon France, the siege and surrender of Paris, the abdication of the Emperor, his banishment to Elba and his return to France in less than a year, his assemblage of the army, and their march northward. Then followed Waterloo. It seems to me like a dream to remember the rejoicings on that occasion — the bands of the militia, the drums and pipes that paraded the town, and the illuminations that followed. Such things make a deep impression on the imagination of a child—"Wax to receive, but marble to retain." Next year, the 42nd Highlanders —the Black Watch—marched through the town. That circumstance stands very clear in my memory. They were received with extraordinary acclamations in every town they passed through; and when they entered Edinburgh the enthusiasm was indescribable.

The talk by our firesides long continued to be about wars, with remembrances of recent campaigns. The barracks round our town were eventually pulled down, and the materials disposed of. My father* bought a large quantity of army stores, principally blankets and greatcoats. I remember seeing the last of the soldiers' greatcoats sold to a ploughman and carried away upon his back.

All articles of food were very dear in those days. Everything was taxed to the utmost extent. Bread

---

* Dr Smiles' father was also Samuel Smiles. He was engaged in trade, first as a paper maker, when paper was made by hand, afterwards as a general merchant in Haddington.—ED.

was sixteen pence the quartern loaf; sugar, ninepence or tenpence; tea, from seven to nine shillings, but oatmeal for porridge, the "staff of life" in Scotland, was moderate; though, compared with present prices, it was dear.

One of the things that struck me very much in my early years, was the illness of my elder brother John. He had an attack of inflammation of the lungs, and Dr John Welsh, who lived close at hand, was called in to visit him. The doctor bled him, and I remember seeing three full cups of blood taken from his arm, lying on the table, waiting for the doctor's next visit. Though the boy was only seven years old, the bleeding at once cured him. Doctors were not afraid to bleed in those days. A few days after, when the boy was downstairs, Dr Welsh called again to see his patient. He put his finger through an unbuttoned hole in the boy's vest, and tickled him. The boy laughed. "Oh!" said the doctor, "his lungs are all right; he will soon be out-of-doors."

Dr Welsh was a most agreeable and cheerful man. Everybody loved him. He had a comely, handsome face, with lively and expressive features. He was the principal practitioner in the town and neighbourhood. Shortly after the above circumstance, Dr Welsh, who had to encounter all sorts of risks, caught typhoid fever from a patient he was attending, and died after a short illness. He was greatly lamented throughout the country.

I remember his widow, Mrs Welsh, who continued for some time to live in the town, and her daughter Jeanie, afterwards Mrs Carlyle. Mrs Welsh was a beautiful woman: tall, dark-haired, and commanding. Jeanie was less lovely; her face was too angular for beauty. Nevertheless, she had many admirers. She might have married well in her native town; but she disliked the place and wished to get away from it. In 1821, two years after her father's death, she wrote, "It is the dimmest, deadest spot in the Creator's universe . . . the very air one breathes is impregnated with stupidity." *

After all, Haddington was not so bad as Miss Welsh painted it. It very much depends upon ourselves whether we are miserable or not in any condition of life. Perhaps Miss Welsh was not of a very contented frame of mind, and her letters seem to show this. She was not pleased with her local surroundings, and was waiting for her Genius.

Mrs Welsh and her daughter, after Dr Welsh's death, occupied the upper flat of Mr Roughead's large mansion, nearly opposite the house in the High Street which my father had bought, and to which we had removed from the house where I was born. I often saw Mrs Welsh and her daughter walking about; but as I was some eleven years younger than Jeanie, and was then but a boy, I had no personal communications with her. It was said that she was fond of Edward Irving, who had been an assistant master in the Burgh School; but he had gone to Kirkcaldy, and become pledged to a minister's daughter there. So Miss Welsh had to wait. But at last the Genius came in the shape of Thomas Carlyle. More than enough has been written about this union, so that it need not be further referred to. Excepting this—that after Mrs Carlyle had removed from Craigenputtock to London, she called upon my mother when she came down to her native place, and gave her to understand that she was quite as

---

* Early letters of Jane Welsh Carlyle. Edited by David G. Ritchie, M.A.

miserable with her Genius as she had ever been at Haddington. There was a reason for this, that cannot be described in this place.

A good education is equivalent to a good fortune. My parents were both of opinion that, though they had comparatively little money to leave to the several members of their large family, the training of their minds in early life was the best possible equipment for their encounter with the struggles and difficulties which they would have to meet in future years. John Knox was a native of the town in which I was born. He was to Scotland what Martin Luther was to Germany. "Let the common people be taught," was one of John Knox's messages. His advice was followed, and the results were great. A poor and sterile country was made strong by its men. The parish and burgh schools of Scotland, and the education given there, are but the lengthened shadow of John Knox. There was a good grammar school in Haddington even in the Reformer's boyhood. He was taught there by the monks, until he went for further training and education to the University of St Andrews.

My first teacher was Patrick Hardie. He had a private school in St Ann's Place, and there I learnt my A B C. In a few years, Mr Hardie was appointed by the Town Council teacher of English and Mathematics at the Burgh School; and I followed him to his new quarters.

Hardie was a good teacher. He taught reading, writing, and arithmetic, very well. He cultivated in his pupils the gift of memory. He made us learn by heart, and recite, poetry and speeches by memorable orators. I remember that I had to learn, with another schoolfellow (Nesbet), an act from

Home's tragedy of Douglas, and a long passage from Campbell's Poems, entitled "The Wizard's Warning," and recite, or rather act the passages with as much eloquence and action as we could muster. All this was very useful; and these passages, learnt at school, remained in our minds for many years.

These are the good points of Hardie's character as a teacher. But he had other points, which were quite the reverse. He was a tyrant and a toady. He had favourites, who were mostly the sons of provosts, bailies, or town councillors, to whom he owed his position; or they were the sons of well-to-do men, who could give him dinners and drink. I was the son of none of these distinguished personages, and not a favourite. My father was an Anti-Burgher—a sort of Quaker Presbyterian, who would not take the Burgess Oath—and therefore not likely to be either a town councillor or a bailie.* Hardie hated Dissenters—he had been one himself—but especially Anti-Burghers.

I was only an average boy, distinguished for nothing but my love of play. I looked forward with delight to my Wednesday and Saturday afternoons, when we had shinty, or football on the sands, or went stravaiging about the country in search of birds' nests, sloes, or haws. I fear I was fonder of frolic than of learning, though I made my way with the rest. I could not have been very bright, for one day,

---

* In the North, provosts and bailies are persons of great importance. They occupied, at that time, what was called "the breest of the laft" at the Parish Church. A man at Peebles had been elected a bailie; he was proceeding along a bye-street, when he encountered a woman driving a cow. "Get out o' the way, man," said the driver. "Woman," said the obstructor, "*I'm no a man; I'M A BAILIE!*"

when Hardie was in one of his tyrannical humours, he uttered this terrible prophecy in a loud voice: "Smiles! you will never be fit for anything but sweeping the streets of your native borough." A nice encouragement for a little scholar!

Schoolboys often imitate the tyranny of their masters. They pick up the brutal words which he has so vehemently uttered, perhaps in a moment of passion; and my schoolfellows nicknamed me after the man who then swept the streets of my "native borough." I shortly after left the school, and had forgotten all about the nickname, when it was recalled to my recollection by Charles Sheriff, son of a farmer at Mungo's Wells. He detested Hardie much more than I did, and said that he had never learnt anything from that teacher. This, however, was a mistake, for, notwithstanding his tyranny and cruelty, in his calmer moments he was an excellent teacher.

Hardie occasionally used the most fearful language in dealing with his pupils. I have heard him say: "I will flog you, sir, within an inch of your life"; "I will dash your brains against the wall"; "I will split your skull into a thousand pieces!" Poor little terrified pupils! I have seen Hardie flog a boy so hard and so long, that he had to hold his sides, and sit down exhausted. Eventually he had to give this up, because of his health!

His favourites, to whom he was always mild and sleek, used to burn the taws (the instrument of torture) at the end, in order to make them black and hard, knowing that the cut thong of leather would never be used to raise wales upon *their* backs.

Hardie did a little surreptitious teaching. He could not very well teach Latin and Greek during

the ordinary school hours, because there was a
classical school, also supported by the borough
magistrates, near at hand; but he could, and he
did, teach Latin after his usual day scholars had
been dismissed. I remained, with some other boys,
to learn Latin. Before we began, Hardie went
upstairs for refreshment, and when he returned to
his Latin pupils, he was frequently very much
excited. On one occasion he was hearing the lesson
of one James Thomson—son of another Anti-Burgher.
The lad was not very bright, and rather dour. Jamie
answered a question wrongly and stupidly; on which
the master became enraged, and violently threw a
book full in the boy's face. One of the boards of the
book hit him on the upper lip and cut it open. His
face was soon covered with blood, and the class was
dismissed. The late President Garfield used to say
of such places: "It is to me a perpetual wonder that
any child's love of knowledge survives the outrages of
the schoolhouse."

A story was told among us at school, which may
be mentioned here. At Haddington, the sons of
provosts and bailies were the favourites, while at the
Edinburgh High School the sons of lords and squires
were toadied by the masters. On one occasion, a
boy was asked by the teacher, "Now, blockhead, can
you construe this: '*Nisi Dominus frustra*'?" the
motto of the city.

"Yes, sir!" answered the boy, with spirit —
"Unless ye be a lord, or a laird's son, ye needna be
here."

Learning is not advanced by harshness and
tyranny on the part of the masters. These are
enough to drive a boy into stupidity and make him
reckless. I have always detested the cowardly

cruelty of exceptional schoolmasters, who, because
they are stronger, use their power in tormenting the
helpless children committed to their charge.

I cannot tell how thankful I was to be taken away
from Hardie's School, and sent to the Classical
School in the adjoining building. Rector Graham
was as much a gentleman as the other was a tyrant.
The two men were very different, in appearance and
character. Hardie was bilious, pale-faced, with hair
of a yellowish-red; his eyes were black, and sparkling
when angry. Graham, on the other hand, was round
and jovial, though a little pompous, full of fun, fond of
quoting Latin, and with a smile for every boy,
whether he was the son of a bailie or not. The taws
were Hardie's instrument of torture; whilst, though
Graham had taws, he never used them. The school
was governed by moral suasion, and yet it was kept
in perfect order. I think every boy in the school
loved old Graham.

The class of boys was no doubt of a better sort
than those at the other school. Many of them were
English, or the sons of Indian officers, or of large
East Lothian farmers. Every branch of learning
was imparted in a pleasant and cheerful way. It was
not made hateful, but was rendered grateful. I
learnt with the rest, and made progress in Greek,
Latin, and French. I still remember some of the
anecdotes with which certain passages were illustrated. I was not a prize boy. At the summer
examinations, besides the bag-full of sweetmeats,
prizes were given to those who stood first and second
in the various classes. Some of the boys took home
armsful of prize books. Two of these were the sons
of a minister, and they had been carefully crammed
at home. But the prizes did not amount to much.

The boys I refer to made no way in the world. One of them became a minister, and broke down completely; the other became a missionary among the negroes.

What became of the favourites at the one school, and the prize boys at the other? I do not think that any of them made a mark in the world. Some became insufferable prigs, stuck up with self-conceit. The prize boys began as prodigies and ended as failures. Forcing at home did no good. In the battle of life, cramming is comparatively useless.

The most successful of my schoolfellows in after years, was originally a dunce. Hardie could not flog arithmetic into him. He learnt little or nothing at school. Teacher after teacher tried him; and the result was the same. At last he was taken from school, and placed under the charge of a private tutor. Then he showed marks of intelligence. His father, who carried on a large business, suddenly died, and the responsibility thrown upon his only son awakened his intellect and conscience at once. He took in hand the conduct of the business which his father had left him. The young fellow was energetic and persevering, and the business rapidly increased. This so-called dunce ended by becoming a public man of considerable social importance, not the least of which was that he was made provost of his native burgh.

On the whole, provided there was perseverance, those young men succeeded the best from whom little was expected. As for myself, if I have done anything worthy of being remembered, it has not been through any superiority of gifts, but only through a moderate portion of them, accompanied, it is true, with energy and the habit of industry and application.

As in the case of everyone else, I had for the most part to teach myself, and I suppose I did so to much better purpose than any schoolmaster could have taught me. Then I enjoyed good health, and health is more excellent than prizes. Exercise, the joy of interest and of activity, the play of the faculties, is the true life of a boy as of a man. I had also the benefit of living in the country, with its many pleasures and wonders.

Heredity had also much to do with my being and instincts. The child is not only father of the man, but the inheritor of the moral and physical condition of his father and mother, and of his ancestors generally, often extending very far back in the family to which he belongs. I have little to say of my ancestry. My parents were sprung from honourable and honest people, who, besides paying their debts, had something to spare for the education of their children. My father's forbears were followers of Richard Cameron. One of them, Samuel Drummond, was at the meeting of the Covenanters at Pentland, in November 1666, when he was cloven down by a Scots Grey—then called The Royal Regiment of Scots Dragoons—under General Dalziel. Fortunately, his life was saved by a religious book which he carried in his bonnet. The family continued to be Cameronians. My grandfather was an elder in that body; I remember being present at a field-preaching at a village within sight of the Pentland Hills, where Samuel Drummond had attended his dangerous field-preaching. My grandfather sent me and my brother John a letter full of good advice, which I still possess. It is not dated, but I think it must have been written in 1821, when I was nine years old.

My mother's ancestors came from the Border.

Her father, Robert Wilson, was descended from a
Major of Foot, who settled near Smailholm in the
reign of Queen Anne. Robert married Elizabeth
Yellowlees, a yeoman's daughter of Cowdenknows,
near Earlston. One of my mother's cousins, George
Yellowlees, was a good artist. While studying at
Edinburgh, he came out to Haddington and painted
portraits of my father and mother, which I now
possess. He afterwards went to London, made considerable progress in his art, and eventually was
appointed Cabinet Portrait-painter to the Duke of
Sussex.

My mother's brothers, the Wilsons of Dalkeith,
were clever mechanics. George invented one of the
first reaping machines, for which he got a prize from
the Dalkeith Farming Club. Robert, the eldest
brother, carried on a large trade as a builder and
carpenter. He was an elder of the Rev. Norman
Macleod, while the latter was Parish Minister of
Dalkeith. I remember his telling me the following
story. An idiot attended the Church, but suddenly
disappeared. The Minister met him one day, and
took him to task for absenting himself from public
worship. He added that there would be no preaching
in the bad place. "Eh, sir," replied the idiot, "it'll
no be for want o' ministers, then!"

My parents enjoyed the portion of Agur.* They
were neither "hauden doon" by poverty, nor
oppressed by riches. Though food was dear, and
taxes were high, they had sufficient for themselves
and their family. They had also enough—though at
some self-sacrifice—for the education of their children.
They were able to start us fair in our journey through
life; though others were better favoured than our-

* "Book of Proverbs," xxx. 1-8.—ED.

selves as regards money and friends. These are
evanescent, whereas the advantages of education are
permanent. I cannot, therefore, be too grateful to
my parents for having so early and so sedulously
started us on the road of knowledge.

There was another example which they set us,
that of industry—more important even than knowledge. My mother was always at her spinning-wheel
in spare hours; she not only wished to keep up the
house store of linen, but to spin for the plenishing of
her daughters. But the family grew rapidly; linen
and cotton became cheaper; and the spinning-wheel
was eventually banished to the lumber-room. Then
the cow had to be provided for, for milk was wanted
as an accompaniment for the porridge, which was the
children's usual breakfast. Hence a byre was built,
attached to the house at the bottom of the garden.
My father was a great gardener, and prided himself
upon his auriculas, tulips, polyanthuses, and other
flowers, which were the favourites in those days. We
had to assist in keeping the garden in order, though
most of us would have preferred being at play on
those Wednesday and Saturday afternoons. Some
would have fished in the Tyne, or sought for bird's
nests, or climbed the Garleton hills, or played at
patriotism in Wallace's Cave, with home-made bows
and arrows. All this, when the opportunity allowed,
used to be enjoyed with much zest and relish.

CHAPTER II

BEFORE I proceed further, I must mention a few recollections of events which specially interested me when a boy. We had comparatively few holidays when at school, excepting in August during harvest time, when we had four or five weeks' rest from learning. The magistrates and parents of the scholars attended the final examination, and as the boys were leaving school, each was presented with a bag of sweetmeats. This was the case at Hardie's, while at Graham's, besides the sweetmeats, prizes were given to the best scholars.

One of our holidays was on the occasion of the Carters' Ploy. There were a number of cart horses in the town, used for conveying corn and goods to and from Edinburgh. The carters joined their funds together, and had a dance in the town hall in summer. One of them was elected to preside over the ploy, and was hailed as "My Lord." The carters dressed themselves up in a singular manner. They sent their hats to their sweethearts, mostly servant maids, who covered them with ribands, round the brim and the crown, and with many angles of ribands between. "My Lord" had generally a velveteen jacket, also decorated. The carters joined in a

procession, and marched through the town, mounted
on their cart-horses.   They stopped at the burgh
schools, when "My Lord" entered, and craved a
holiday for the scholars.   This was always granted,
and the boys went to see the race.   It took place on
the high road between Lawrence House and Begbie
Coach Works.   After the race, there was the dance;
when "My Lady," the servant maid who had
adorned "My Lord's" hat, opened the ball.   I
remember one of our servants being "My Lady."

This curious custom has entirely disappeared.
Frightful accidents sometimes happened.   A cart-
horse was quite unfitted for galloping on a macadam-
ized road.   Occasionally the poor brute fell, and
sustained such injuries that it had to be shot.   The
riders also occasionally suffered, in broken arms or
legs.   So the carters' ploy was discontinued, all
the more surely, when the advent of railways
greatly diminished the number of cart-horses in
the town.

We had also holidays on the king's birthday, on
the New Year's day, and on the annual Fast Day.
On the first named of these festivals, the whole of
the Burgesses met at the cross, and drank the king's
health; and at night there was a bonfire in the streets,
with much squib-firing, and reports of big and little
cannon.

I must also mention another sight which struck
me with horror.   That was whipping house-breakers
in public at the cart's tail.   No doubt the burglars
deserved their punishment; but it took place on
market days, in order to have the fullest audience—
when men, women, and children looked on.   The
whipping, with a knotted lash, took place at about
six or eight appointed places; and then the criminal

B

was taken to the gaol to have his bloody back dressed.

There was another exhibition at our meeting house, quite as offensive as whipping men at the cart's tail. That was, publicly rebuking men and women on the cutty stool.* It was usually the women only; the men could not stand it, and fled. Fortunately, the children could not understand the meaning of the rebukes : they were often sent home.

The town had then its piper and drummer. It had been an ancient custom, and the magistrates revived it in my younger days. Donald Macgregor, the piper, skirled the Highland tunes while marching round the town. Old Baird, the drummer, called the attention of the public to roups, sales, and such like. He was sometimes very drunk, and stuttered and havered, so that the people could not hear his announcements. He was at length dismissed, and "Hangie" was appointed in his place. "Hangie" was one of the town's officers, and, being in debt, he accepted £10 to lash one of the above burglars through the town at the cart's tail. He was ever afterwards called "Hangie." On Sundays, he used to march with the other officers in front of the magistrates from the Town Hall to the Established Church, where the latter took their places in the front of the "laft."

This special officer had another work to do. The town had been burnt down several times during the border wars between the Scots and English, and another great conflagration occurred through the

---

* "The cutty stool," said Sir John Sinclair, "is a kind of pillory, erected for the punishment of those who have transgressed in the article of chastity." Dr Jamieson, in his *Scottish Dictionary*, says, "It is the stool of repentance, on which offenders were seated in church, now generally disused."

carelessness of a servant, when the town was half burnt down. As a precaution to future servants, the following proclamation was made once a week, towards dark, for six weeks between Christmas and Candlemas :

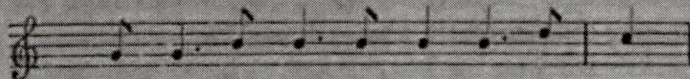

> " A' gud men servants where'er ye be,
> Keep coal an' candle for charitie ;
> Your bakehouse, brewhouse, barns, and byres,
> It's for your sakes, keep weel your fires,
> For oftentimes a little spark
> Brings mony hands to muckle wark ;
> Ye nourises that ha'e bairns to keep,
> See that ye fa' nae ower sound asleep,
> For losing o' your good renown,
> An' banishin' o' this burrow's town ;
> It's for your sakes that I do cry,
> Take warnin' from your neighbours by."

The old gentlemen "residenters" wore toupées, a kind of peruke tied with a riband, hanging down the back of the neck. Their hair was powdered, and knee-breeches and buckles on the shoes were common. I saw the last of the Spencers—named after the third Lord Spencer, who first wore it; it was used either by men or women ; and modern fashion seems trying to restore this article of dress.

Although I have written a book about "Thrift" when a man, I was not at all thrifty when a boy. We children had all penny-pigs, or thrift boxes, to implant the idea of saving spare money. But I was never a saver. I thought that the principal use of money was to be spent. I occasionally put a few pennies into the slit, but I soon worked them out again by means of a table knife. My brother Jack filled his to the top, and when it was quite filled the pig had to be broken to get out the contents. Mine was usually empty. I suppose years and discretion brought the idea of "Thrift," but I continued to spend money pretty freely.

I remember, when a little boy, getting my first introduction to the novels of Walter Scott—then the "Great Unknown." One of my sisters, when an infant, was sent to the country to be nursed; and I used to accompany Peg Nielson, our servant, to see the child on Saturday afternoons. Our way was through Clerkington Park, a charming place about a mile from the town, with the river Tyne meandering through the demesne. Peg was a capital story-teller, and many a time did she entertain us with "auld-warld" tales of brownies, fairies, ghosts, and witches, often making our flesh creep. But she could also be amusing and cheerful in the adventures she narrated. While on the way to Clerkington Mains, I asked her to tell me a story. "Yes, she would: it was a story of a gypsy woman and a little boy who was carried away in a ship by the smugglers." And then she began, and told me, in a manner that seemed most graphic, the wonderful adventures of Harry Bertram and Meg Merrilies, as related in the well-known novel of *Guy Mannering.* Many years after I read the book, and found that she had omitted nothing of the story: her memory was so good and her power of narration so excellent.

When a boy, I was taken by my father to see the Parliament House at Edinburgh. The courts were then sitting, and in one of them I saw the "Great Unknown." He was then Clerk to the Court of Session, and sat, with another clerk opposite him, beneath the Judges, of whom Charles Hope was Lord President—a handsome, splendid-looking man,

with an admirable voice. I saw Walter Scott rise,
and limp round the table to his fellow-clerk; then,
leaving the Court, he proceeded down Parliament
House. He used to be called Peveril of the Peak,
because of the loftiness of his head. I saw also in the
Court, Francis Jeffrey and Henry Cockburn; the
former a bright, keen-sighted little man, with a finely
chiselled face; and the latter distinguished for the
penetrating darkness of his eyes.

I return to the description of my native town.
Haddington lies in the valley of the Tyne, at the foot
of the southern slopes of the Garleton Hills. There
is a pleasant walk up the first Plantain to the top of
the Kayheughs. From the summit, not far from an
ancient British earthwork, and looking to the south,
a splendid view is to be seen. In the bottom of the
valley winds the river Tyne. In the hollow lies the
old town, with its ancient cathedral, the Lamp of
Lothian, with its massive central tower, rising
above all. There sleeps the hallowed dust of many
generations.

To the west, lies the richly wooded fertile valley,
over the woods of Saltoun, once the seat of The
Patriot, Andrew Fletcher, towards Moorfoot and
Soutra Hill. Looking due south, the eye stretches
over the plantations surrounding the ancient fortalice
of Lethington, once the residence of Chancellor
Maitland (the astute secretary and adviser of Mary,
Queen of Scots), where the "Political's Walk"
is still to be seen. The eye wanders south, over
the swelling wooded country about Eaglescarnie,
Coulston, and Gifford, with the "Goblin Ha'"
amongst the trees, until the view ends in the lofty
range of the Lammermuirs with their blue summits
against the sky.

Down the valley of the Tyne, towards the east, the landscape extends over Amisfield, Whitting-hame, towards Hailes Castle, where the ill-fated Queen Mary took temporary refuge with her third husband, after spending the night at Bothwell House, Haddington. Waprain Law shuts out part of the view to the east. The Law is a huge dome, having no connection with any other mountain range. It is a mass of trap rock, which doubtless resisted, in some remote age, the mighty current of water and glacier ice which rolled over the country from the westward.

But fine though the view is from the southern side of the Garleton Hills, it is still finer from the northern. From the Skidhill there stretches out a far-reaching plain, containing some of the finest agri-cultural land in East Lothian. It extends from beyond Dunbar in the east to Musselburgh in the west. All round this smiling country, lies the Firth of Forth, and in the northern distance the blue hills of Fife. Beyond Musselburgh Bay, Arthur's Seat lies like an elephant at rest, with the pillars of the National Monument on Calton Hill, and the smoke of Edinburgh in the distance. The view is infinite and varied. Looking northward, some five miles off, we see the woods of Gosford (the seat of the Earl of Wemyss), Aberlady Bay—where Napoleon was to effect his landing—Gullane Hill, and still east-wards, the ruins of Dirleton Castle, Balgonie, the Red House, North Berwick Law (a long extinct volcano), the Bass Rock, the crumbling ruins of Tantallon — one of the strongest castles of the Douglases, and the last which remained in their possession ; and far out at sea, at the mouth of the Forth, the Isle of May, crowned with its lighthouse.

One fine afternoon, in August 1822, I went up to the Garleton Hills to see the Royal Fleet on its voyage up the Forth to Leith. Beyond Gullane Hill, three ships were seen nearly close to each other ; and we were told by some naval men, who had their spy-glasses with them, that the centre ship had George the Fourth on board, on his way to Leith and Edinburgh. For many weeks before our town had been in a state of excitement. The Mail and the Union were loaded from day to day. Carts and waggons passed through the streets, full of heather, the national badge at the time. Everybody must go to Edinburgh to see the famous procession, and the welcoming of the king. I was considered too young to go, but my eldest brother went with my father, to witness the wonderful sight.

We had our August vacation, and I afterwards went to see my numerous relations at Dalkeith while the king was still residing with the Duke of Buccleuch. I saw the "curled darling" pass along the High Street, on his way from the duke's palace, to visit the Marquis of Lothian at Newbattle Abbey. I had merely a sight of the king in passing, for his carriage drove on at a rapid rate. The Scots Greys were then at Dalkeith, and their band played nearly every morning in front of the Parish Church. The grey horses were terribly used up by their frequent gallop-ings to and from Edinburgh when escorting the king.

After I had seen my relatives at Dalkeith, I went to Lasswade, Loanhead, Hawthornden, and Rosslyn, to visit other friends there. The scenery along the North Esk is very charming ; and the walk by Poulton, through Hawthornden to Rosslyn, is almost unsurpassed in river scenery. The remains of the old castle at Rosslyn and the exquisitely restored chapel—a marvel of architectural art—attract strangers from far and near.

My grandfather was still alive. He was still acting as an elder of the Cameronians. Some years before my last visit to him, I was present at a field-preaching of the congregation. The people came from great distances. They sat or lay about on the grass; and the preachers succeeded each other, with intervals, during which psalms were sung; the services lasted until near sunset.

I fear I must have been a great "tease" to these old people during my holidays. I had a little cannon and gunpowder, and kept firing away nearly all day long. The neighbours complained, but still I went on; at length I burnt my hands with an explosion of gunpowder, and then I was cured.

My grandfather was a fine-looking old man. He was very gentle in nature. His long, white hair fell over his shoulders. At my last visit, he accompanied me down the loan for about a mile. He was evidently growing weak and feeble. He bore his ninety years well, but age was telling upon him. At last he said, "I am weary," and sat down upon the milestone. After he had got his breath, he went on, "My dear laddie, I shall never see you any more. I am getting very frail. There is only one thing I have got to do, and that is—to dee. Ye are very young, but ye will hae to do the same, and follow me. Now, be a good boy; read your Bible; obey your parents; farewell, Samuel."

And so, taking a loving farewell of the old man, I left him there. On looking back, I saw him toddling feebly up the hill. I never saw him alive again. The next time I witnessed his placid face, he was in his coffin. I attended his funeral at the end of the same year, on a snowy winter's day. He was buried in Lasswade churchyard, near the monument erected to General Sir Archdale Wilson (the victor of Delhi), which overlooks the beautiful valley of the Esk.

CHAPTER III

A STUDENT OF MEDICINE

I HAD reached my fourteenth year, when the question arose, what was I to be? We were a large and growing family, and every one of us must do something, and eventually work for our own living.

Adolphus Trollope, in his *Recollections*, mentions the case of a boy who was asked what he would like to be when he grew up? The boy's answer was, " I should like to be a giant or a retired stockbroker! " I was not so ambitious as this ; but when my mother asked me, " What would you like to be, Sam? " I answered, " I would like to be a painter "—I meant an artist. I had a taste for drawing and colour, and many years after illustrated one of my own books.

I had perhaps been inspired by the art of my cousin Yellowlees, who painted the portraits of my father and mother ; and I greatly admired the drawings of the Union and Mail coaches, which he rapidly threw off. But my mother thought that I wished to be a *house*-painter. " Oh no! " said she, " that is a dirty business." I did not answer ; and the matter slept for a time.

On a future day, she again asked me, " Would you no like to be a minister? " " Oh, no! " I said decidedly, " I'll no be a minister." " What for no? "

I could not very well explain then, but I can now. We children were surfeited with preaching and ministering. Sunday, the "day of rest," was to us the most exhausting and unpleasant of the week. Our preacher was a combative man. He preached the narrowest Calvinism, and there was far more fear than love in his sermons.

We had to work very hard on the so-called day of rest. In the morning, after prayers, we had to learn the "carritch" and a "paraphrage." Then we went to the kirk, and after singing and prayers, we listened to a sermon often more than an hour long, and got out at one. After refreshment, we went to kirk again at two; heard another sermon, and were dismissed at four. Then we had to say our catechism and paraphrase. There was actually a *third* sermon at six o'clock; we got home at eight, and said our catechism and paraphrase. We had no sort of recreation on Sundays. Walking, except to the kirk, was forbidden. Books were interdicted, excepting the Bible, the Catechism, and the Secession Magazine, or perhaps some book of Evangelical sermons.

I have no doubt it was all intended for our good; but I never in my youth had any agreeable recollections of Sundays. Our minister was a good and hard-working man. He, no doubt, gave us all that he had to give; but he was wearisome and unsympathetic; and his doctrines, though intended to frighten us into goodness, had perhaps the very reverse effect. There was no wonder, therefore, that I should not wish to be a minister.

The next question put to me by my mother was this: "Would you no like to be a doctor?" The question was rather startling at first. There were many prejudices about doctors in my younger days.

Our servants used to tell the trembling children about the "black doctors" that were ready to clap a plaster over our mouths, and carry us away no one knew whither. Then, a regular watch and ward was held over the parish burying-ground, to prevent the "doctors" rifling the graves, for the purposes of the dissecting-rooms at Edinburgh. I remember going with my father, when he was on the watch, to take the first turn with him round the churchyard. There were three or four men, I think, one of whom was elected the foreman. They were supplied with some old muskets, mounted with bayonets, to give the resurrectionists a warm reception. This frightful state of things culminated a few years later, in the murders by Burke and Hare of living "subjects" for Dr Knox's anatomy class at Edinburgh.

But doctors were necessary for many reasons. It so happened that I fell down a hatchway, and tore open my groin, very near the femoral artery. The doctor was sent for, and put in two stitches, and I was soon well again. This doctor was Robert Lewins, a very pleasant, kindly man, full of anecdote. His partner was Dr Robert Lorimer, eldest son of the minister of the Parish Church, also an excellent person. When I was recovering from my wound, my mother asked Dr Lewins if he could take me as an apprentice. "Yes," he answered, "my apprentice, James Dorward, is just leaving me for Edinburgh, to attend the classes there; so that I have an opening for your son." It was arranged accordingly; and on the 6th November 1826, I was bound apprentice to Drs Lewins and Lorimer for five years.

There was not much to be done in my new vocation. I had to learn the nature and the qualities of drugs, and how to make up prescriptions, pills, mixtures, potions, ointments, blisters, infusions, tinctures, and such like. In course of time, I learnt the arts of bleeding and bandaging. I had to assist in attending the poorer class of patients. I also went on with my own education. There were plenty of libraries in the town, and I used them freely. There was the Town's Library—a collection of books that had been made over to the burgh by the Rev. John Gray, together with an endowment, about a hundred and fifty years before. Most of the books were theological, but some of the recent additions were valuable. But I did not make much use of the library. Patrick Hardie, the master of the English School, was the librarian; and when I took out Gibbon's *Decline and Fall*, he havered a bit to me, in his dictatorial way, as to how I was to read it. I did not like this, and went to other libraries.

There was another popular collection of books, called " Begbie's Library," left by some native of the town for general use, together with a small salary for the person who kept it and gave out the books. But the library that I made the most use of was the East Lothian Itinerating Library, founded and worked by that most excellent man, the late Samuel Brown. Having been laid up by illness, he derived great consolation, during his protracted recovery, from the perusal of good and entertaining books. It occurred to him that he might help to give the same consolation to others, who were less able to provide it. It seems that a number of " balances of militia insurance" remained in his hands, for which he could find no claimants. With part of these balances he procured two hundred select volumes, some of which were of a moral and religious tendency, and the others books of travels, agriculture, the mechanical arts, and general science. He divided these into four assorted sets of fifty volumes each, and stationed them in four large villages, under the superintendence of gratuitous librarians. After the books had remained there for a certain time, they were removed to other districts. The interest of the readers was thus kept alive in these itinerating books; and the habit of reading was developed and fostered.

In order to maintain and extend the libraries, subscriptions were invited. The newly-purchased books were kept for two years in the three principal towns of the county, for the use of the annual subscribers of five shillings; after which they were merged in the general circulation. In this manner, after some twenty years of well-sustained devotion to his enterprise, and by dint of much personal sacrifice, Samuel Brown had set forty-seven excellent libraries in circulatory motion through the county; and there was scarcely an inhabitant who was not within a mile and a half from one of these institutions. As Haddington was the centre of the movement, I had the advantage of perusing all the new books as they came out; and in this way I greatly added to my store of knowledge.

There were other libraries in the town, besides these: the Subscription Library, to which I did not then belong; and two circulating libraries—Tait's and Niell's—from which all the novels and miscellaneous works of the day might be obtained. There was thus no want of reading, for those who might be disposed to dip into the vast stores of accumulated knowledge, poetry, literature, fiction, and theology.

There was another excellent institution that Samuel Brown was mainly instrumental in founding: and that was the " Haddington School of

Arts," which very shortly followed the formation of a similar school at Edinburgh. My master and friend, Dr Robert Lorimer, was one of the first to give lectures to the members, on the principles of Mechanics, and on Chemistry. The lectures were well attended by the leading mechanics of the town. I remember three of them, who worked as carpenters for the Messrs Scoular of Sunnybank. They made carts, ploughs, and agricultural implements. Two of these men saved money enough during the summer to pay for their class instruction at Edinburgh University during the winter. One became the minister of a Presbyterian congregation at Blackburn; another became master of a large public school at Hull; and the third, who remained a mechanic, rose higher than the others. His name was Andrew Lamb. He was an enthusiastic student at the School of Arts. I remember him well, for he used to attend the committee meeting of the Juvenile Missionary Society, for which I was a rather irregular collector. He shortly after left Haddington; but many years after, he called upon me at the London Bridge Station. He was then General Manager of the Peninsular and Oriental Steamship Company, and the dispenser of considerable political power at Southampton, where he then resided.

Dr Lorimer gave several courses of Lectures on Chemistry and the Arts at Haddington and Dunbar during the time that I was under him; and he did me the honour to select me as his assistant. He was a most kind man, and instructed me faithfully, giving me much good advice. He put me in the way of preparing all kinds of gases for the lectures; and while he was absent visiting his patients, I went on with the work. There was both interest and instruction in all this; and it helped me much in my future studies. Dr Lewins was also very kind. I had access to his library. He had a finely assorted stock of the old English novelists—Fielding, Richardson, and Smollett; and I fear I paid more attention to these than to the scientific works which his library contained. Yet it was well to know what had been done by the great men who lived before us.

I once witnessed the doctor in the throes of literary composition. It was a tremendous business. We went into a back bedroom in the furthest corner of the house, so as not to be disturbed by the noises in the kitchen. The doctor dressed himself in his long, hanging shawl-gown; strode about the floor, and dictated. The product was an article on Infantile Remittent Fever. I knew it thoroughly, for I wrote it over three or four times. It was full of rather long words, such as "intromittent," "exacerbations," and so on. The paper appeared a few years later in the *Edinburgh Medical Journal.*

I went on with my education at the same time. For this purpose, I attended Mr Johnstone, master of the Parish School, in the evening. I took instructions from him in Mathematics, French, and Latin. Johnstone was a most accomplished man, full of accumulated knowledge; he was a good linguist, a good mathematician, and stored with information, which ebbed out in every word of his discourses. I did not know at the time, but I afterwards ascertained, that he was an intimate friend and correspondent of Thomas Carlyle. It came out in this way. Many years after (in 1882), when Carlyle's name had become distinguished, Mr Johnstone's daughter—then living at Lockerby, in Dumfriesshire —sent me a large number of letters from Carlyle to

her father; asking me to edit them, and give them to
the public. As I knew that Mr Froude was then
busy with Carlyle's Life, I recommended her to send
them to him, for the purpose of being included in the
biography. But I presume she did not take my
advice, as, at the time at which I write, they have
not yet been published.

Perhaps they scarcely merited a separate publication. They consisted principally of letters written by
Carlyle to Johnstone, after the former had left Eccle-
fechan (where Johnstone's father was the burgher
minister) for Edinburgh, down to the period of
Johnstone's becoming the parish teacher at Haddington. The letters are written in an ordinary English
style, and not in the Carlylese language which was
afterwards invented. The first letter was the best:
it described Carlyle's journey by coach to Edinburgh
in the midst of a snowstorm.

In one of the later letters, after Johnstone had
intimated his intention of applying for the office of
parish teacher at Haddington, Carlyle recommended
his friend to visit Miss Jeanie Welsh, and secure her
influence. Miss Welsh knew a Mr Gilbert Burns,
brother of the poet, who had considerable influence
with the "heritors" of the parish, who elected the
teacher. Gilbert Burns had first come into the
neighbourhood as steward for Mr Dunlop of West
Morham, whose wife, Mrs Dunlop of Dunlop, in
Ayrshire, was an intimate friend and correspondent
of Robert Burns in 1786-96. Some of Burns' most
powerful letters were addressed to that amiable and
accomplished lady. After the estate in East Lothian
had been sold by her son, Captain Dunlop, Gilbert
Burns was appointed factor of Lord Blantyre's estate
of Lennoxton (formerly Lethington), and removed to

Grantsbraes, where he resided till his death in 1827. The result of the application to Gilbert Burns, through Jeanie Welsh, proved successful. Johnstone was appointed parish school teacher, and I became his pupil. Miss Welsh shortly after married the modern Jeremiah. It was thought that she might have done better. Her friends were of opinion that she had thrown herself away "upon a dominie"! Carlyle had been a teacher, with Irving, at Kirkcaldy.

At the end of the third year of my apprenticeship, Dr Lewins removed to Leith, for the purpose of succeeding Dr Kellie, his former master. He took me with him, and I then began to attend the medical classes in the University of Edinburgh. I matriculated in November, 1829, and attended the lectures of Dr Duncan for Materia Medica, Dr Hope for Chemistry, and Mr Lizars for Anatomy. The lectures began at 9 A.M., and I walked up from Leith to Edinburgh—a distance of about three miles. In the dead of winter, I used to breakfast in the dark, and then push up the hill in time to be present at the beginning of the lecture. Chemistry followed, then Anatomy. I returned to Leith by midday, to give such assistance as I could to Dr Lewins.

My life then was very pleasant. There was the bustle of the seaport, the scenery by the seaside, the daily walks to and from the College, the picturesque beauty of Edinburgh, which never tires, and the friends and acquaintances I made—all of these made life very agreeable and enjoyable. One of my most treasured friends was Adam Hope—a most active, energetic, and sensible fellow—the brother of George Hope. He was then learning his business at the extensive engineering works and sawmills of Burstall

& Co. He afterwards went out to Canada, where he founded a town, and made a reputation.

In the following year, I took lodgings in Edinburgh, near the College, and went on with my studies—more especially in Anatomy. I also attended the lectures of Liston on Surgery and Dr Fletcher on the Institutions of Medicine. Both were very able men. The first was perhaps the most dexterous surgeon of his time; the other was a most profound lecturer on his branch of science. He was an extensive reader, and brought the science of all Europe to bear upon his subject. When the works of Darwin afterwards came out, I felt that Fletcher had long before expounded very much the same views; or, at all events, had heralded his approach. After his death, which happened a few years later, Dr Lewins, who was his intimate friend, edited his Lectures, which fully show the calibre and genius of the man.

One of my friends, a fellow-attendant at Dr Fletcher's lectures, was John Brown—afterwards the celebrated author of *Rab and his Friends*. He was then in a jacket, a fellow of infinite humour, though very shy. It was some time before one could get into his nature. But when once there, it was impossible not to love him. I knew his cousin Samuel better than himself. Samuel Brown was a native of my own town, and I had much controversy and correspondence with him. He represented Shelley's ideal character—"a pard-like spirit, beautiful and swift." Even when a boy, he was full of theories—not always well grounded. He was rapid and impetuous, and came to his conclusions in too sudden a manner. I shall return to him later on.

CHAPTER IV

REFORM—THE LAUDER RAID—THE CHOLERA

ABOUT this time "Reform" was in the air. The three days at Paris in July 1830 had wakened up Europe, and excited a general desire for change. In England and Scotland there was much distress, and in the south of Ireland, the people, as usual, were in trouble. There were rick-burnings in Kent and the southern counties, machine-breaking in the manufacturing districts, trials of radicals at Glasgow, and distress among the working-classes generally. It was thought that Reform of Parliament was paramount above all other reforms. The sailor king had ascended the throne, and was favourable to the new views. The Duke of Wellington retired from office, and Earl Grey came into power. Parliament met on the 3rd of February 1831, and on the 1st of March following Lord John Russell brought forward his measure for Parliamentary Reform. The whole country was roused by the proposal. Shoals of petitions were sent in from all quarters; political unions were formed; and a state very nearly approaching "the Revolutionary Epoch" seemed to be on foot. The second reading was carried by a majority of ONE.

There was a great illumination at Edinburgh on that occasion. The city lights up brilliantly, especially when seen from the Calton Hill or the North Bridge. There is the long vista of Princes Street on the one hand, and the lofty lighted-up houses of the Old Town on the other. But the mob—always the biggest of despots—proved unruly. Everybody must agree with the mob, or take the consequences. On this occasion it proceeded to break the windows of those who did not light up. There was a large quantity of metal laid down for the repair of the macadamised road along Princes Street, which suited them handily. They took up the stones, and, notwithstanding the charges of the police, smashed many windows.

I think it was in George Street, where the mob went careering along, that they came to a large house not lit up. They began to smash, when suddenly three beautiful women came forward, on to the balcony, each with a lighted candle in her hand. They saved the house. The mob worships beauty and courage. They set up a loud cheer, and went on in their wild fury. "The glorious majority of one" was displayed in many places. Some thought it was a satire.

The ministers were eventually left in a minority. The king dissolved Parliament, and the members went back to their constituents. And now followed a desperate struggle. The country was in a whirlwind of excitement. The new writs were made returnable on the 14th of June, and the turmoil of the election of the new Parliament proceeded in town and country. The cry was, "The Bill, the whole Bill, and nothing but the Bill." A monster meeting was held in the King's Park, Edinburgh, at which I was present as a spectator, when enthusiastic resolutions were unanimously carried. At the close of the

University Classes at the end of April, 1831, I returned to Haddington, where I found the same excitement prevailing about the Bill.

Haddington was one of a group of five burghs returning a member to Parliament. They took it in turn to be the returning burgh. This time it was the turn of Lauder, a little town on the other side of the Lammermuir Hills. Haddington and Jedburgh, the two largest burghs, had declared in favour of the Reform Candidate; Dunbar and North Berwick in favour of the Tory; but Lauder was considered doubtful. It depended upon its decision whether Robert Stewart, of Alderston, the Reformer, should be returned to Parliament, or Sir A. J. Dalrymple, the nominee of Lord Lauderdale, the Anti-Reformer. I do not know what arrangements were made, but I knew that a strong detachment of the Haddington Reformers intended to march to Lauder, and take steps to secure the return of their candidate in one way or another. I accordingly resolved to go across the Lammermuir Hills and witness the proceedings.

It was a fine day in May, and I greatly enjoyed the walk to Lammerlaw. I had been at the top of the cairn on the hill-top the year before, and enjoyed the glorious view. I went by Gifford, past the Woods of Yester, and through Long Yester farm, up the track through the heather; skirting the many remains of camps of ancient tribes who had occupied the country long before the inroads of the Scots and Picts, who, after all, were but interlopers. The air was sharp, crisp, and bracing, as I ascended the hill; near the summit I descended the rounded slopes of the Lammermuirs—a perfect sea of hills— lying silent and sublime, as far as the eye could reach. Not a sound was heard, except the whirr of a moorfowl on its way to cover, or the occasional cry of a startled sheep.

Amidst the stillness of nature, which was impressive in its loneliness, I went onward to Tullis Hill. Here I met the first man I had encountered for many miles—a shepherd. He was standing signaling with his arms to a dog on the opposite hill, which was divided from us by a deep glen. I could scarcely see the dog at first. It looked like a moving spot of dark upon the green; and the sheep looked like white bits of wool upon the hillside. But the dog was at work. As the shepherd near me lifted his arms and signalled, the dog, watching him, ran up the hill in one direction or the other as he had pointed; and in course of time he brought the flock all together, home to the sheep-farm.

Descending the mountain on the southern side I went on to Hazeldean, passing several more of the ancient camps already mentioned, and after skirting along the burn on its way to join the river Leader, I struck the high road from Edinburgh, and after about ten miles more walking from the summit of Lammerlaw, reached the town of Lauder—the scene of the intended election on the following day. I took up my quarters with a friend, and shortly after went into the streets to see the new arrivals from the adjoining towns. I met the two law agents— Messrs Stobie and Younger—and was invited by them to join their party in a room upstairs, in the second inn of the town—the principal inn, the Lauderdale Arms, being appropriated by the other party.

I found the little room hot and fuming with the steam of whisky toddy. The leading reformers were all there; and Robert Stewart, the candidate, was present. It was a sort of free-and-easy, and in the midst of conversation, songs were given. Deacon Melville, the Haddington tailor, sang his song, beginning, "Away ye gay landskips, ye gardings of roses," and ending with "dark Loch na Garr." Other songs followed, but I did not wait until the close of the sitting.

On the following morning, crowds of strangers entered the town. The principal procession came from Haddington. It consisted of a lot of reformers, headed by "General" Badger, and accompanied by a public speaker, "Orator" Maclauchlan—a diminutive baker of the Newgate. As the time for the election approached, a crowd of men assembled opposite the Lauderdale Arms. Lord Maitland, Sir Anthony Maitland, and others, issued from the inn, and proceeded across the street to the Council Room, escorted by their gamekeepers and farm stewards. The Maitlands were allowed to pass; but a tussle took place with the gamekeepers. I saw a young Haddington carpenter bring down the thick end of his stick on the bald crown of the head gamekeeper. He went down like a shot. It was a most cruel assault. Sir Anthony Maitland went up the outside stairs of the Council Room, and shook his fist at the foaming crowd, vowing vengeance.

The most important event, however, occurred at some distance from the town. One of the councillors, Bailie Simpson, was in a delicate state of health, and did not intend to vote. A post-chaise was sent for him by the Lauderdale party; but another chaise was also in readiness, with a fleet pair of horses. At a corner of the road, the carriage containing the bailie was stopped, the bailie was hustled out and put in the new chaise. The one which had contained him was upset in the ditch by a powerful flesher of Haddington, and the voter was driven rapidly away towards Blainslie. The time for the election had now arrived. It could not be postponed. The voting took place, and Robert Stewart was declared elected by a majority of one—again "the glorious majority of one!"

The procession again re-formed and marched off to Haddington, elated with their victory. I did not return until the following day, when I again crossed the mountains; but I was informed that on the arrival of the procession at Haddington, they were headed by several men with blazing tar-barrels on their heads; and in the darkness of the night, the scene had been very startling. The people were perfectly frantic with joy and excitement.

A few days later, the new member made his entry into the town. He was enthusiastically received at Laurencehouse, about a mile out of the town, by men, women, and boys—for boys are always on the winning side. They are a perspiring phalanx in the van of all public movements. During the Reform era every boy was a reformer. To please the boys and the people generally, and perhaps to show the general enthusiasm, an extempore band was got up and headed the procession. It consisted principally of a splendid big drum, which used to belong to the Haddington Militia. It was lent by Peter Martine, who, though a Tory, showed his liberality by lending the drum, which was beaten by a lame Radical weaver, who in his early days had been a big drummer. There were, however, other instruments. There were two key buglers, one Hugh Shields, the parish precentor, who played very well; the other, a carpenter, who played very badly. There was also Tom Muat, the shoemaker, who played the clarionet. The music was shockingly bad; but it didn't matter. The crowd made up for it by their enthusiasm. Then there were speeches, made by the orators, and received with immense applause by the multitude.

Of course the election could not stand. It was petitioned against, and Robert Stewart was unseated, when Sir A. J. Dalrymple became the sitting member for the burgh during the expiring days of the old parliamentary system. Attempts were made to detect the authors of the outrage at Lauder. The chaise driver, who drove away the voter, was apprehended and imprisoned for twelve months. But the powerful flesher of Haddington, who had been the main instrument, was never found out. The young carpenter who smote down the gamekeeper was, by some means, enabled to leave the town, and was never afterwards heard of. One of the leading councillors received his reward. He was made a magistrate in the West Indies. Such was the outcome of "The Lauder Raid." Robert Stewart was returned to Parliament without opposition at the first election under the Reform Act; and he continued to be member for the burghs until he was unseated by Balfour of Whittinghame some ten years later.

To return to my own personal history, I went back to Edinburgh in the following November. This was my third session. I attended the Anatomical Classes and Practical Surgery under the two Messrs Lizars; Practice of Physic under Dr Mackintosh; and walked the Infirmary at midday. Here Liston was the principal surgeon when any important operation was to be performed.

Asiatic cholera was now travelling north-west-

wards through Europe, in the direction of England.
It had reached Hamburg, and was about to visit
this country. The first cases, I think, occurred at
Gateshead : and the next at Haddington. Early one
morning in January 1832, I was roused by a loud
knocking at the door of my lodging at Edinburgh. I
had been suffering from a frightful dream. I knew
at once that something must be wrong at home, and
feared the worst. I opened the window myself, and
asked what was wanted. I was told that I must go
out to Haddington immediately, as my father was ill
of cholera. A gig was at the door to carry me out.
I got ready at once, and was on my way within a
quarter of an hour. It was a fine winter morning,
and the sun came up over the Forth, as we drove over
Birslae Brae. Though Forsyth, the livery stable
master, drove fast, we arrived too late. My father
was dead when I entered the room where he lay in
his last placid sleep. I recognised the strong likeness
to my grandfather when I had last seen him. I had
never witnessed the likeness before; but family
resemblance often comes out in the moment of
death.

Cholera was very deadly in the town at that time.
Many died in the front street, near where my father
lived. The cause of the fatality was afterwards discovered—want of wholesome water, and utter want of
drainage. The defect was at length remedied, after
many years' delay. My father was buried in the choir
of the old Cathedral at Haddington, close by the
burial place of Dr John Welsh, whose daughter, Mrs
Carlyle, was afterwards interred there.

There was great sorrow and lamentation at home.
A family of eleven children had to be provided for
—the youngest an infant, only three months old.

I remained at home for some time, as a consolation to my mother. I did not know at first whether I was to go on with my medical education or not. It might possibly be too costly—looking to the circumstances in which we were placed. Then, another serious circumstance occurred. My father had been surety, with two others, for his elder brother John, who was a paper manufacturer at Colinton, near Edinburgh. He had got into some dilemma with the Excise; the mill was stopped; and a security for some £800 had to be paid. One of the first things to be done, after the death of my father, was to raise the third of this money, and pay it to the lawyer at Edinburgh. Part of the sum was borrowed, and I went in to pay the money. It proved a total loss, and it was felt to be very distressing at such a time.

After remaining at home for some time, I professed my willingness to abandon my profession. But my mother would not hear of it. "No, no," she said, "you must go back to Edinburgh, and do as your father desired: God will provide." She had the most perfect faith in Providence, and believed that if she did her duty she would be supported to the end. She had wonderful pluck, and abundant common-sense. Her character seemed to develop with the calls made upon her. Difficulties only brought out the essence of her nature. I could not fail to be influenced by so good a mother. I was inspired by her, and obeyed her.

I went back to Edinburgh accordingly, finished my third winter session at the University; and after remaining during the summer session, studying Clinical Surgery under Mr Syme, Midwifery under Dr Mackintosh, and Practical Anatomy under Mr

Alexander Lizars, I submitted myself for examination.
It was common, in those days, to have a "grinder,"
or coach. But I dispensed with that expensive preliminary, and met daily a student of about my own
age, Henry Smith—afterwards a thriving chemical
manufacturer; and with him I went carefully through
all the necessary coaching.

We went together to be examined. After waiting
in the ante-rooms of the New College of Surgeons,
first one and then another candidate came out—
rejected! One was much older than myself. I
thought that if he had not been able to pass, there
was little chance for me. Then Henry Smith was
called in. After what I thought a very long time of
"heckling"—so long that I feared he would never
come out—he made his appearance with a beaming
face. "I have passed," he said. "Is it difficult?"
"No, not at all. I know what you can do. You will
find it easy!" Accordingly, when I was next called
in, I went with good heart.

Although the examinations were in those days
conducted *viva voce*, and without any written
papers, the examiners soon got at the gist of the
students' knowledge. First one, and then another,
took me in hand, and after examining me in special
topics, came to a rapid conclusion. There was Dr
Huie, a difficult examiner, Dr Simson, Dr Begbie,
Dr Maclagan, and others. First, there was a paragraph of Gregory's *Conspectus* in Latin to be
construed, or a passage of *Celsus*. Then Materia
Medica, when the method of preparing Antimonial
Powder and Calomel had to be explained. Then
anatomy, when the arteries, nerves, and muscles at
the base of the scull, had to be described. I knew
this well, for I was well grounded in anatomy. Then

surgery, with a description of reducing a hernia and performing amputation of a leg. And so on with the details of the practice of surgery and medicine. By taking the candidate on such subjects unawares, and ascertaining exactly what he knew about them, the examiners were enabled to come to a conclusion as to the other subjects on which he had not been examined. After about an hour of such inquiries, a large mass of facts had been ascertained as to the competency and the knowledge of the student. I got through without difficulty; and had the pleasure of receiving my diploma, dated the 6th of November, 1832—six years exactly, after the date of the indenture of my apprenticeship.

CHAPTER V

"WHAT are we to do with our boys?" is a difficult question to answer. One thing which my parents did for me, was to give me a good education. It was better than if they had given me a fortune. But what use was I to make of it? There was I, a passed surgeon, before I had completed my twentieth year. I was too young to start business for myself. If I did, who would have employed me? I looked even younger than I was.

Unfortunately, at that time, the number of surgeons was greatly in excess of the public demand. Europe was at peace. The army, instead of absorbing surgeons, discharged them; and in Haddington, as elsewhere, there were experienced army surgeons on half pay, competing with the local practitioners. The navy was also on a reduced scale; and with the demand for reform, it was likely that it would be still further reduced. There were to be no more wars. Some surgeons went to India, but I could not find my way thither, for I had no influence. Besides, as I was the son whom my mother most relied on for assistance, and as she wished me to remain at home for some years, I finally consented.

I did go to Galashiels in 1833 to visit my relations

there, and to look about me for an opening. There
I found an old college friend who had just commenced
business. He said, "If you come, I will go!" As
he had first obtained possession of the ground, I
retired and returned homeward. I came back by
way of Abbotsford, which I visited for the first
time. It was the year after Sir Walter's death,
and the place looked very sad and silent. I also
went to see my relatives, the Yellowlees, at Cowden
Knowes Farm, and was hospitably entertained by
them, then home by Lauder, the scene of the raid
a few years before.

But I could not be idle. I was requested by
Provost Brown (the first provost under the Municipal Reform Act), and by Mr Davie, the Secretary
to the School of Arts, to deliver a course of Lectures
on Chemistry to the members. This was a pleasant
occupation. It took up a considerable portion of
the summer; and I wrote out twelve lectures—
the longest spell of writing I had ever undertaken.
I had the use of the excellent apparatus belonging
to the institution; and whether I improved my hearers
or not, I know that I greatly improved myself in my
practical knowledge of Chemistry, Heat, Electricity,
and Galvanism. My former teacher, Mr Johnstone,
gave a course of lectures, on alternate evenings,
on Mathematical and Physical Geography; and Mr
Archibald gave another course on Mineralogy and
Geology. These lectures were delivered in the Parish
School. It was used for the education of children
during the daytime, and for the education of adults
in the evening—a very proper manner of using public
buildings for the benefit of all classes. The lectures
were exceedingly well attended.

Eventually, I determined to settle at Haddington,

and practise medicine there—at least for a time. I scarcely expected much success, for the population of the town and neighbourhood was small and stationary, and I was the youngest of eight practitioners. There were the two Dr Howdens, father and son, who had an old established business; Drs Lorimer and Cruickshank, with the former of whom I had served; Dr Black, a retired army surgeon; Dr Burton; Mr Anderson, surgeon; and lastly myself, the youngest of them all. Still, I got some remnants of practice, mostly among the poorer people.

The life of a country doctor, though varied, becomes monotonous. Dr John Brown has given a good account of the profession in his essay, "Our Gideon Grays." He introduces it with the motto, taken from Mungo Park, who was originally a country doctor: "I would rather go back to Africa than practise again at Peebles." The doctor has to be at everybody's bidding, and must ride out to the country, wet or dry, far or near, whether paid or not. In my case, much of my work was done gratuitously—as is the case with every young country doctor. Still, I met with a great deal of kindness, among the farm-servants as well as among the farmers. The latter were always willing to give me entertainment while attending their people, as well as a glass of whisky toddy. This is one of the perils of the profession; and one which I often found it necessary to shirk. There was much to admire in the poorer class of people among whom my lot was cast. As a lady who had travelled much said to me, "The East Lothian peasantry are not *picturesque*, like those we meet abroad." No! but they are wonderfully well

D

educated at their parish school; and they have a
great deal of shrewd common-sense—a sort of
mother wit, which goes further than any amount of
picturesqueness. The Lowlander is hardy, economical, and industrious—rather reticent of speech,
but opinionated and argumentative—somewhat un-
compromising and self-assertive.

I knew some of these men who were full of
sagacity, the result of treasured experience—though
their income was not more than ten shillings a week.
Out of their little earnings, they would send their
children to school. But how little remained for the
doctor who attended them in their trials and troubles?
One thing they were rich in, and that was Contentment. They were fairly satisfied with what they
had, and tried to make the best of it. The rich
man is he who is contented with what he has: for
all men, as every wise person knows, cannot have
a front seat in the social circle. Fortunately, goodness does not belong to any special class, and I
have found some of the best men, and the best-
mannered men, among those whom we call the poor.
Manner is, after all, the expression of the nature
of the man; and doing to others as you would
be done by, quiet self-possession, tact, and courtesy,
the essentials of a gentleman, are to be found
amongst all classes, even in the most secluded
districts. An old saint said, "One little turn of
the eye sets a man either in the sun or in the
shadow of his own body."

Though the poor man may know that he cannot
be a hero, yet he can always be a man—and the Man
is the true thing after all. It is not the quality of the
coat, but the heart that beats under it. He is the
true gentleman who possesses and displays the refined

qualities of human nature; and such men I have
found everywhere. I have seen them in sorrow and
suffering—when the house was dark with the shadow
of death; and yet never found them wanting in
thankfulness and gratitude for the mercies that were
vouchsafed to them. Here, for instance, is the
record of the life of an old gentleman—the like of
whom I have often known during my brief pilgrimage
on earth. And yet he was only a shepherd, working
through life for a wage of not more than ten or
twelve shillings a week.

The local journal said of him :—

"A feeling of tender regret and old remembrance
will be awakened in many minds by the announcement
in our obituary list to-day of the death of Mr John
Wood, shepherd, Long Yester, who, after no special
illness or suffering, but the exhaustion of extreme old
age, expired on Friday last. He was the oldest sur-
vivor of a race of worthy men in their day and calling; an experienced, skilful, and faithful shepherd,
who, though disabled for many years for active work,
took an anxious interest to the last in his sheep; a
man of honest principle and sterling worth, he could
not speak or act an untruth. Exemplary in all the
duties and relations of life, he lived and worked as
ever in the great Taskmaster's eye, and thus, after
'life's long day,' near the place where he was born, and
where, eighty years ago, he first tended the flocks, with
life's taper burning slowly to its close, the fine old
man has passed away. Of him it may be truly said
in the words of the sage—

> "'His virtues walked their narrow round,
> Nor made a pause, nor left a void,
> And sure the Eternal Master found
> His single talent well employed.'"*

It is unnecessary for me to go into all the details
of my life while practising as a country surgeon.

* This record, "*In Memoriam*," is taken from the *Haddingtonshire
Courier* of 2nd January 1882.

My employment was very fitful. Sometimes I was out of bed for two or three nights together; at other times I had little to do. How to employ my spare time? I set to work at my French; bought French books, and read and studied them. The works of Aimé-Martin were amongst my favourites, as well as those of Degerando. The former gave me new views about woman's power in the world, which I afterwards turned to good account. I had many amusements too. I studied music, practised violin-playing, and got up a quartette party. We even went the length of giving charitable concerts. I also revived my old study of drawing, and began painting in oil and water colours. I proceeded to prepare a course of lectures on Physiology and the Conditions of Health, and illustrated them with paintings, like my old instructor, Dr Fletcher of Edinburgh. The preparation of these not only filled up my time, but gave me much pleasure. I gave about fifteen lectures in the Sheriff's Court-room, and they were well attended.

I had many good friends. One of the most attached was Tom Todrick,* a most genial, honest, sensible fellow. We were boys, and became men together. We took the London *Examiner* in its best days, while Albany Fonblanque was the editor; as well as the *Monthly Repository*, with Fox, Sarah Flower Adams, Dr Southwood Smith, and Mrs Leman Grimstone, as principal contributors. I devoured poetry, especially Shelley and Keats. I afterwards rose to Coleridge and Wordsworth, for each age has its special poetical attractions. The highest of all is, I think, Shakespeare. From this, it will be seen that I made good use of my time.

Another friend was Samuel Brown. He was a

* Afterwards Banker, in succession to his father.

most able, though vehement and impulsive, young
fellow, a splendid talker, and afterwards an impressive lecturer. Great things were expected of him;
but somehow he missed his way. While studying chemistry, in which he was proficient, he fell
upon some new views of atoms and the constituent
elements of bodies, to the development of which he
gave his life. As he himself said in one of his
subsequent writings :—

"It is the first step that is the heroic step. It
has to be taken in the dark, it has to be taken alone;
it can be taken only by a man who is capable of taking all the past along with him, and it cannot be
taken by him on whom the bounded present has
already crystallised, changing him into a pillar of
salt."

This will give an idea of the fibre of the man.
While he was still a student at Edinburgh, he wrote
to me as follows :—

"Your views regarding theorising accord with
mine. [I forget what my views were, but probably
they meant that theorising, as is implied by the word,
meant to *see* clearly.] I verily believe, and am prepared
to prove that, notwithstanding the sound and fury that
is eternally raised in our ears by modern writers
regarding the inductive philosophy, very few of the
great discoveries since Bacon's time have been made
by analysis. Many who make such a *fracas* about
the connection of cause and effect, and the *Novum
Organum* in these fruitless and laboured prefaces, are
knaves who would, though asses, dress themselves in
the lion's hide, and palm off their bastard products as
legitimate. Others, again, after they have discovered
by synthesis, go on (half unconsciously) to erect a
fabric from foundation upwards, just as the architect,
after seeing in the perspective of his brain the beauty
and grandeur of a fancied edifice, commences and pur-
sues its construction. The common, and I believe

the most successful, way of philosophising proceeds in
this manner. A man endowed with genius surveys
a pile of facts which has been collected partly by
former theorisers in order to stablish their vantage
ground, and partly by the myriads of idiots who
crowd the highways of science. He conceives (or
perceives, if you will) a bond of union whereby they
may be all linked together in a glorious series of
relations. He generalises; he in fact forms a theory;
he applies the touchstone of truth; it bears the touch
in the manner in which it has been applied; it is
accepted; and what if it go the way of all living;
what if it crumble into nullity like its predecessors?
Has he not added to the number of known facts, as
former theorisers had done, and pointed out mines
(perhaps of gold) for the unmotived to work? Is
not all human knowledge valuable only for its facts?
Is not the cause of humanity thus eminently served
by this disposition to speculate? Did Davy not conceive that the alkalis and earths are metallic oxides,
and then prove it? Did not Œrsted perceive that
electricity and magnetism were identical, and then
prove it? Did Newton not conceive the identity of
terrestrial attraction and the celestial forces, and then
throw around this conception the gorgeous illumination of mathematical evidence?

"The theories of a day are the expression of
what is *known* in that day, and are the moving
springs of that knowledge's progression. Theories,
like empires, pass away, and are no more known upon
the earth. That of yesterday is mocked, and to-day's
may share its fate to-morrow! And must we ever
grope on in miserable doubt? Shall we never arrive
at ultimate principles as well as ultimate facts? Shall
no granite be found which shall stand the wear of
time? Have we *no* test whereby we may ascertain
when we have clasped the golden things we looked
for, *when* we may revel in intellectual luxury in the
bosom of eternal truth, without the dread of some
monster with his MORE FACTS saying, 'What do ye?'
Aye! there is *one*, there *is* one: *Mathematical
demonstration*, and that alone. What is proved by
mathematics *must* be. No science shall, can ever, be
perfect till reduced to the absolute logic of mathematics. Astronomy, statics, hydraulics, acoustics,

and so on, are perfect, *because* they are mathematised. For instance, we shall never be certain that we have gained a last and infallible generalisation of the wondrous alchemy of our world and its grandeur, till we can reason mathematically on chemical questions. Is there any hope that we shall ever be able to do so? Yes! you and I *will* yet see that jubilee day of corpuscular science! It *shall* be proved that all the varieties of matter issue from *one* elementary atom—that the fifty-five elements at present recognised are all isomeric compounds of this one with itself, increasing in an arithmetical progression; that the affinities of each are in the ratio of their bulk, which shall *then* be known; that——shall I go on? No! It would hurt you, and it would hurt myself. If this consummation, so much to be desired, were brought about, how many thousand thousand grandeurs would it expose in every branch of human knowledge! How it would bear on the great metaphysical questions! . . . I believe firmly that no great extension of metaphysical physiology can take place until corpuscular science is perfected."

I have given this lengthy extract from Samuel Brown's letter, as it explains the dream of his life, on which his fortunes were wrecked. But I may be wrong. His dream may yet be realised; for we do not know what science may have in store for us. At all events, if he was right, he was long before his time. It is curious that the estimable Professor Robison of Edinburgh—a man of profound knowledge in physical science—entertained a belief in the possible transmutation of bodies. "The analysis of the alkalis and alkaline earths," he said, "by Guyton, Henry, and others, will presently lead, I think, to the doctrine of a reciprocal convertibility of all things into all."

Samuel Brown afterwards endeavoured to explain the doctrine to me in his chemical laboratory at Haddington, when he had the use of the apparatus

of the School of Arts, with which I was so familiar;
but I could never see my way into the gist or facts of
his theory. He had a method of converting starch
into iodine, by which he said the quantity of iodine
might be continually increased; and this was a
matter to be determined by weighing the final result.
But I never had the proofs put before me. Shortly
after, full of his supposed discovery, he brought the
subject under the notice of Faraday, one of the first
men of the day. But Faraday never put out his hand
further than he could draw it back. Though far-
reaching and imaginative, he was yet humble in his
speculation. He might have overlooked or neglected
the young inquirer; but he kindly answered him as
follows:—

"I have no hesitation in advising you to experi-
ment in support of your views, because, whether you
confirm or confute them, good must come out of your
experiments. With regard to the views themselves,
I can say nothing of them except that they are useful
in exciting the mind to inquiry. A very brief consideration of the progress of experimental philosophy
will show you that it is a great disturber of pre-
conceived theories. I have thought long and closely
on the theories of attraction and of particles and
atoms of matter, and the more I think, in association
with experiments, the less distinct does my idea of an
atom or particle of matter become."

Nothing further could be got out of Faraday.
But Samuel Brown still adhered to his opinions.
He gave a brilliant course of lectures on the Philosophy of the Sciences, in conjunction with Edward
Forbes, before the Philosophical Institution of Edinburgh. He made many friends, for everybody
admired him. The Professorship of Chemistry in
the University became vacant, and the young lecturer

appeared as a candidate. There is little doubt that he
would have been elected, for his religio-political sup-
porters were in a majority at the council. But he was
twitted with his absurd and unscientific views (for so
they were thought) about atoms and the convertibility
of matter. He was very honest, and took his stand
upon his views. He burnt his boats, blew up his
bridges, and cut off his retreat. He would bring
them under the notice of Liebig, admitted to be one
of the greatest chemists of the day. He went to
Giessen accordingly, and saw Liebig; but nothing
was ever heard of the interview. It was unsatisfactory—unconfirmatory. The election at length
took place at Edinburgh; and, as Samuel Brown had
retired, another professor was appointed.

He was still determined to wrest from Nature her
secret. I was afterwards informed by a young
chemist who had joined him, that the two took rooms
together at Blackheath, near London, and there
entered upon a series of elaborate investigations. In
order that they might confine themselves sedulously
and exclusively to their work, the two agreed to shave
off half the hair from their heads, and thus taboo
themselves, as it were, from the charms of society.
But Nature could not thus be conquered.

The next thing I saw of Brown's, was a remark-
ably clever essay on the Smallness of Doses in
Homœopathic Medicine. He seems to have been
attracted by the new treatment. After this, he wrote
many vigorous articles for the *North British Review;*
but he left for a time, or at least he did not pursue,
his old walk of science. His cousin, Dr John Brown
(of *Rab and his Friends*), says of him :—

"His wings were too much for him. He was for
ever climbing the Mount Sinais and Pisgahs of

Science, to speak with Him whose haunt they were—climbing there all alone and in the dark, and with much peril, if haply he might descry the break of day and the promised land. . . . His fate has been a mournful and a strange one; but he knew it, and encountered it with a full knowledge of what it entailed."

During the later years of Samuel Brown's life, he was seized with a fatal disease from which there was little hope of recovery. He went to Derbyshire (where he tried mesmerism), then to London, and finally returned to Edinburgh. The last letter I had from him was towards the end of his life. I had written an article about his father, the founder of Itinerating Libraries, in a London Journal, and he desired to have a copy of it. He said he was ill, fatally ill, but he desired to do a little duty to his father before he died. The Memoir afterwards appeared. Poor Brown died in his thirty-ninth year. He was most lovable—as a boy and as a man. He was perhaps too bright for daily use. He was fascinatingly brilliant—impulsive in his speculations —and, as many thought, a great deal too rapid in his conclusions. And yet his cousin, Dr John Brown, said of him and his theories :—

"Some of us may live to see '*Resurgam*' inscribed over Samuel Brown's untimely grave, and applied with gratitude and honour to him whose eyes closed in darkness on the one great object of his life, and the hopes of whose 'unaccomplished years' lie buried with him."

Note.—Though he "could not see his way into" these speculations of Samuel Brown, the modern theory of electrons and the recently discovered phenomena of radio activity, which they vaguely anticipate, seem to justify Dr Smiles' recognition of genius in the striking personality of his friend.—ED.

CHAPTER VI

A ROLLING STONE GATHERS NO MOSS

ONE of my intimate friends in Haddington was George Scoular—a man of whom a great deal might have been made. Though constitutionally delicate, he had a vigorous mind, which teemed with imagination. Like everybody else in those days, he was a great politician, and took an immense interest in the reform cause. He first came to light at a public meeting held to petition Parliament in aid of Municipal Reform. To the surprise of his friends, who before had seen nothing in that pale, delicate man, with his face overshadowed by his massive forehead, he made a powerful speech. He carried the meeting with him, and the petition was enthusiastically adopted. He spoke again and again, always improving. But his constitution was too weak for mental work. He was taken ill of a form of mesenteric disease, and sent for me. For change of air, I sent him, with his sister, to Portobello, near Edinburgh; and there I had my old teacher, Dr Mackintosh, called in as consulting physician. The doctor did what he could, but the case was hopeless; and shortly after George Scoular returned to Haddington, became worse, and died quite peacefully.

During my interview with Dr Mackintosh at

Portobello, he asked me how I was getting on at Haddington.

"I am not getting on," I said, "I am going off."

"How is that?"

"Too many doctors," I answered; "more than enough to doctor double the population."

"Well," he rejoined, "remember that a rolling stone gathers no moss."

"Very true," I said; "but while I have been settled there, I have gathered none whatever: I think I had better begin *to roll*."

"Well, of course, you are the best judge."

And so we parted.

Another of my friends was Dr Carstairs of North Berwick, about nine miles off. He was of about my own age, and was, like myself, struggling for a practice. He was settled on the coast, having the sea on one side and the land on the other; so that he had less country to travel over. While laid up, on one occasion, by an inflamed throat, he asked me if I could come down and assist him with his patients. I did so, and remained a few days. While there, I was sent for to attend a remarkable character named Jock Whitecross. He was a fisherman at Canty Bay, a little fishing village lying almost immediately under the ruins of the ancient castle of Tantallon. Jock had a lease of the Bass Rock, which lay, a big round rock in the Firth of Forth, screaming with solan geese and flights of sea-birds, only a few miles off.

Not long before, Jock had lost his son—a finely-built young fellow—whose boat had been upset in a stormy sea, and his body was washed ashore on the strand almost in front of his father's door. Jock, on speaking of the sad event, said to a neighbour, "Eh, man, the Lord's gien me a sair whup the day." Jock had to deliver twelve solan geese a year to the minister of the parish, as his "teinds." But the minister of the parish having complained about the deliveries of the geese, and the fishy taste of the birds, Jock delivered the whole of them one day together; on which the minister was worse satisfied than ever.

"I canna make them into butcher meat," said Jock, "nor can I be fashed to deliver them as ye like, so there they are, helter skelter."

There were many similar stories told about Jock; but this was to be the last of him. I found him attacked with cholera of a bad sort. He was dying when I entered his cottage, and when I left, his last breath had departed. Such are the scenes that country doctors have often to witness.

Whether it was because of my frequent visits to the neighbourhood of North Berwick, or how it was I know not, but one night I was sent for to attend a case at Redhouse, on the way thither, about seven miles from Haddington. After attending to it—and it was altogether a gratuitous case—I was riding homeward on my old mare. It was about two o'clock in the morning, and having been up for two nights previously, I was very sleepy. While going down hill, the horse put its foot on a stone and tumbled down. I fell over its head, and lit upon my white hat, which was crushed; but it saved my head. I got up, thoroughly awakened, but the horse was off. I walked after it for some four miles, where I found the poor creature, with its broken knees, standing at a door where I had called a few days before. I parted with the horse, and did not buy another. "The game was not worth the candle."

Among the various things which I did to fill up

my abundant time, was to write a book! That was a difficult matter. But I made up my mind, read and studied diligently, and prepared the sheets for the printer. My subject was *Physical Education*—not a bad idea. Dr Combe's work on *The Principles of Physiology applied to the Preservation of Health*, had been found of great use; and it occurred to me that a work devoted more particularly to instructions as to the Nurture and Management of Children might be equally useful. It was, at all events, beginning at the beginning, with the education of the human creature. For philosophy has been in the wrong in not descending more deeply into physical man, for it is there that the moral man lies concealed. I took for my motto the following passage from Paley: "The health and virtue of a child's future life are considerations so superior to all others, that whatever is likely to have the smallest influence upon these, deserves the parents' first attention." I accordingly treated of nursing, air, and exercise; and endeavoured to show that the due education of the body was the basis of moral and intellectual culture; protesting, at the same time, against cramming the youthful mind with unnecessary knowledge.

I did the best that I could in preparing the work. It might have been better done. Indeed, it *was* shortly after much better done by Dr Andrew Combe himself, in his *Treatise on the Physiological and Moral Management of Infancy*. But I did not know, at the time I wrote my book, that that excellent man was engaged in such a treatise. When finished, I took my manuscript to the Messrs Chambers of Edinburgh, who were engaged at that time in bringing out many entertaining and useful works. I saw William Chambers, and he told me that he expected Dr

Combe would prepare for their house a similar work. As I had the MS. with me, I went to Mr Boyd (of Oliver & Boyd), whom I knew, and asked him to furnish me with an estimate of the cost of printing and publishing my little treatise. The result was, that it was shortly after in the hands of the printer. But before it appeared, I received a letter from William Chambers, saying that he had been disappointed in Dr Combe—that he was about to publish a treatise on his own account, and asking for the perusal of my manuscript. It was too late, and my book came out, and was well reviewed in the *Athenæum, Chambers's Journal*, and other periodicals.

I only printed 750 copies. The book sold fairly well, but if it paid its expenses, that was all. During the last few years, the advertisements swallowed up the proceeds of the sales. At last there remained about 100 copies of the unbound sheets. These I disposed of in the following manner. There was a Mr Slater, related to a friend of mine, who had brought out a cheap series of books in London, including Emerson's Essays, and Frederica Bremer's Tales—(the last very much to the disgust of William Howitt, who was left with a whole room full of printed and unsold volumes, translated by Mary Howitt)—and these were well known at the time as "Slater's Shilling Series." Though the books had a large sale, they were too cheap, and eventually ruined the publisher. Slater gathered his traps together, and was about to leave for Australia to pursue his trade as a bookseller. He asked me if I could give him a lift. I made him a present of all the unsold copies of my book; and I hope they proved of use to the colonists and their children. I afterwards found that the emigrant had married a young wife and settled at Geelong, where, with her help, he brought out a new series of Slater.

The last of my occupations to which I must refer, as it had some influence on my future life, was the writing of leading articles for an Edinburgh newspaper. Dr Thomas Murray, a Lecturer on Political Economy, was at that time editor of the *Edinburgh Weekly Chronicle.* I knew the doctor, and he asked me occasionally to send him paragraphs of intelligence. I went a little further, and sent him regular articles. In course of time, he promoted these to the leading columns; and I wrote with the "we," as if I were the editor. I became a regular, and as Dr Murray afterwards said, "a much-prized contributor." Might not this prove an opening into the press? I thought so at the time, and when an advertisement appeared in *Tait's Magazine* for an editor of the *Leeds Times* in the room of Robert Nicoll, the poet, who died in December 1837, I applied for the position.

I received an answer from the proprietor, requesting me to send a specimen of my powers, and mentioning as the subject, an article on the Suffrage. I wrote one, and sent it by return of post. It was approved, but I was informed that, on further consideration—as the *Leeds Times* was strongly opposed by a new paper, the *Northern Star,* the organ of the Chartists or extreme Radicals—it was thought necessary to appoint as editor a gentleman of great newspaper experience, one who had recently been editor of the *True Sun,* a Mr Charles Hooton. He was certainly a most accomplished man, an able writer, the author of the *Adventures of Bilberry Thurland, Colin Clink,* and other clever works of fiction. I could not complain of this, and I accord-

ingly altogether gave up the prospect. Something
else would, without doubt, turn up.

In the meantime I arranged for the collection of
my accounts, sold off my stock of drugs, and prepared to leave Haddington. I did so in May 1838.
My intention was to proceed to Leyden or Heidelberg, and take the degree of M.D.; and, besides,
to learn the German language and improve my knowledge of French. With that view I took leave of my
old town, and set out for Hull by sea, accompanied
with testimonials—from the Rev. Mr Hogg, my
revered minister; Mr Graham, my old teacher;
Dr Burton, my attached friend; Provost Lea, my
neighbour and fellow-violoncello player, and many
more dear friends and acquaintances.

Dr Burton truly said that, "in a limited and not
increasing population, under the professional care of
old-established practitioners, the opportunities for a
young medical man, however talented, to display his
skill and attainments, are so few that they do not
merit a sacrifice of the time necessary for the trial;
and I believe you have done wisely in the step you
have taken, and that you deserve to succeed, and
will succeed, wherever you settle." I may add that
Dr Carstairs had already left North Berwick, and
had settled at Sheffield, where he was doing well;
that Dr Cruickshank afterwards left Haddington
to practise in North Berwick, and eventually in
Australia; and that Dr Burton himself shortly after
left for Walsall, and entered upon a large practice—
thereby reducing the number of practitioners in
Haddington to something like the proper average
number.

I may add that, before I left Haddington, I was
elected a member of the Town Council, and that,

E

had I waited, I might even have been made a Bailie!
But I could not wait any longer. I wanted to make
a living; and for that purpose it was necessary for
me to look out for some other field of labour.

I left Leith for Hull by steamer about the middle
of May 1838. As we passed down the Firth of
Forth by the Bass Rock, the gulls and solan geese
were screaming more loudly than usual, and wheel-
ing in wild convulsions round the cliffs. A storm
was evidently brewing, and by the time we reached
St Abb's Head it had come on furiously. It was a
very wild night. The winds blew, the rain fell, and
the storm raged. The waves swept the deck, and as
I was unwilling to go to my sleeping-berth, I went
down to the engine-room behind the boilers for
warmth. At length, I found it necessary to go to
my cabin—and then I felt very ill—the first and only
time I have ever been discomforted when at sea.

In the early morning I went on deck. The waves
were still surging and the wind blowing furiously.
I noticed the captain peering through the mist at
some object behind us. What was he looking for?
It was for the *Pegasus*, the rival steamer. He feared
that she had gone down during the night, for she was
not so good a sea boat as the one we were in. But
there she was behind us, with her white funnel and
red hull, far away in the distance. Only five years
after, the *Pegasus* was wrecked on the Fern Islands,
and lost nearly all her passengers.

We reached Hull in safety, and after resting there
for a few days, I embarked on the *Sea Horse* for
Rotterdam, which was reached after a pleasant
voyage of twenty-four hours. I took up my lodgings
in an English hotel for a few days. After admiring
the Boomjees—the quay which extends for about a

mile and a quarter along the river side—and taking a
general view of the town, its public buildings, canals,
and bridges, I called upon the Rev. Mr Stevens, the
Scotch minister, to whom I had a letter of introduction. He received me kindly and gave me much
information as to the University of Leyden, which
decided me, although I had a letter to Professor
Tiedemann of Heidelberg, to go on to Leyden to take
my degree. I went thither by the Trekschuyt, on
canal boat, then the popular mode of conveyance.

We travelled to Leyden through a rich flat
district, past country houses, villages, windmills,
gardens, green pastures, and canals spanned by
bridges stretching in all directions. Then came the
old collegiate city with its tall spires standing black
against the setting sun. I was taken by a fellow-
passenger to a *logement* in a retired part of the town,
where I remained for a few weeks. The family consisted of host and hostess, two sons, and three
daughters. They kept a small private hotel, in which
I was the only boarder. The father and two of the
daughters were very musical; and I greatly enjoyed
their performances. I soon felt quite at home, and
got to know a great deal about Dutch manners and
customs.

In due course of time I submitted myself to an
examination by Professor Van der Hoeven, Dean of
the Faculty of Medicine, and other gentlemen. It
was by no means so thorough as the one at Edinburgh some years before. Being conducted in a sort
of dog Latin, the same amount of information could
not be educed. It was, however, more costly than I
had expected, and nearly emptied my purse. But I
had still enough money left after the first examination
to enable me to make my proposed walking tour

through Holland and up the Rhine. Leaving my luggage behind me, I shouldered a knapsack containing a change of linen and some books, and left Leyden by the eastern gate on the morning of the 15th of June.

It was a very fine day, bright and sunny. Of all the ways of seeing a country, commend me to the Walk. A staff in hand, and kit on back, and away along the high road, turning into the byeways, if you like; resting occasionally under the porch of a village hostel; then on again, hearing the bells tolling far away across the plain ; watching the passing changes of the clouds, and how they cast their purple shadows on the foreground, while through an opening in the skies a stream of bright sunshine illumines the white sails of a distant windmill, or of the Dutch boats as they work their way among the farmsteads and cattle-fields. This is the true way to see and enjoy a country. To appreciate thoroughly the fresh and healthy and beautiful in Nature, you must walk; and those only can enjoy the pleasure who are willing to give to the work the requisite amount of physical exercise.*

* I may mention I took copious notes during my residence abroad. I afterwards worked them up into a series of articles which were published in a London Journal. They form enough to make a book ; but they are not worthy of republication.

CHAPTER VII

I HAD performed my little tour. I had enjoyed my little holiday. It was all very pleasant. I had made many friends while I was abroad. They had been very kind to me. I had learnt something of modern languages : and a good deal of human nature. Now I was about to enter on the active business of life. I desired first to get to London, in order to make inquiries about the NEW WORLD on the other side of the globe. Hence my voyage to the Thames, instead of to the Humber.

Our steamer reached the shores of England on a misty morning in the beginning of September 1838. I was awakened early by the ringing of the bell aboveboard—indicating a fog. On making my way on deck, I found we were enveloped in mist. The snortings of the steamer ceased for a time, and the sailors heaved the lead to ascertain the depth of water beneath us. We groped our way ; "go on slowly" was shouted by the captain, then "stop her." And there we lay, hearing many bells about us from adjoining ships, which told us that we were approaching the mouth of the river.

After about an hour, the mist slowly cleared away. It rolled past us in banks of cloud ; and then we saw where we were. The low shores of the English coast lay on either side, Essex on the north, Kent on the south. "That is the Nore light!" We were now in the mouth of the Thames, nearly opposite Sheerness. We could see the great hulls lying in the mouth of the Medway, and a paddle-wheel steamer, the *Black Eagle* (I think), one of the first used by the Government, throwing out clouds of black smoke. The river became busier. Steamers, wherries, ships—their sails bellied out by the wind—came down the Thames in numbers; some were coasters, some were foreign bound, some were destined for the furthest ends of the earth.

We passed the Hope, and the old fort of Tilbury on one side, and the town of Gravesend on the other. Here many vessels were lying anchored in the stream, awaiting their complements of seamen or passengers. Some of them were three-masted East Indian ships, and loomed large in the distance. Boats were plying between them and the pier; and the whole scene presented a busy appearance. This was the outer boundary of the port of London, where outward-bound vessels received their final clearances. And here the revenue officers came on board to take custody of our luggage, as well as the river pilot to navigate our steamer up the river.

From this point the Thames became busier and busier. We passed numbers of colliers floated up by the tide, and met outward-bound ships sailing down, fishing-boats, yawls, wherries, lighters, smacks, and vessels of all kinds, were seen on every side; while along the banks were workshops and manufactories, the scenes of busy industry. We saw comparatively little of the inland country after passing Greenhithe —the river being shut in by embankments—until we

passed Plumstead Marshes and reached Woolwich.
There we observed rows of cannon and cannon-balls
piled along the Royal Dockyard wharf, in front
of the long range of manufacturing workshops.
Above Woolwich, a stretch of low wooded hills
was seen extending over the lower ground, the tower
of Charlton Church forming a picturesque object.

Now Millwall was reached—the river still alive
with craft of every sort. From this point upward,
the banks present an almost continuous range of
buildings. The noble front of the Greenwich
Hospital—more like a palace than a hospital—
stood before us in its glory, one of the finest works
of Sir Christopher Wren. Behind the hospital I
could see the Royal Observatory, situated on the
elevated grounds amidst the trees of the park—the
Observatory from which British seamen reckon their
longitude all over the world. Then we sailed
past Deptford Dockyard, and up Limehouse Reach,
to the Pool, which was crowded with shipping. We
reached the point under which the Thames Tunnel
crossed the river, and then the old tumble-down
houses of Wapping, almost overhanging the water.
Behind were the magnificent docks, with masts
shooting up like a forest for miles. Then the
venerable Tower! And this was London, the great
city which is the centre of so many aspirations.

I was alone in the place, though in the midst of
millions. I knew nobody, and nobody knew me. A
feeling of melancholy is apt to intrude upon one in
the midst of a crowd of the unknown. The only
people who regarded me, and seemed to care for me,
were the 'bus conductors, who beckoned to me, and
wished me to patronise their vehicles. But youth is
vigorous, hopeful, and naturally cheerful. I made

my way to a boarding-house in Poland Street, Oxford Street, to which I had been recommended by my brother, who had lodged there the year before. The landlady was willing to accommodate me for a week or two, and I took up my abode there.

It was a pleasure to me to make the acquaintance of Mazzini, who was then boarding in the house. It was during the period of his first exile in England. I was struck by his noble yet melancholy countenance. He was then suffering from the loss of his young Italian friends, but still more from disappointment and loss of hope in the future of his country. He had sought refuge at first in Switzerland, but his persecutors having tracked him thither, the Swiss Government, terrified by the threats of its despotic neighbours, urged him to leave the country, and he eventually took refuge in England—still, as ever, the land of the free.

"Never shall I forget it while I live," said Mazzini himself, "nor ever utter without a throb of gratitude the name of the land wherein I now write, which became to me almost as a second country, and in which I found the lasting consolation of affection, in a life embittered by delusions and destitute of all joy."

And yet he continued devoted to the idea of the united nationality of his country, and still spoke hopefully of the revival of cosmopolitanism, of the brotherhood of all men, and the amelioration of all through the work of all.

I understood that he was then supporting himself as well as some other Italian exiles, by writing articles in the English reviews—for he understood the English language thoroughly—and that he was thus drawing the attention of the English people to the Italian question. Finding, also, a number of poor Italian boys about the streets of London— mostly playing for their *padres*, who treated them savagely — Mazzini started a school, and en- deavoured to teach them something that was good. He himself supplied the greater part of the funds from the proceeds of his literary labours, and took his full share of the teaching of young people, in what was likely to promote their moral and intellectual progress. He also lectured to them, as well as to Italian working men, on Italian history, the outlines of natural philosophy, and the lives of great men, so as to elevate them above subjection and poverty, and fortify their minds in serious thought and earnest purpose.

But to return to my own special business in London. I called upon Mr Rowland Hill at his offices in the Adelphi Terrace, and presented my letter of introduction from his uncle, Provost Lea of Haddington. Mr Hill received me very kindly. The provost had told me all about his history. Rowland Hill had first been a teacher at Hill Top School, Hazelwood, near Birmingham; and a very effective teacher he was. He had there published a work on *Public Education*, and *The Hazelwood Magazine*. In 1826, at the suggestion of Lord Brougham and others, he and his brothers founded a similar school at Bruce Castle, near London. This undertaking proved satisfactory, but the work con- nected with it broke down Mr Hill's health, and he left it and travelled abroad for a time. But being a man of great activity and ingenuity, he sought for new work on his return home. He was one of the founders of the Society for the Diffusion of Useful Knowledge, the inventor of a Printing Press, the author of a paper, prepared for Lord Brougham, on "Home Colonies" for the gradual extinction of pauperism and the diminution of crime. He was also devising his great scheme of Postal Reform. But, meanwhile, a project had been formed for the colonisation of the then unoccupied territory of South Australia; an Act for the purpose was obtained; commissioners were appointed, and of this body Mr Rowland Hill was appointed secretary. It was in reference to the position that he held in this project, that I called upon him.

In his usual kindly manner, he gave me much good advice. He did not think that South Australia as yet held out any inducements to professional men. It was capitalists who would invest money in the lands of the Colony—labourers of all kinds, skilled and otherwise—ploughmen, servants, and shepherds who knew something about flocks. I had no pretensions to take rank amongst any of these classes, and I felt it necessary to abandon my idea of emigrating to that part of the world.

"Stay at home," said Rowland Hill; "with an active mind like yours, there is plenty of room for you here. I find that, like myself, you have written about Education. I have read your book—it is very good: my uncle sent it me. Go on in the same direction: there is plenty of room." I thanked him for his encouragement. He concluded by asking me to come and dine with him at 2 Burton Crescent, where he then lived. He would introduce me to Mrs Hill and his family, and I should meet Dr Bowring.

I went accordingly, and had the pleasure of making Mrs Hill's acquaintance, and that of her two charming little girls. I also met Dr Bowring. He was then distinguished as a philologist, political writer, and statistician. He had been editor of the *Westminster Review*, and for some time member of Parliament for the Kilmarnock Burghs. Much of the conversation was new to me, and very interesting, ranging over a wide field of topics. While I had been abroad in Germany, the queen had been crowned, a rebellion had broken out in Canada, stormy proceedings had taken place in Parliament, and the agitation for the Charter had begun at Birmingham. The conversation turned upon the scheme of Postal Reform, about which Mr Rowland Hill had already published his pamphlet. Indeed, on the 13th of August, the preceding month, the select committee had reported in favour of the scheme. I could not fail to spend a pleasant and most instructive evening in such society.

A few days later I went to the public meeting held in New Palace Yard, on the 17th of September. The object was to petition Parliament in favour of the People's Charter, the movement in favour of which had been initiated at Birmingham a few days before. The chief speaker was Feargus O'Connor, who was loud and mouthing. Richardson, his disciple, also spoke. Hetherington, Lovett, Fraser of Edinburgh, and Ebenezer Elliott of Sheffield, were there. The proceedings were marred by the physical force swagger of some of the speakers. I did not much admire the London crowd. They seemed loafers and idlers, not working men. Palace Yard then formed a square. Opposite the platform in front of the hotel, from which the orators spoke, was the entrance to Westminster Hall, towards which the speakers often pointed. I kept clear of the crowd, and looked after my pockets. Of course, everything

passed off with "loud cheers." The movement was
fairly begun.

The next visit I paid was to a dear and estimable
lady, whose contributions to the *Monthly Repository*
I had read and re-read—I mean Mrs M. Leman
Gillies. Before leaving Haddington, I had received
the following letter from her :—

"43 ALLSOP TERRACE, REGENT PARK,
"LONDON, 4th January 1838.

"DEAR SIR,—A few days ago, I was gratified by
the receipt of your excellent little work on Physical
Education, and the very flattering letter by which it
was accompanied. My first impulse was to write to
you immediately, for I feared that I might already
lie justly open to the charge of ingratitude or
negligence, your letter being dated as far back as
the twelfth of last month. But it was suggested
to me that I had better first read the work, and that
so doing would enable me to reply with more
pleasure and satisfaction both to the author and
myself. This advice (which you will not think the
worse of me for taking so readily, as it was given
by my husband—the brother of an oftentimes near
neighbour of yours, Lord Gillies), I acted upon;
and I have read your book with great pleasure and
advantage, for the advice and instruction which it contains admit of application beyond the beautiful little
atoms of humanity for whom it is designed. I shall
send the work immediately to a sister of mine, now
staying at Jersey, who has a large and lovely family
of children, and also to another married sister,
yet more remote, who, like myself, has become a
graft upon a Scottish family. Your name is a fit
harbinger of your useful and benevolent work, and
it will be welcomed everywhere with that mute but
bright language which your name expresses.

"I am delighted that you say so much on these
important and much neglected matters—Ventilation
and the Skin. No building should be erected
without immediate reference to the first—no being

exist without great regard to the latter. Well-constructed dwellings and an easy access to warm baths would, I am persuaded, beyond anything else, improve the useful classes of these kingdoms, and form essential auxiliaries to the Schools and Institutes, which, from the depths of my heart, I rejoice to see rising everywhere. Free lungs and pure skin would introduce that cheerfulness and suavity of manner in which the working people of England, at least, are so deficient. That universal instrument of Divine Benevolence—the Air, which no set of Exclusionists have yet been able to appropriate—awakens, when it is permitted to permeate the frame, feelings analogous to itself—activity, the handmaid of industry, springs up, and cheerfulness, the inspirer of sociality, goes forth.

"Greatly, also, is the human family indebted to you for your advocacy of Singing as a means of health and branch of education. Ignorantly and ungratefully have we neglected one of the most beautiful gifts of a bountiful God. How many hundred years have the birds on every bough breathed to us admonition and example—yet all that has been effected in this country has been to make Music a sickly exotic in the homes of luxury, and even there ministering more to vanity than anything else.

"Let me not forget to tell you that 'C'* is the daughter of Dr Southwood Smith, and is now Mrs Hill, of Wisbeach, near Cambridge. I have given you this information without consulting her, but I cannot imagine that I do wrong.

"I hope, my dear sir, that your book will meet all the success which it merits—your *best* reward is certain; of *that* it is impossible you should be defrauded.

"Pray accept my thanks, and believe me respectfully yours,

"M. LEMAN GILLIES."

---

* I may mention that a series of very interesting articles appeared in the *Monthly Repository* entitled, " Memoranda of Observations and Experiments in Education." They were signed "C," and were afterwards republished collectively by "Caroline Southwood Hill." My interest in the articles led me to inquire of Mrs L. Gillies as to the author.

It was the least I could do, while in London, to visit the lady who had been so polite to me. I did so, and had much pleasant conversation with her.

At the house of her relative, Miss Margaret Gillies, in Millfield Lane, Highgate, besides Mrs Leman Gillies, I had the pleasure of meeting Dr Southwood Smith, who lived near at hand, author of the *Philosophy of Health*, and the friend of Jeremy Bentham; Edwin Chadwick, already becoming distinguished in connection with the Sanitary movement; Miss Mary Gillies, an amiable and most accomplished lady; and a charming girl, very much made of by everybody. I thought she was precocious, but she was merely quick and cultivated, from mixing much in the best society. She was Dr Smith's granddaughter, and the daughter of " C," referred to in Mrs Leman Gillies's letter to me. She became afterwards extensively known and beloved; and many now bless the name of Miss Octavia Hill.

I need not go through the sights I saw during my first visit to London. But it was not the "sights" I saw, but the enormous size of London, that impressed me. I had been brought up in a country town where I knew everybody, even the cocks and hens running about the streets. Now I was in a great city of some three millions of people, where I was only a stray unit, knowing nobody. The busy throng of the streets, the rush of life through the thoroughfares, the tide of human necessity which rolled along from day to day, could not fail to excite my sense of wonder. London was a new world, unlike everything I had before seen, or even imagined. It filled my mind, and took possession of my being.

Such is the bulk of London; it is impossible for

any one to see it all, to know it all, to understand it
all, outgrowing, as it daily does, all possible means
of seeing and knowing it. Londoners themselves,
who spend their daily life in it, often know as little
about it as country people do. The inhabitant of
the West End knows as little of those of the East
End, as the latter do of Wales or the Highlands. To
most men, London may be an utter solitude, if they
wish it. They may live there unknowing and
unknown. In the midst of millions they may be
alone, far more than they can possibly be in the
country town, where every man's life and concerns
become the business of everybody. In London, there
is an entire emancipation from tattlers and busy-
bodies. Hazlitt says that you can enjoy the greatest
personal freedom in the world there; and that
"personal merit is at a prodigious discount in the
provinces." That may be; but at the same time in
London there is a want of personal sympathy.
Though there is no scandal, there is no help. The
people are strangers to each other; each is intent
upon his own business, knowing nothing, and caring
less about what his neighbours are doing, or feeling,
or suffering. Jostling each other in the streets, they
press forward eagerly in pursuit of their special
object. The country big man feels himself nobody
in London. There is, indeed, no such remedy for
provincial vanity and self-importance as a visit to
London. When the Highland chief paid his first
visit, his retainers thought that London would be
thrown into commotion by the event. But London
took no notice. To account for it, the chief explained
that "London was quite in a state of confusion when
I was there!" It was, however, only its ordinary
state of confusion.

There is one thing that Londoners may boast of —extreme mental liberty. A man may think and speak as he likes—within the law. No man is muzzled or shouted down on account of his opinions, or exposed to the petty persecutions he has sometimes to endure in the provinces. He need not be a hypocrite; he has no pretence for being a hypocrite. Public opinion in London may be inactive and slow to manifest itself; but private opinion is active, free, and independent. This, to my mind, forms one of the chief attractions of London life, for it is one of the greatest privileges which free-minded men can desire.

One word more, before I leave London. Dr Epps had so strongly eulogised my little book on Physical Education, in his published lectures on Physiology, that I thought it right to call upon him and thank him for his good services. He received me kindly; and, amongst other things, he told me that he had a great many applications from the country for homeopathic practitioners. "I recommend you to study the subject," he said; "and I can send you down to Leeds, where there is a splendid opening." He spoke with absolute confidence of the truth of the new views, as if not a word could be said on the opposite side. Dr Epps was always a man to be "cock-sure." And yet, homeopathy, as first presented, never seemed to me entirely acceptable. I was told in Germany that if a grain of opium in solution were dropped into the Rhine at Schaffhausen, it could only have reached sufficient dilution to be administered in the millionth-grain dose by the time it reached Coblentz. No doubt small doses of poisons as well as medicines often produce powerful effects. But I had been accustomed to very appreciable doses of most things, and I could not, for mere personal interest, give up my views. I promised, however, to look further into the matter, but meanwhile declined the kind invitation. I parted with Dr Epps, the best of friends.

I then proceeded to Sheffield, to see my friend Carstairs, whom I had known and assisted at North Berwick. There was no railway then through the Midlands. The London and Birmingham railway had been opened throughout on the 17th of September, the day on which the Chartist meeting had been held in Palace Yard. I preferred, however, to go round by sea; and accordingly proceeded to Hull. I had a pleasant voyage, and went to the boarding-house overlooking the Humber, where I had been well accommodated some five months before.

From Hull, I went by steamer up the Humber to Thorne, on the river Don. Here a coach was waiting to take us on to Sheffield. We went by Doncaster—a bright little town. The day was fine and sunny. The trees were tipped with gold, and already assuming their autumnal look. We passed Coningsburgh Castle, the famous place described in *Ivanhoe*, supposed to have been the home of Athelstan the Unready. It stands on a wooded hill close by the road. Its round towers and flying buttresses had a romantic effect, and the scenery around was most charming. It was true English scenery.

The coach took us through Rotherham to Sheffield, over which hung a pall of dark smoke. We went along the banks of the Don, which became filthy and black as we proceeded upwards. Collieries,

F

quarries, and iron works, were on every side. The
houses became continuous, until we reached the
great teeming centre of the cutlery manufacture.
Tilt hammers were beating, grinding mills were
turning, and chimneys were vomiting forth their
smoke.

My friend was ready to receive me. He made
me welcome, and I soon felt at home. He was
working his way into a good practice, and in his
leisure hours he was writing articles for the *Sheffield
Iris*, which he found to be a pleasant as well as a
profitable employment. One of the first persons to
whom I was introduced was John Bridgeford, the por-
prietor of that journal—a genial, honest man, whose
friendship I then made. Through him I got to know
his friends, who were large-hearted like himself,
among others James Montgomery, the poet, who
looked thin and old. He still continued to write,
though not for the *Iris*, of which he had at one
time been editor. But perhaps still more interesting was my introduction to Ebenezer Elliott,
the Corn-law Rhymer, with whom I afterwards
became much better acquainted. I had seen him
before at the meeting in Palace Yard; but now I
saw him in his own warehouse.

I was taken up a flight of wooden stairs to his
office in Gibraltar Street, and there I found him
standing behind the counter. The place was somewhat dingy—fit enough for iron and steel dealing,
but scarcely giving one the indication of a poet's
study. I was introduced; and though quiet at first,
he soon opened up, and, pacing up and down, talked
bitterly of "those dirt-kings—the tax-gorged lords
of land." He was rather slightly formed; his
features were somewhat marked by the smallpox;

his very shaggy eyebrows overhung his blue eyes;
and his head was covered with thick grey hair. The
thing uppermost in his mind was "The Bread Tax."
He had already been publishing vehement poetry on
the subject; and he soon became well known as
"The Corn-law Rhymer."

I mentioned the fact of his appearance on the
platform in Palace Yard.

"Ah!" he said, "were you there? that fellow
Feargus O'Connor will ruin that cause. The threat
of physical force will never do: we want the power
of public opinion. In the long run, it must
prevail."

I referred to his poems on the Bread Tax.

"People think me ferocious," he said, "but I
cannot write gently on that great crime. And yet
I could not hurt a fly, even if it stung me."

Elliott was the Burns of his time. He lived in a
manufacturing town, instead of in the country; and
he saw industry hampered, and working people
distressed, by what he thought to be a law against
nature and humanity. Hence the vehemence of his
songs against the Corn Laws. The more beautiful
side of the poet's nature is revealed when he takes to
the Green Lawn, the Open Heath, or the Wild
Mountain, and writes about "The Wonders of the
Lawn," "The Excursion, "The Dying Boy to the
Sloe-blossom," or "Don and Rother." Then his
anger is disarmed, and he takes nature to his
bosom. Yet there is reason to believe that he
gained little reputation by his tender and gentler
effusions; for it was only when he became in a
manner notorious as "The Corn-law Rhymer"
that his merits as a true poet began to be
discovered.

Before leaving Sheffield, my friends Carstairs and Bridgeford strongly recommended me to settle down at Doncaster, where there was then a good opening for a general practitioner. I was disposed to take their advice, and returned home for the purpose of making the necessary arrangements. Bridgeford accompanied me on the top of the coach as far as Hathersage, on my way to Manchester. I knew nobody in Manchester, and proceeded to Liverpool by the railway, which had been opened a few years before. The ride was something surprising; and the speed was then thought unrivalled. I little thought that in a future year I should write the life of the engineer of that railway.

After staying for a few days with a relative in Liverpool, I took steamer for Glasgow. From Glasgow, I returned home to Haddington, for it was still home; but only for a month. I collected all my "things" about me—my clothes, my instruments, my books (such as I wished to preserve), and set out again for Doncaster, for the purpose of settling down there.

I had desired any letters that might arrive for me after I left, to be sent to me, care of Mr. Scott, architect (of Gilbert and Scott), who was then living at Doncaster. On calling there, a letter was presented to me, the perusal of which had an important influence on my future career. It was from Mr Bingley, reporter for the *Leeds Times*, and was written on behalf of Mr Hobson, the proprietor of that newspaper.

The letter was to this effect: that the prosperity of the *Leeds Times* had not continued since the death of Robert Nicoll; that its circulation had fallen off, partly through the competition of the Chartist

organ, the *Northern Star*, conducted by Feargus
O'Connor; and that, though Mr Hooton was a
most able man, of great literary finish, he had
somehow not entered freely into the political movements of the neighbourhood, and that, in short, he
was about to leave, and Mr Hobson wished to
supply his place with another Scotsman.

This was certainly a great move. Dr Epps had
proposed to send me down to Leeds as a homeopathic
doctor. That offer I could not accept; as I had no
faith in homeopathy. But now came another
proposal that I should go to Leeds. It seemed as
if Leeds were to be my fate. I could not come to a
conclusion on the moment. But I would go over to
Sheffield again, and consult my friends Carstairs
and Bridgeford. When I mentioned the matter to
them, they were delighted. They recommended me
at once to accept the proposal: "it was a fine field,"
they said, "and even if you do not succeed as an
editor, the trial will afford you an opportunity of
looking about you and finding some other opening
where you can eventually succeed."

I certainly hesitated, before stepping into the
shoes of Robert Nicoll and Charles Hooton, the
one an enthusiastic poet and able editor, the other
an accomplished literary man; but, as Bridgeford
said, "You can but try," and Carstairs added, "I
know you can do it, if you use your full mind and
vigour," I came to the conclusion to abide by
their recommendation, and accordingly wrote to
the proprietor of the *Leeds Times* accepting his
proposal.

I went over to Leeds by coach, passing through
Barnsby and Wakefield, and duly arrived at the
great manufacturing town, overhung by clouds of

smoke. There I was to remain for nearly twenty years ; there I married, there all my children were born ; and there I spent about the happiest and most fruitful period of my life.

And now for the life of the provincial editor.

CHAPTER VIII

I ARRIVED in Leeds towards the end of November 1838. I had still about six weeks to spend before I began my work as editor. There was time to make acquaintance with the place, to understand the local politics, and prepare for the work to be done.

Leeds forms the centre of an immense manufacturing district. It is the heart of the woollen trade. The people are distinguished for their energy in business, commerce, and politics. They are robust, manly, industrious, shrewd, and hard-headed. When Köhl, the traveller, visited the town, he gave a very poor account of its art and architecture. It has become more ornamented since then. But though there was little art, there was a great deal of common sense and public spirit.

At the time I entered Leeds, there was a considerable amount of distress among the working people. The price of food was high, and wages were low. Good wheat was from 80s. to 86s. the quarter. In fact, the price of corn had not been so high for twenty years. All this told upon the labouring classes. The *Northern Star* was furiously preaching the Charter. Feargus O'Connor was holding torchlight meetings in the manufacturing districts, and approaching more and more to the doctrines of physical force. On the other hand, the Corn Law repealers were beginning to move, though only by very tentative steps.

The first lecture on the subject was given by Mr Paulton at Leeds on the 29th December 1838. Though Mr Baines, one of the members for the borough, was in the chair, the meeting was very thinly attended. The lecture was read, with not much force; and though the lecturer was thanked, but little effect was produced. A fortnight later, a public meeting was held in the Cloth Hall Yard, for the repeal of the Corn Laws. The meeting was largely attended, partly because Feargus O'Connor was to be there. Mr George Goodman introduced the motion for repeal, and was opposed by the Chartist leader. I presented myself for the first time before a Leeds audience, and moved the previous question. "Who is he? What is he?" I heard asked on every side. "It's the new editor of the *Leeds Times!*" In this way, I soon got to be known. I may add that, after a long palaver, Feargus O'Connor was defeated, and the resolutions were carried by a considerable majority.

I may mention that a meeting had been held at Manchester a few days before, at which the Anti-Corn-Law Association had been formed. Mr Cobden appeared at this meeting, and recommended those present to invest part of their property in the fund, to save the rest from confiscation. Subscriptions were at once put down for large sums; the *Anti-Corn-Law Circular* was started; and the movement was fairly initiated.

Meanwhile I proceeded with my own work—the editing of the paper. I had perhaps some of the qualities necessary for an editor. I had plenty of energy, and ability for work. I was ready for it at all times—early in the morning, at midday, and at midnight. When a country doctor, I had always been ready to ride at any minute, in all weathers; now I was equally ready to write.

It was pleasant work too. I had to read no end of newspapers, periodicals, and reviews. My pair of scissors took the place of my lancet. I clipped and cut, and made piles of extracts, without fear of injury to any human life. Then I used the paste pot with effect, and made up my slips for the paper. Much of my reading was skimming, but I was soon able to get the gist of a thing.

Readiness and quickness were great points. A newspaper editor cannot be a writer of "moods." He must be ready at noon, ready at night; quick of apprehension, quick at expression. These qualities did not come suddenly. They came by degrees, with constant use and experience. I was willing to work, and was always working.

I used to write about four columns of leader a week, besides subleaders and paragraphs. Then I wrote a column or two of reviews of books. This, with looking over the correspondence, filled up my time pretty well. I had plenty to do, moreover, in my spare minutes. I read many papers before the Literary Institutes, took part in public meetings, and attended at the soirees of Mechanics Institutes throughout the West Riding.

The distress continued to increase in 1839. Flour was 3s. 10d. a stone. This means a great deal to a man who lives by his labour and the eating of bread. To many families it meant destitution, especially at a time when work was scarce. I think it was about this time that my friend Colonel Thompson wrote his

famous little paper on "The Siege of Bolton." It
first appeared in the *Sun*, and was spread broadcast
through the country on the wings of the press. It
was a most vivid account of the intense suffering
endured from want of food by the hungry population
of that manufacturing town. Of course it pointed a
moral. As in O'Connell's celebrated story of the
horse, "Will they try Corn?" that was the remedy for
starvation.

The Chartists, however, insisted on their own
remedy. Nothing but the Charter could answer their
purpose: nothing but universal suffrage. They went
to all manner of lengths to force their measure before
the public. They mustered in the churches, and
crowded out the regular congregations. At Manchester, they took possession of the Cathedral, but
when the preacher announced his text, "My house is
the house of prayer, but ye have made it a den of
thieves," they left the place abruptly. They mustered
at public meetings, and insisted upon the Charter. I
was present at a meeting of the British and Foreign
School Society held in the Commercial Buildings on
the 4th September 1839, at which the publisher of
the *Northern Star* and his followers were present.
Mr Baines, M.P., was in the chair; but a motion was
proposed that Joshua Hobson should preside; and a
vigorous contest took place. Mr Baines stood firmly
to his post, though Hobson tried to push him out of
the chair. The quiet Quaker ladies sat still and
looked in amazement. Of course, nothing could be
done. The members of the Society eventually
retired. The gas was turned off; and the meeting
broke up in disorder.

The working people suffered much. Towards the
close of the year, at least 10,000 persons were out of

employment in the burgh of Leeds. Though the people complained, they did not riot. It was different elsewhere. There were riots at Birmingham, Manchester, Newcastle, and other places. At Newport, in Wales, a Chartist insurrection took place, which ended in the capture of Frost and a number of rioters. At Bradford, men openly practised military evolutions on Fairweather Green, furnished with pikes and firearms. Sixteen of them were apprehended by the police, and were sentenced to various terms of imprisonment. Feargus O'Connor himself was sentenced to eighteen months' imprisonment for inciting to insurrection and plunder in the *Northern Star*.

The Anti-Corn-Law movement had as yet made no real progress. The Whig ministry, then in office, was dead against it. The Chartists commanded the multitude, and they, or at least the noisiest part of them, were equally opposed to the repealers. In March 1840, a deputation of Anti-Corn-Law men appeared in London, and waited upon the leading ministers. Having stated to Lord Melbourne, then Premier, their object—the repeal of the Corn Law—his lordship curtly remarked, "You know that to be quite impracticable." Their interviews with the others were equally unsatisfactory. Multitudes of petitions for the repeal were of no use. On the 26th of May, the House of Commons, by a majority of 123, refused to consider the question of the Corn Laws.

What was to be done? My friend, Mr Hamer Stansfeld of Leeds, thought that the true method was to infuse some new blood into Parliament by the extension of the franchise. The ten pound suffrage introduced by the Reform Bill had only enfranchised the middle classes. Why not extend the suffrage to the industrious people—the working power of the country? After conferring with Mr James Garth Marshall—the friend and correspondent of the late Dr Arnold—it was arranged that a society should be established for this purpose.

Mr Stansfeld was a man for whom I had the greatest esteem. He was frank, free, and open, in all that he did. He possessed the courtesy of the true gentleman; and withal he was intelligent, enlightened, and firm to his purpose. He was full of industry, integrity, and excellence. In a word, his character was sterling. As was said of some one— he had the *whitest* soul that ever I knew.

I felt it to be a great honour to be consulted by such a man. He was pleased to say that he had read and approved my views as to "levelling up" the people as a mass, by education and the extension of privileges—so as to do away with the idea of social exclusiveness. He had read my "Appeal to the Middle Classes," which had appeared in the *Leeds Times* of 10th August; and suggested that an association should be formed for the extension and redistribution of the franchise. He asked me to write out an address on the subject, which I proceeded to do. This was approved by his friends, and published. A number of leading men subscribed their names, and a public meeting was held in the Music Hall, on the 31st of August 1840, to initiate the new association, James Garth Marshall in the Chair.

The first meeting was very successful. The chairman made an admirable speech. It was quiet, but emphatic. Among other things, he said that "the more immediate cause which originated this association was the late unanimous refusal, by a large majority of the House of Commons, to remove or modify the iniquitous tax on the people's food—a refusal sullen, unreasoning, without the decency of inquiry, and almost without the formality of a debate." He pointed out the greatest of social dangers that threatens us—the long, unrelieved misery, the long, unredeemed wrongs, which divided society into hostile classes, each by open violence and wrong struggling to preserve their own selfish interests, regardless of the rights of others. He concluded by stating that the mode by which the Society proposed to proceed, was vigorous and well-directed agitation, discussion, and support of such great practical measures as the Repeal of the Corn Laws, National Education, Inquiry into the Condition of the Working Classes—all in reference to, and in strict subordination to, the great special object of Parliamentary Reform.

Mr Hamer Stansfeld followed in a vigorous speech. Alderman George Goodman — afterwards mayor and representative of the borough in Parliament —insisted upon cheap and equal justice for all classes of the community. Councillor Joshua Bower, Mr Joseph Middleton, barrister, and others (of whom I was one), addressed the meeting; and the resolutions were unanimously adopted.

I was afterwards requested to act as Honorary Secretary, and wrote the first address, which was issued to the public. In that address, the disproportionate representation of the people was strongly pointed out. For instance, it was shown that twenty-five small boroughs, of no importance whatever, sent fifty members to Parliament, whilst Leeds, with 20,000 more population than all these boroughs combined, sent only two. It was the same with the towns and cities in Ireland.

Mr Marshall followed this up with other addresses
—one to Daniel O'Connell and the Repealers of
Ireland, announcing the motto of "Justice for each
and for all"—and arguing that "the people should
make the Government, and that to the people the
Government should be responsible for all its acts."
By these publications, and especially by the proposal
to have a conference of friends of the movement in
Leeds, a considerable amount of interest was excited
in the proceedings of the association. When it became
known that Hamer Stansfeld had declined the
office of mayor of Leeds, in order to devote himself
more effectually to the work of the association, the
editor of the *Leeds Mercury*—then ably conducted
by Mr Edward Baines, junior (afterwards Sir
Edward Baines)—proceeded to address him in a
· series of letters in opposition to the movement, which
were published in the columns of that paper on the
21st November, and 12th December, 1840; and the
2nd of January 1841.

It is unnecessary to go at any length into the
details of this controversy. But it may be briefly
mentioned that Mr Baines opposed the proposed
measures—Household Suffrage, The Ballot, Redistribution of the Representation, Triennial Parlia-
ments, and Absolution of the Property Qualification
—on the grounds principally that they would "let
in the Tories"—that they would "destroy the
influence of towns," "strengthen the aristocracy,"
and "perpetuate the Corn Law." The pamphlet
in which the letters were afterwards published, bore
this argument on its front. Mr Baines held, no doubt
truly, that a great portion of the working people to
whom the franchise was to be extended ("perhaps a
majority ") could not write their own names; that the

measure would thus be transferring power from the
educated to the uneducated classes; and that the
redistribution of the suffrage would, by including so
many more of the county voters, diminish the
ascendency of the towns, and give to the county
population "an immense and unassailable preponder-
ance."

Mr Hamer Stansfeld defended himself, also in
the columns of the *Mercury;* and his letters were
afterwards published in a pamphlet form. Mr
Stansfeld denied the justice of refusing the suffrage
to the people of the counties, on the grounds stated
by his opponent. He would trust them, and believed
that the Ballot would sufficiently protect them in the
exercise of the franchise. Mr Roebuck also gave
an admirable lecture before the association, in which
he clearly and brightly illustrated "The Science of
Government." Later the controversy became merged
in the proceedings of the great Suffrage Festival,
which took place in Messrs Marshall's new mill at
Holbeck, on the 21st of January 1841.

The mill had just been erected, and was not yet
supplied with machinery. It was built in the style
of an Egyptian temple, with an immense chimney
like an elongated pyramid. The great roof was
supported on iron pillars—there being grass enough
on the top for sheep to feed—and the room itself
covered five times as much space as Westminster
Hall, extending over nearly two acres of ground. It
was certainly the largest room in the world; and on
this occasion was densely packed. The proceedings, on account of the heterogeneous audience, and
the frequent howlings of the Chartists, were very
confused.

The object was to have a friendly conference with

the working people, and to exchange thoughts freely with them about the extension of the franchise. Their leaders were invited to be present, and to address the meeting. The speakers on the side of the Household Suffrage Association were, Mr James Garth Marshall, the Chairman, Mr Joseph Hume, M.P., Sir George Strickland, M.P., Mr John Arthur Roebuck, Mr Sharman Crawford, Mr Williams, M.P., and Col. Perronet Thompson; and on the part of the Chartists, Messrs Moir, delegate from Glasgow, O'Neil from Birmingham, Lowry from Newcastle, Mason from the Midland Counties, and Deegan from Sunderland. The resolutions were passed, some of them amidst howling; and though they all went in the direction of a large extension of the franchise, the speakers differed to a large extent with respect to the various "points" of the Charter.

Dan O'Connell was expected to attend the meeting, in which case the Chartists intended to shout him down; but he did not make his appearance until the following day—when there was a conference in the Cloth Hall Rotunda in the morning, and a dinner in the evening—at which the great Dan made one of his best speeches. Hume, Roebuck, and Col. Thompson also spoke.

Although the Household Suffrage Association continued its operations, and started a Working Man's Club in Albion Street, where a library was established, lectures delivered, and discussions held, nothing came of the movement. It was like flogging a dead horse to make it rise and go. It would neither rise nor go. After the lapse of two or three years, the association expired of inanition. Another movement took its place, and the rapidly growing distress compelled the country to take into consideration the question of the Corn Laws.

It was about the beginning of 1841 that I had my first communication from Mr Cobden. He had declined to attend the Household Suffrage meeting in Marshall's mill, although (he said) "the principles so ably advocated by the Leeds Association had always had his humble advocacy, and he should continue, individually, to give them all the support in his power," but that "his engagements during the next month, in the cause of Corn Law abolition, would occupy every moment of his leisure." Shortly after, a communication appeared in the *Anti-Corn-Law Circular*, addressed to me by name, in which the editor virtually assailed the attitude taken by the Leeds Suffrage Reformers. To this I sent a letter in reply, requesting its insertion in the *Circular*. Mr Ballantyne, who was then the editor, handed my letter to Mr Cobden, who wrote to me, requesting me not to press for the insertion of my communication.

He said : " The letter in the *Circular* addressed to you, expressly draws a distinction between the readers of the *Star*, and the working classes generally. Under such a state of things as 12,000 or 15,000 copies of a Chartist paper (insidiously opposing the Anti-Corn-Law Party) selling weekly in Leeds, it was merely argued that that was a proof of the necessity for advocating the Repeal of the Corn Laws. You will judge whether you would wish your letter to appear. I think it would be hardly fair, and might be calculated to do harm. Why should we even *appear* to be at variance, when the Anti-Corn-Law Party, and rational radicals are really identically the same in politics? Our only difference is as to the means of carrying out our objects. We think *time* must be regarded, along with labour, as essential

G

means to the obtaining of Corn Law Repeal, and are
willing to give a further trial of both. I wish the
Leeds A. C. L. men had held on to the question
for a year or two more. When the Whigs go out,
then will be the time for a new combination of parties,
with a chance of getting some aristocratic leaders.
Unhappily, we are not fit to run alone without the
guidance of the latter. By the way, do you see
Dan's abuse of the Anti-Corn-Law League for inter-
fering with the Whigs at Walsall? Observe, too,
that he says in the same speech, that he is for Universal Suffrage. Although joining you, he is preparing for a retreat upon the *Charter*. The artful
dodger!"

The Chartists continued their uproarious proceedings at public meetings. It became almost impossible
to hold an assemblage on any subject without their
interference. They were especially violent against
the Corn Law men, assuming that if their movement succeeded, the Chartists would be nowhere.
At a meeting at Deptford in April, the Chartists were
ejected by force; but at a meeting in the Cloth Hall
at Leeds they succeeded, and forced the mayor from
the chair. It was the same at Edinburgh and elsewhere.

In the face of the increasing distress, the Whig
Ministry proposed, in May 1841, to revise the Corn
Laws, and the Premier (Lord Melbourne) acknowledged that he had "changed the opinion which he
formerly held — grounded as that opinion was on
purely temporary interests." The new proposal was to
fix the duty on wheat at 8s. a quarter, and to reduce
the duties on timber and sugar. A meeting of Leeds
Delegates was held on the 7th of May in the Rotunda
of the Coloured Cloth Hall, when it was resolved to
petition Parliament "in favour of the abolition of
monopolies generally, and especially for the reduction

of the sugar and timber duties, and the repeal of the Corn Laws."

Upon this Mr Cobden wrote to me the following letter :—

"MANCHESTER, *Saturday.*

"MY DEAR SIR,—

"I fear from the tenor of the *Mercury* that the Anti-Corn-Law deputies will be preparing themselves for Monday next to support Ministers and desert our League. We are determined in Manchester to stick to total and immediate repeal, and wherever a branch association drops off from us, we will do our best to rear up another in its place. The proposal to unite the agitation against the timber duties, sugar duties, etc., will be a virtual secession from our League. It will be an infringement upon the rules, which restrict us exclusively to the subject of total and immediate repeal. My object in writing is to beg that you will stand up for us at the Monday's meeting, and prevent any rupture. I see by the *Mercury* that Members of Parliament and others have advised us to enlarge our objects. Yes! *we* are very troublesome to M.P.'s, both Whig and Tory, and they would be glad to turn us into anything but what we are. They know if we become mere *tariff-reformers* they may pass muster—just as Stanley, Graham, and Co., passed off as excellent Parliamentary Reformers before the Reform Bill. But when we come to the test of Total Repeal of the Bread Tax, they can't shuffle, and so they dislike us, and would willingly separate us from one another to weaken us.—Believe me, yours faithfully,

"RICHARD COBDEN."

The proposals of Ministers were lost in the House of Commons. A motion by Sir Robert Peel, expressing want of confidence in the Ministry, was defeated by a majority of only one. A succession of defeats at length compelled them to resign, and Parliament was dissolved on the 22nd of June 1841.

We were now in for a new election. Mr Baines

had expressed his intention of not offering himself
again to the constituency; Sir William Molesworth
had lost the confidence of the electors; and it was
consequently necessary to find two new candidates.
Probably in deference to the Household Suffrage
Association, Joseph Hume was selected as the
strongest man; and a comparatively unknown
gentleman, Mr Aldam, a mild Whig, as the other.
The two Tory candidates were Mr William Beckett,
the well-known banker, and Lord Jocelyn.

To aid in the election, I started a little penny paper
entitled *The Movement.* It passed through four
numbers. In the first I gave a biography of Joseph
Hume, which he himself said was exceedingly well
done: "he did not know how I could have picked up
so many facts about his character and history." A
native of Montrose, he was educated as a surgeon—
principally through the efforts of his mother, who was
a person of equally strong character with himself—
and went out to India in the service of the East
India Company. He soon displayed his extraordinary perseverance and capacity for labour.
During the Mahratta War, he was with Lord Lake's
army; and in the bustle of the camp, and while
engaged in the laborious duties of his profession, he
studied the language. When Colonel Achmuty—at
that time interpreter to the army—became disabled,
the only person found able to hold communication
with the natives was the indefatigable surgeon from
Montrose, who was immediately promoted to the
office of interpreter. Besides continuing his medical
duties, he was requested to fill the offices of Pay-
master and Postmaster of the troops! He performed
all his duties with such activity and industry as to
secure for him the marked approbation of the

Commander-in-Chief, as well as his private friendship.

After a period of industrious prosperity, he returned to England. He travelled through Great Britain; made himself acquainted with every place of manufacturing celebrity in England, Scotland, and Ireland; then he travelled abroad, in Spain and Portugal, Turkey, Greece, Egypt, Italy, and France. By the temper of his mind, his experience and information, his habits of patient industry and research, and the solidity of his fortunes, he was now well able to fill with effect a seat in the legislature of his country. He was elected for Weymouth in 1812—three years before the battle of Waterloo.

From the time that he took his seat in Parliament, down to the year 1841, when he offered himself to the Leeds constituency, Joseph Hume distinguished himself by his indefatigable industry. There is scarcely a page of the parliamentary register which does not contain some record of his sayings and doings. In the finances, the revenue, the excise, the public accounts, the army and navy, the representation of the people, the removal of religious disabilities, he was always at work. He was the most regular attender, the most consistent voter, the most laborious investigator, the most active and useful member, perhaps, who ever sat in Parliament. Financial questions were his favourites. Shortly after he entered the House, he found that the public accounts were imperfect; and that frauds to an immense amount might be (and probably were) committed without the possibility of detection. He was defeated again and again, but stuck to his text. Attention was at last awakened; converts came slowly dropping in; and in 1822, the Select Committee, which had been appointed at his urgent desire, reported in favour of his method of so preparing the accounts, that the true balance might be struck between income and expenditure. For twenty years more he continued on his unpaid mission, checking the accounts, and advocating all manner of improvements, in trade, in commerce, in reducing taxation, and in extending freedom. And now he offered himself to the largest manufacturing town in Yorkshire.

But he was not good enough for Leeds. Mr William Beckett, an able man no doubt, was at the top of the poll; Mr Aldam was second; and Joseph Hume third. He was accordingly defeated. To show the pleasant way in which things were done in the North, a coffin was carried in front of the hustings, which was openly proclaimed to be the coffin in which Mr Hume was to be buried. He was not buried, however, but lived to do a great deal of useful work. He was at once returned to Parliament by his fellow townsmen of Montrose, and took his seat as usual. He lived to see the end of the Corn Laws; and during the later years of his life, he devoted his energies to throwing open public places—the British Museum, National Gallery, the Tower, the Houses of Parliament, Westminster Abbey, Kew Gardens, and such like—to the people at large. It seemed only reasonable that they should be permitted to see the collections maintained by the public taxes. Now, thanks to the persevering tenacity of Joseph Hume, they were at length enabled to enjoy the sight of their own property.*

* I have endeavoured to bear my testimony to Mr Hume's philanthropic efforts in *Self-Help*, pp. 115-117 ; and *Duty*, pp. 317-320. I wonder that no Life of Joseph Hume has been published. It would form a fine record of indefatigable and useful perseverance.

CHAPTER IX

I FOUND a great deal of life, industry, and energy among the population of Leeds. Although trade was bad, and they had much misery to contend with, they were anxious to help themselves by all conceivable and rightful methods. Some thought that politics might help them, others placed their reliance on co-operation. They might be seen groping, perhaps blindly, in the dark, after some grand principle, which they thought would lead them to fresh life, and liberty, and happiness. But disappointments too often befell them. The disposition to co-operate together for mutual benefit and defence, first manifested itself in strikes and combinations — its most imperfect form. Although these efforts were for the most part failures, the energy they displayed was nevertheless immense. During the strikes which occurred about 1840 in the manufacturing districts — including Manchester, Stockport, Preston, Bradford, and Leeds—not less than three millions sterling in wages had been virtually thrown away by the working people. Think of such an amount of capital being expended on land, buildings, establishments for co-operative production, or on the means of physical, moral, and intellectual improvement—what great results might not have been anticipated from it! At the same time, this union of efforts showed what a great moral power they had at their command in their beneficent principle of co-operation.

It was indeed already shown in the matter of benefit societies. I became a member of the Manchester Unity of Oddfellows, and of the Ancient Order of Foresters. Although they have "words" and "signs," and are invested with some show of secrecy, they are really and truly societies for mutual benefit and support. Not fewer than 8000 working men of Leeds belonged to the Manchester Unity; but there were many other societies—Independent Oddfellows, Gardeners, Foresters, Ancient Druids, Order of the Ark and of the Peaceful Dove, the Knights Templar, the Ancient Romans, Knights of Malta, Loyal Ancient Shepherds and Shepherdesses, and even an Order of Ancient Buffaloes! Looking at the number of members these various lodges contained, I found it was quite within the mark to calculate that the working people of Leeds alone subscribed not less than £15,000 annually for mutual assurance against sickness and accident. Ten shillings was paid weekly to a member while sick; medical attendance was also provided; £10 was allowed on the death of a member, and £5 to the widow, if the deceased brother was married.

With these objects some lodges combined schemes for moral and intellectual improvement. They formed libraries, and had courses of instructive lectures delivered before them. Doubtless there were imperfections in these societies, for no human institution can be perfect; but in the cultivation of friendly brotherhood, and in the practice of mutual help, they were admirable as beginnings. They were managed on the whole with practical and business-like sagacity. There may have been some waste; possibly also, full advantage was not taken of the organisation which most of the societies displayed; but that the general result was most improving to the condition of the working classes, could not for a moment be called in question.*

There was another movement going on in Leeds at the time I settled there, perhaps of a more questionable description. At the same time, the persons who took part in it were by no means of an unintelligent character. I allude to the Socialist movement. Leeds, like other large towns, had a Socialist Hall. This had formerly been Walton's Music Saloon, in East Parade; and it was afterwards taken by the Mechanics Institute. But when I first knew it, the place was used for Socialist meetings and lectures. I went there occasionally to see what was done and said. The body had preachers or lecturers who could talk cleverly and well. But unfortunately, they mixed up a great deal of atheism with their views of co-operation. It was not until the Revs. Charles Kingsley, Frederick Denison Maurice, and Edward Larken, developed the practice of Christian Socialism that the co-operators were dragged out of this frightful pit.

Robert Owen had been the beginner of the movement. He held that in the competitive system was found the root of all the miseries of society. He proclaimed the negation of all religious belief as essential

* I may mention that I afterwards gave a full account of these movements in the *Quarterly Review*. See articles, No. 212, October 1859, on "Strikes," etc.; No. 232, October 1864, on "Workmen's Benefit Societies."

to the establishment of his system. His doctrines were economical, metaphysical, and anti-theological. The political economy of Socialism contemplated nothing else than the total abolition of poverty. Productive labour was not to be required of any one after the age of twenty-five. Society was to be composed of communities, each possessing land sufficient for the support, *for ever*, of all its members. The philosopher's stone was a child's toy compared to this arrangement.

The metaphysics of Socialism were comprised in the maxim that character is formed *for*, not *by*, the individual; and that society may so arrange "circumstances" as to produce whatever character it pleases. Man's active agency in the formation of his character was altogether disallowed. There was to be no religion in the new society. "Superior external circumstances alone were to be permitted to act upon and to influence each individual will." The only deity recognised by Mr Owen, as stated in his *Outline of the Rational System of Society*, was "an incomprehensible power which acts in and through all nature, everlastingly composing, decomposing, and recomposing the materials of the universe." Such was his idea of moral sublimity. One had better be "a Pagan suckled in a creed outworn," than believe in this spinning jenny of a universe, with its "decomposing and recomposing."

The preachers or lecturers at the Socialist Hall did their best to illustrate these views. They would read a chapter of the Bible, mock it, and raise a laugh at it. The audiences seemed to be kept together by these means. Tom Paine was the writer most quoted. The lecturers were varied from time to time. The Socialists here borrowed a wrinkle from the

Wesleyan Methodists: they went from circuit to circuit. Among the lecturers I heard, were Lloyd Jones from Wales, Buchanan from Glasgow, and Fleming from Berwick-on-Tweed. Their principal business was to preach against religion, and to cut up the parsons. At the same time, there were some practical heads amongst them, and in course of time lectures were delivered upon home colonisation and co-operation. The members proceeded to collect money for the purpose of buying an estate, to exhibit these principles in active operation. They did collect enough money to purchase a small estate in Hampshire, called Tytherly. A good deal of money was spent on buildings; but after a few years, they found they could not make the place yield a profit, and it came to grief. The estate was, I believe, eventually bought by Lord Ashburton.

But their efforts in co-operation were much more successful. Some of the members started an Operative Land and Building Society, others a Redemption Society. They bought land, erected dwellings, built mills, and by clubbing their means, began to manufacture, and to grind corn for themselves. Such associations were conducted under the provisions of the Friendly Societies Act, and many of them proved very successful.*

But to return to the political movements of the time. When Parliament met, after the general election of 1841, it was found that the Anti-Corn-Law men were greatly outnumbered. In the debate on the Address, Ministers found themselves in a minority of 91, in a House of 629. They accordingly resigned; when Sir Robert Peel was sent for by the Queen, and undertook to construct a new ministry.

* I have given an account of these in *Thrift*, pp. 102-9.

And yet this was the Prime Minister, and this the
House of Commons, that afterwards abolished the
Corn Laws.

It was left for distress to do the work, though the
Anti-Corn-Law leaders did not abate their efforts.
Cobden had been returned for Stockport, and was
now the recognised parliamentary leader of the
League. He made his maiden speech, which was
well received; but the main work was done out of
doors. Before he went to London, to take his seat
in Parliament, he sent me the following letter:—

"MANCHESTER, 3rd *August* 1841.

"MY DEAR SIR,—
          "Mr Stansfeld called on me to-day, and I
mentioned to him how important it is that the great
towns, and Leeds in the number, should be prepared
to hold simultaneous meetings at the time when the
Corn Laws become the practical question in the House
of Commons. It is quite clear that the repeal can
not be carried in any other way than that by which
the Reform Bill and the Emancipation of the
Catholics were wrung from the Aristocracy. The
process of the Registration Courts will not effect
our purpose unless aided by the masses. In fact,
we can't wait the years which would be requisite
to turn the eighty Tory majority into a minority.
Everything then depends upon our securing the
hearty co-operation of the people, and this can only
be done by a steady perseverance in the agitation of
the question *as a bread tax*, and as it affects the
wages of labour. Too much has been said about
the interests of capitalists, farmers, and landlords;
and too little stress has been laid upon the rights of
labour. The process of enlightenment is slow but
sure, if we treat the Corn Law as a Wages question.
This simplifies the matter, and gets rid of all the
rubbish about the protection of interests. *What
protection has the labourer?*—should be the Socratic
mode of answering any argument in favour of
protecting this or that interest. The labourer has

no legislative protection excepting the Union Workhouse which the landlord, farmer, and capitalist may
equally, in case of need, enjoy.

"But I am arguing the case, when I merely
wanted to urge the necessity of organising ourselves
for the conflict. How stands Leeds? Have the
Corn Law repealers such an influence that you
could join in a unanimous demonstration at a public
meeting against the bread tax, without interference
from the Chartists or Tories? We are in that position
here, and unless the other large towns can be worked
into the same sound state we shall not be in a
situation to take advantage of the chapter of accidents
during the ensuing parliamentary campaign, or in
the event of a bad harvest. We can hope nothing
from Parliament unless influenced from without. In
this opinion, the best of our friends in the House
concur. When in London, on Friday last, I met
Villiers, Warburton, and others; and in talking over
the future tactics of the Opposition in Parliament, they
expressed a very decided opinion that the course to
be pursued indoors must depend altogether upon the
movement in the *North*. I very much fear that we
are, on the contrary, looking too much for help from
the House of Commons, and too little from ourselves.
The whole matter lies in a single enquiry—*Can we
unite with the people around us?* If not, the game
is up, and we deserve no pity if the fate of the house
divided against itself falls upon us. If we do unite
amongst ourselves now, I think circumstances are
conspiring to lead us on to speedy victory. The
Corn Law will be the great practical question of the
next session. Peel will, or rather *may*, be forced
to tamper with the present scale. *Then* will be the
time to rouse the people to coerce the party into a
full, or at least a fair, amelioration of the law. But
we must be preparing NOW for the occasion. I told
you long ago my conviction that a vast amount of
ignorance existed even in Leeds upon the subject
of the Bread Tax. Did not the late election convince
you that I was right? That ignorance still remains,
and you must remove it ere you can rouse the people
into zealous action. I shall only add, that no other
question but that of Corn Law Repeal and Free
Trade will take practical hold of the public mind

during the next session. I mean that the suffrage
extension question is not at present a practical one.
Nothing definite on the subject is before the electoral
body, as a body. Is not the agitation of the question
a waste of power *now?* And will it not be in fact
best forwarded by sticking to the Corn Law, which
is as democratic as the most ultra Chartist can desire.
Go then incessantly for total and immediate repeal
of the Bread Tax. Rouse young and old—rich and
poor—men and women, to action, by pressing home
the injustice, the wickedness, the foul impiety, of the
starvation law. Ever yours truly,
                                        "R. COBDEN."

I quote this and the following letters of Mr
Cobden to show the intense active interest which he
took in the question he had taken in hand. If he
wrote such letters to me—a comparatively unknown
person, both as regards position and influence—what
must he not have done to others in all parts of the
country, who possessed a much greater amount of
both. He continued to urge the necessity of union of
parties against the Bread Tax.

After Parliament had been prorogued, Mr Cobden
wrote to me again, on the subject of a proposed con-
ciliatory meeting in Leeds, which Colonel Thompson
was to attend. In this letter, he said :—

" I have never found good to come out of formal
attempts at reconciliation with the leaders of the
Chartist party. In fact, we have long ago given up
the attempt to compromise matters with these
worthies, and have rather preferred to work up a
party of Corn Law repealers independent of the old
leaders. This requires laborious effort on the part of
one or two middle class men, but they must not be
obnoxious *as politicians* to the Chartists. With
proper exertions you will be sure of success. I must
reiterate my old song—the people are in nine cases
out of ten profoundly ignorant of the nature and

effects of the Bread Tax. I have never been able to join in the unmeasured censures of the working class which I occasionally hear from my friends. The fault lies in the apathy of the middle class. When the latter are fairly up, the working class instinctively fall into their places as the allies of the middle man."

Nevertheless, our public meeting was held. It was summoned by the Parliamentary Reform Association which still continued to exist. The meeting was held in the large room of the Commercial buildings, and was full to overflowing. The Chartists were present in great numbers, and the meeting was occasionally a scene of great uproar and confusion. Colonel Thompson, Mr Jelinger, C. Symons, and others spoke; and Dr Lees, the Temperance Advocate, who on this occasion appeared on the side of the Chartists, addressed the meeting. The occasion was distinguished by an excellent, manly speech from Mr James Garth Marshall, the chairman, who never spoke more admirably nor acquitted himself better. But as a whole the meeting was a failure. Nobody was conciliated, and everything went on as before. Mr Cobden then addressed to me the following remarkable letter :—

"LEAMINGTON, 21st October 1841.

"MY DEAR SIR,—
              "There is nothing that is more untoward than your present state in Leeds. At the very time when we want a complete phalanx for the crowning struggle against Monopoly, you are broken into sections waging war against each other. In looking back to your past position—three years ago, when you could hold great and unanimous meetings upon the Corn Law—I fear you are in a worse dilemma just now than at any former period of the Corn Law agitation.

"I confess when I think of the materials you have had to work with in Leeds, compared with ours in Manchester, I cannot acquit you of having made a very bad use of them. In almost every respect Leeds stood better than Manchester three years ago, or even later. The *Leeds Mercury* sided with the League, whilst the *Manchester Guardian* was, up to the Whig dissolution, the bitter and malignant foe to our out-and-out agitation in Manchester. It is no compliment to you to say that the *Leeds Times* is immeasurably superior to its Manchester namesake. So much for the Whig and Radical press.

"As for Men, we have not one of the standing of Mr Marshall, possessing his moral courage, right-mindedness, and liberality. We have not one possessing the never failing generosity, and the talent (judging him by his controversy with Mr Baines) of Mr Stansfeld.

"Then for the people to lead. *You* had an orderly community, quite an example, at your public meetings, for intelligence and good behaviour. Manchester, on the contrary, had not for eight years been able to call a public meeting on any political question. The huge factories of the Cotton district, with three *thousand* hands under *one* capitalist, give to our state of society the worst possible tone, by placing an impassable gulf between master and operative.

"Such was your condition and such ours when we began the Anti-Corn-Law agitation. The question now is—why does the cause stand so well in Manchester, and why so adversely in Leeds? I can attribute it to no other reason than that it has been *worked* incessantly in the former place, *apart altogether from party politics.*

"The work has been done by a very few, so few that we have been the laughing-stock even of ourselves, as we sat and chuckled over the splutter we were making in the name of THE LEAGUE! You have not an idea how insignificant a body the working members of The League really comprise. Still we worked. When we could not hold public meetings we got up little hole and corner meetings. Two years and a half ago, we called a public meeting. The Chartist leaders attacked us on the platform at the head of their deluded followers. We were nearly the victims of physical force. I lost my hat, and all but had my head split open with the leg of a stool. In retaliation for this, we deluged the town with short tracts printed for the purpose. We called meetings of each trade, and held conferences with them at their own lodges. We found ready listeners, and many secret allies, even amongst the Chartists. We resolutely abstained from discussing the Charter or any other party question. We stuck to our subject, and the right-minded amongst the working-men gave us credit for being in earnest, which is all that is necessary to secure the confidence of the people.

"Our strength grew, and the result is that we can now hold a public meeting at any moment. Nay: the repealers carried the war into the Chartist camp on Monday last (see Wednesday's *Guardian*) by upsetting their meeting in retaliation for their interruption of the meeting at the Corn Exchange, at which Colonel Thompson was present. We shall work on in Manchester, for much remains to be done.

"Why do I go over our exploits? Not for egotistical display. We have done no more than our duty: but simply to give you the assurance that everything may be done in Leeds by working perseveringly in the cause of Corn Law repeal. But you are right in saying that the agitation must be separated from the plans of political parties. May not your Young Men's Anti-Monopoly Society— aided by the presence of ministers—tend to rescue the question from the contamination of party?

"I cannot go at length into my reasons for thinking that the only chance open to such as you and me for effecting any amelioration in the condition of the people, is by adhering to the advocacy of practical reform rather than attempting organic changes. I am strongly of opinion that unless commercial reform be effected before, *long before*, political reform can be carried, this country will have received its death warrant at the hands of the aristocracy. We are much nearer the accomplishment of tariff reform than of organic change. Public opinion has decreed the one, whilst there is scarcely an organised public movement for the other.

H

"Let us work, then, for the practical good, giving all possible countenance and help to the advance of political reform. Believe me, yours very truly,

"R. COBDEN."

The wisdom embodied in this letter may be judged by the after result of the movement. Although no public meeting was held during the later part of 1841 on the subject of the Corn Laws, a much more important investigation took place. This was the appointment by the operatives of Leeds of an Enumeration Committee, for the purpose of ascertaining the number of unemployed persons in the borough, and the extent of the distress from which they were suffering from want of employment. The principal person who had to do with the initiation of this committee was James Rattray, an operative stuff printer, who consulted me on the subject. James Speed, a handloom weaver, was also connected with it. Rattray acted as secretary, and Speed as the chairman of the committee. The whole proceedings were conducted by the working people themselves. On several occasions I accompanied the enumerators when making their visits, and I witnessed many sad sights. Men, women, and children "clamouring" for food—willing to work, but with no work to do; not angry, not furious, at the laws which kept them idle; but patient, long-suffering, and very helpless. This was the time when a distinguished and compassionate person, hearing of the existence of distress in the manufacturing districts, recommended the operative classes, who were suffering from hunger, to take an occasional pinch of curry powder in a little water to allay the craving for food. What these poor creatures wanted was, not curry, but bread, not warm water, but mutton and beef.

The results of the inquiry were remarkable. It was ascertained by personal visitation, that out of 4752 families examined, consisting of 19,936 individuals, only 3780 persons were in work, while 16,156 were out of work; and that the average earnings per head amounted to only 11¼d. weekly for each individual. Distress continued to increase all over the West Riding. The position of the handloom weavers was especially distressing. Three months later, 16,000 individuals were on the books of the Leeds Workhouse as receiving parochial relief. In addition to this, 10,000 persons had received relief from a fund of £7000 raised by voluntary subscription. Meetings were held to "make known the unparalleled distress which prevailed in the borough, and the gradual decay of trade consequent thereon," and more money was collected for the relief of the sufferers. From the Manufacturers Relief Committee in London, £500 was also obtained for the relief of the Leeds poor. It may be mentioned that at the beginning of August 1841, wheat was quoted at 86s. the quarter.

All this was steadily working for the repeal of the bread tax. Cobden did not fail to take advantage of the situation. He summoned together a meeting of ministers of every denomination at Manchester, to consider the condition of the labouring classes. They were 650 in number; their proceedings were conducted with great order; but they did not fail to protest against the Corn and Provision Laws. Resolutions were carried, unanimously approving of their abolition. Then an Anti-Corn-Law Bazaar was held in Manchester, at which about £10,000 was collected by the sale of goods, for the support of the League. It was not merely the working people who suffered. Mills were being closed in all the manufacturing districts; bankruptcies were increasingly numerous; and thousands of operatives were reduced to a state of pauperism. Cobden, though he saw his prophecies being fulfilled, was by no means over-sanguine. Let me give another of his letters, to show his views at this time. The first part of his communication, it will be observed, relates to a matter entirely different from the chief subject of his thoughts.

"LEAMINGTON, 6th *November* 1841.

"MY DEAR SIR,—
        "An aunt of mine sojourning here, who is 'great' in theology, and deeply versed in Evangelism, Voluntaryism, Puseyism, and all the other *isms*, has been much edified by the perusal of your account of a certain pipe in Dr Hook's church for carrying the remains of the sacred elements into consecrated ground; and her conscience, or rather her curiosity, is so much troubled that I have promised to ascertain if it be a veritable account, or only a wicked invention of a witty editor. Pray, therefore, oblige me with a line by return to this place, that I may settle her pious longings upon the momentous affair.*
        "What an ominous lull there is in the public mind! Political opinion seems for the moment to be

* In March 1841 the Chartists elected working men as church-wardens at Leeds. Some of them were dissenters. It happened that the excellent vicar, Dr Hook, was at that time very much given to High Churchism. He had a *piscina* provided in the New Parish Church, such as is used in Roman Catholic churches, when the priest rinses the chalice or pours away the remains at the celebration of the Mass. This *piscina* consisted of a shallow stone basin with a pipe or drain leading directly to the consecrated ground outside the building. Whether by accident or design, this pipe became choked up with lime, so that the wine poured into the basin accumulated there, and could not get away; hence the necessity for repairs, and the paragraph in the local paper.

at a deadlock. It can't be denied that we are plunged into the profoundest apathy upon the subject of parties. The Whigs are just as unpopular as the Tories—nay, rather more so—and is there any other party even in embryo? As for leaders, the masses have just as much love for Peel as for Russell; and I very much fear that the old radical leaders are damaged past redemption. Hume, Grote, and Warburton, and their followers, might have constituted a party five years ago, but they have since been drummed through Coventry at the heels of 'finality' Lord John, and are now suffering the penalty. I had hoped that Roebuck would have taken the fullest advantage of his fortunate exemption from this ordeal. His four years parliamentary quarantine gave him great advantage at the late sitting of Parliament. I am afraid the country will think with me that he has not made the most of his opportunities. The opposition to Sharman Crawford's motion, and his personal affair with the *Times*, were mistakes; and mistakes, even with honest intentions, are too severely scrutinised nowadays to be committed by a leader without serious injury to his reputation. His indiscretions have, I suspect, impaired public confidence in *Radical* leaders. Wakley's conduct in the House has very much increased this feeling. And the truth must be allowed to be told—we are without political leadership. Parties in the House and out of it are chaotic, and will, I suspect, continue to be so for some time to come.

"In the meantime, all we can hope for is to educate the public mind on practical questions, inoculate the people with sound principles of political economy, draw them from the worship of men to the admiration of abstract truths, and thus prepare them to take advantage of the chapter of accidents. When I was at the annual meeting of the Stockport Mechanics Institute a few days ago, I promised a prize for the best essays on *Machinery*, and on *Capital and Labour*. Couldn't you give a hint of this kind to Mr Marshall?

"You will see that we are going to have a meeting of deputies in Manchester on the 17th, to concoct plans for the winter. We shall thus ascertain in Manchester what are the feelings in different parts of

the kingdom. I am told from all sides that, unless we
do something, *i.e.*, strike a blow, we shall lose public
confidence. *What can we do?* There is always
danger of being made ridiculous by showing one's
teeth before one is *able* to bite. If we were to
attempt a *coup*, and it were to fail like the Chartist
sacred holiday, we should be laughed at for ever.
Should some practical measures not be speedily
carried, they will come too late; and what rational
man can say that we are in a fair way for doing
anything very soon?

"Still, what more can we do? At least we are
not standing in the way of a more hopeful movement;
for, of the three questions that now agitate the people
—Repeal of Corn Law, Repeal of Union, and
Charter—I can't help thinking that our question
stands in the place of the favourite in the public
mind. Bad is the prospect, even of the best; but so
long as there is no better to which to resign the
course, we must work away with whip and spur,
keeping our head steadily towards the far-distant
winning post.

"My opinion is every day strengthened, that we
must not seek *official* alliance with Chartists or any
other party. The leaders of the Anti-Corn-Law
party ought to take every opportunity of avowing
their sympathy as individuals for the Suffrage men;
but any formal coalition is unwise and unpracticable.
Many of the Chartists, as, for instance, O'Connor
and Colonel Napier, have their own views upon
Corn Laws, which must prevent their joining us;
and this ought to satisfy every honest man of their
party that it would be quite impossible for the two
bodies to coalesce. We must insist upon our right
to carry on an independent agitation, and if the
hired knaves who interrupt our meetings persevere,
we must harass them out in their own way. Our
Manchester operative Anti-Corn-Law men have
declared the *lex talionis* in force, even to sticks and
stones; and so formidable was their preparation for
the last meeting, that the Feargus men did not
venture even to lift their voices in opposition.
Indeed, I am told that, since that evening, their
committee have passed a resolution against further
interference. But I have no faith in those who

follow the 'Star' excepting in their weakness.
They are, after all, contemptible in numbers.—Yours
very truly,   R. Cobden."

At length the new ministry met the House of
Commons. The Queen opened Parliament in person
on the 3rd of February 1842. In the royal speech,
she acknowledged, "with deep regret, the continued
distress in the manufacturing districts of the country,"
admitting that the sufferings and privations which
had resulted from it "had been borne with
exemplary patience and fortitude," and recommended to the consideration of both Houses "the
laws which affect the imports of corn and other
articles."

Mr William Beckett, one of the members for
Leeds, moved the address. Sir Robert Peel is said
to have selected him on account of the condition of
the Leeds operatives, and more particularly because
of the Report of the Enumeration Committee. Mr
Rattray, the operative stuff printer, who initiated
that movement, afterwards wrote to me as follows,
when settled in Glasgow :—"There is no retrospec-
tive incident which affords me more real gratification
than the fact that Mr William Beckett informed
myself and Mr Speed, that it was our report which
induced Sir Robert Peel to select him to move the
address at the opening of the session of 1842, when
the Tariff wedge was put in that was to dislocate
the entire fabric of monopoly ; and, as I have never
forgotten the valuable and hearty assistance which
you personally and by the *Times* rendered to that
committee, I have taken the first favourable
opportunity to express my sense of your worth as a
gentleman ; and I trust that in a personal and

literary sense, you will not chide me, nor object to the original style of my dedication." *

Sir Robert Peel introduced his new measures on the 9th of February. A total repeal of the Corn Law, he said, would add agricultural to manufacturing distress, and he thought it well to be independent of foreign countries for bread. He accordingly proposed the new *sliding scale* of corn duties, with numerous amendments in the tariff. The alterations in the Corn Law did not satisfy Mr Cobden : he denounced the scheme as an insult to a suffering people. It met with no better success in the north, where it was generally denounced. It unsettled everything, and settled nothing. Thousands of meetings were held, and thousands of petitions were sent in to Parliament. Nevertheless, the ministers carried their measure by a large majority. Cobden went back to the country, to rouse not only the manufacturing but the agricultural classes against the Corn Laws. Meanwhile, an alarming outbreak occurred in the manufacturing districts, which at one time threatened to assume the form of an insurrection.

Southey once said that "the nation that builds upon manufactures sleeps upon gunpowder." The events in progress seemed to prove the truth of the statement. The working people had become restless. They had long been promised a "sacred month" by Feargus O'Connor. It had been postponed from month to month ; and now they were about to take the matter into their own hands. Some of the poorer loom weavers at Staleybridge who were unemployed, or on strike, compelled all other branches

* The truth is, that after Mr Rattray left Leeds, he travelled about the world a good deal, and wrote a book, which he dedicated to me.

of trade in the town to follow their example. Most
of the principal towns in Lancashire caught the contagion, and all the factory district became suddenly idle.
The "sacred month," in which nobody was to work,
had at last begun. Crowds of men and women went
from place to place, stopping the mills, and turning
out the working people. It was comparatively easy
to do this. The knowing hands, getting access to
the boiler of the factory steam engine, and forcing in
the plugs, caused the water to escape over the flames
in the furnace. The fire was extinguished; the
steam engine stopped: and the hands turned out.
In many cases valuable machinery was destroyed.

The contagion spread. By the middle of
August crowds of unemployed factory people surged
into Yorkshire. They came by the roads leading
over Blackstone Edge, down towards Huddersfield
and Halifax. Leeds was thrown into a state of great
excitement. The magistrates issued 30,000 staves for
the use of special constables. The police buckled
cutlasses to their sides, and several thousand extra
men were sworn in. In hot haste, a dispatch was
sent to the Horse Guards for military: and one fine
evening in August, the 32nd Regiment of Infantry,
a fine body of men, arrived from Weedon, and went
marching up Briggate to the tune of "All is lost
now" from *Sonnambula*. Prince George of Cambridge was also in the town, at the head of a detachment of Lancers, and a troop of Horse Artillery with
their field pieces.

By this time, the manufacturing towns in West
Yorkshire were the scene of riotous proceedings.
Boiler plugs were forced in, and thousands of unem-
ployed crowded the streets of Dewsbury, Halifax,
Holmforth, and Bradford. A remarkable sight was

to be seen in Skircoates Moor, in the neighbourhood of Halifax. About fifteen thousand "turn-outs" assembled there, passed resolutions in favour of the People's Charter, and spent the night on the purple heather of the moor. They consisted of men, women, and children. It was a sad sight. The greater number of them were arranged in circular groups, and as night fell, they sang Chartist songs. The women were especially excited. Some prisoners had been taken, and they exclaimed, "If we wor men, they wudn't be long there"—that is, in the police station. Others said, "Ye're soft, if ye don't fetch 'em out to-neet."

The women entered Halifax on the following day almost at the head of the mob. When they reached the North Bridge, where the military were drawn up to oppose their progress, numbers of women sprang forward and seized the horses' bridles to turn them aside, exclaiming to the soldiers, "You wouldn't hurt women, would you!" One of the infantry presented his bayonet to a woman; she put it aside and said, "No, no! we want, not bayonets, but bread." The whole scene reminded one of the French Revolution, which, in the language of Burke, arose "amid the fierce cries and violence of women."

The crowd surged onward to Bradford, and then to Leeds. On the morning of the 17th, the report reached the town that a number of rioters were on the road from Bradford. It was true. At Stanningley, they forced the boiler plugs of Varley's mill, and compelled the people to leave the factory. They next proceeded to Bramley, and stopped all the mills in that out-township. Then to Armley, Wortley, and Farnley; and now they were approaching Leeds. The mob reached Holbeck and the immense mills of the Messrs Marshall. The yard-door leading to the boiler of the new mill was strongly barricaded and defended by Mr J. G. Marshall and his workmen. Yet the mob, by repeated efforts, broke in the door, and rushed into the yard. They could not, however, find the boiler plug, and left the place without stopping the mill, or doing further mischief. The soldiers were now called out, and Prince George and his Lancers, together with the Artillery and their field pieces, were formed in a line in Camp Field. The Riot Act was read. The pieces were loaded, and ready to fire; but, fortunately, the mob was dispersed without loss of life. A number of prisoners were taken, and led off to the court-house by the military. The back of the strike was broken; and the "sacred month" ended in about 2000 persons suffering imprisonment for being concerned in these riots in the county of York.

The way was now open for the leaders of the Anti-Corn-Law movement. They renewed their conferences, held public meetings, engaged lecturers to enlighten the people, printed and distributed throughout the country millions of tracts, invaded the agricultural districts and held discussions with the farmers, and worked the movement in the most vigorous manner possible. I was a very humble volunteer and worker in the same cause; and I remember having addressed public meetings at Huddersfield, Halifax, Skipton, and Ossett. At the last place I mounted the pulpit in a Baptist Chapel—the first and only time I have spoken from so elevated a place. Of course, Cobden was the soul and centre of the movement. He spoke often in Leeds and the neighbouring towns. It is not necessary for me to go further into this history,

as the whole question is fully discussed in Mr
Morley's *Life of Cobden.*

I remember, however, a story being told me by
Mr Rawson of Manchester, which is worthy of being
remembered. Mr Thomasson of Bolton had gone
with Cobden and Rawson to a country town, to hold
a discussion with the farmers in the market-place.
Mr Thomasson was a dyspeptic man, and had a
very delicate stomach. He could not digest wheat
bread, but was driven to the use of bran bread.
When he arrived at the country inn, he asked the
landlady if she could get him some bran to make
bread with. She had never heard of such a thing!
But the bran was got, and the bread was made.
Next morning, the ostler and the grooms had a horse
nose-bag stuffed with bran, and carried it about
the streets, followed by a crowd, crying, "This is
what these Manchester sweeps would feed us on!
This is what they want to bring us to!"

Before bringing this chapter to an end, I may
mention that the Corn Laws were repealed by the
ministry of Sir Robert Peel in June 1846; and that,
of the other two movements above mentioned, the
Chartist one collapsed in April 1848, after the
Kennington Common procession, and the Household
Suffrage one triumphed in August 1867, so far as
the residents in towns were concerned, by the "dish-
ing of the Whigs" by the Tories. The Ballot and
abolition of property qualification for members
followed. But no party has yet had the courage to
tackle the far more difficult question—the extension
of the Franchise to the agricultural labourer.[*]
Possibly the bogey predicted by Mr Baines in 1841

* This point was, however, afterwards settled in the session of
1884-85.

may be a bogey after all.   By giving the agricultural
population a fair and equal share in the suffrage, the
towns may lose a portion of their political influence,
and "the Tories may come in," to the horror of
Whigs and Radicals.

CHAPTER X

I LEAVE POLITICAL LIFE

By the end of 1842, I had had enough of newspaper editing. I found it a rather unquiet life. Yet it was in many respects pleasant. I was introduced to good society, was invited out a good deal, and made many friends. But it seemed to lead to nothing. There was the perpetual grinding, the threshing of straw that had been a thousand times threshed, the constant excitement, the wonder whether I was doing good or harm by my efforts. I wished to pursue some quieter course, and to have more time for reading and study.

Besides, I had got engaged to be married, and would now have to work for two instead of one. I had never before thought much of money or of money-making. It was sufficient for me if I earned enough to pay my way and save a little besides. But now I was about to give "hostages to fortune," and I required to consider the future. To marry, one must have means, as well as the prospect of increasing means. As Keats says :—

> "Strange ! that honey
> Can't be got without hard money."

Accordingly, I considered whether I might not resume my former profession. With the consent of my affianced, I did so. I took a house in Holbeck, an out-township of Leeds, and put my surgeon's address on the door. In course of time, I was occupied in many ways. I attended the members of several of the Benefit Lodges, and in this way became known amongst the working people. On Sundays I taught young men, and sometimes gave addresses, in the Zion School, New Wortley. Nor did I give up my connection with the newspaper. I continued to write articles so long as was necessary, and until I could dispense with doing so. Moreover, I was kept constantly busy by a Leeds publisher, who engaged me to write various guides and pamphlets. Some of these had an immense circulation. Among them were Guides to America and the various English colonies. The *Guide to America* was especially successful.

Mr Mann, the publisher in question, also requested me to write a *History of Ireland*. This was an entirely new field of work. I looked into the materials for such a history. Unfortunately, they were not very numerous. The Leeds Library, to which I had access, contained very few books about Ireland. Moore's History only brought it down to the period of the Reformation; Leland's to the Revolution of 1688; Taylor's gave the Civil Wars of Ireland; and so on, but there was nothing very good or complete. I wished to give a summary down to the present day. I ought to have had access to the State Paper Office; and there I might have been able to produce something good. But I had no such access. Yet I did the best that I could.

The work was produced in monthly numbers in 1843. I must confess that it was written too hurriedly, and scarcely deserved the success it obtained. The arrangement with the publisher was half profits, but, so far as I was concerned, I received nothing in return for my labour and trouble. The work had a large circulation; but the failure of the Dublin bookseller through whom the principal portion of the book was sold, prevented the publisher deriving any profit from the work, and I shared his bad fortune.

After I had got out the last number of the *History*, I married, on the 7th December 1843; and the Christmas of that year saw my once solitary home lighted up with love and cheerfulness. I never regretted my marriage. My wife and I were altogether united through life. I obtained a cheerful and affectionate companion, and I hope that she obtained a devoted and equally affectionate husband. But these are things over which we draw the curtain. The happiness of married life cannot be babbled about to all the world.*

To return. The *History of Ireland* was published as a whole in 1844, and was well reviewed by the *Eclectic Magazine*, the *Nonconformist*, and the best of the Irish reviews. The *Athenæum*, while praising the book, said that "the author has made but little use of the documents published from the State Paper Office. Notwithstanding these drawbacks, his work claims the merit of honesty and impartiality; his views of policy are sound and philosophical; his sympathies are on the side of the oppressed; and his opinions are the result of careful examination." No one could be better aware than myself of the imperfections of the work, arising, in a great measure, from my having to work at a distance from the best

* Dr Smiles married Sarah Anne Holmes, daughter of a contractor in Leeds. She was born in 1823, and was educated at Liverpool by Miss Martineau, a sister of the well-known Dr James Martineau. Mrs Smiles died on the 14th February 1900.—Ed.

authorities. I was afterwards urged by William Howitt to republish the work; but that would have occasioned me too much trouble, and my labours besides were turned in an altogether different direction.

I think 1843 was my heaviest year of work. I was well and healthy, took plenty of exercise, and my mind was always alive and active. I found work, plenty of work, necessary for my happiness and welfare. I had always a lot of business laid out beforehand. So soon as I had finished *Ireland*, I prepared six lectures on the "Men and Times of the Commonwealth," which I delivered gratuitously to the members of the Leeds Mechanics Institution and Literary Society, the first four in February 1844, and the last two in December 1845. I afterwards delivered these, reduced to four, at the Manchester Athenæum, and the Liverpool Mechanics Institution. I was very proud of this period of history, and often afterwards thought of devoting myself to its study. But it is only men of sufficient means and fortune who can devote themselves to the pursuit of any branch of history.

In the year 1844, I moved over to Wellington Street, Leeds, and there my eldest child was born. I was still near my old friends in Holbeck. Yet, by the removal, I to a certain extent separated myself from them. I still continued my literary pursuits, but I had given up the idea of living by literature. I liked to regard it as my staff and not—my crutch. It had hitherto failed me. "Dinna be an author," said Robert Nicoll's aunt to him, "they're aye puir." And so Robert had experienced at Leeds, in the position which he occupied, and in which I succeeded him. I recognised the truth of Coleridge's statement in his *Biographia Literaria*—"With the exception of one extraordinary man," he says, "I have never known an individual of genius healthy or happy without a profession: *i.e.*, some regular employment which does not depend on the will of the moment, and which can be carried on so far mechanically, that an average quantum only of health, spirits, and intellectual exertion, are requisite to its faithful discharge. Three hours of leisure unalloyed by any alien anxiety, and looked forward to with delight as a change and recreation, will suffice to realise in literature a larger product of what is truly genial, than many weeks of compulsion." I found this to be true, in spirit and in fact. My future literary efforts were conceived in joy, and executed with pleasure. Whether they had any pecuniary results mattered little, for I had another occupation to live by.

I remember being called upon one day, at the office of the *Leeds Times*, by a gentleman from Armley, who introduced his son, a strong young fellow of about twenty, and said he wished him trained "as an editor." "An editor!" I said, "I never heard of such a thing. Why an editor?" "Well," he answered, "there are professions of doctors, barristers, and so on: why not editors?" "Simply because, like poets, editors are born, not made. A young man cannot be trained for an editor, as he can be for a doctor, or a manufacturer, or any other business." "But he *hates* business! he is a capital speaker, and wants to be an editor." "We have no openings, and we don't take apprentices." "Never mind," the father said, "let my son be admitted to the office, and let him try to do his best." We allowed him to look over the papers, and cut out paragraphs of news, and, if he could, to make a para-

graph by himself. But he was above that. The
young fellow wanted to make speeches, and write
articles! Of course, that could not be allowed. He
soon tired of looking over the papers and cutting out
bits of news; and then he disappeared. The next
time I saw his name, I found he had got among the
Chartists and made speeches. He could certainly
speak by the yard, but there was nothing in it. He
should have had his nose held to the grindstone for
some years, and then probably something might
have been made of him. What became of him afterwards, I do not know.

In March 1845, I was waited upon by a deputation of young men, who requested me to give them
a lecture, or at all events "to talk to them a bit," at
the Mutual Improvement Society which they had
established in what had before been a Cholera
Hospital, in St Peter's Square, Leeds. I complied
with their request, and delivered an address which
was afterwards published under the title of *The Education of the Working Classes.*

After citing the instances of men of worth and
valour who, in the face of the greatest difficulties, had
contributed to the honour of their race, enriched the
literature, and advanced the science, art, and commerce of their country, I observed :—

" Now, I would not have any one here to think,
that because I have mentioned a number of individuals who have raised themselves, by means of
self-education, from poverty to social eminence, and
even to great wealth—that these are the chief marks
to be aimed at; and that the cultivation of knowledge
is to be regarded only as a means of gaining a higher
position in society than that which you now hold.
This would be a great fallacy; and the encouragement of it could only end in disappointment.

"My object, in citing these instances, has been merely to show that adverse circumstances—even the barrenest poverty—cannot repress the human intellect and character, if it be determined to rise: that man can triumph over circumstances, and subject them to his will: that knowledge is no exclusive inheritance of the rich and the leisure classes, but may be attained by all : or, at all events, that no difficulties of situation, however great, can furnish any reason for despair.

"The education of the working-classes is to be regarded, in its highest aspect, not as a means of raising up a few clever and talented men into a higher rank of life, but of elevating and improving the whole class—of raising the entire condition of the working man. The grand object aimed at should be to make the great mass of the people virtuous, intelligent, well-informed, and well-conducted ; and to open up to them new sources of pleasure and happiness. Knowledge is, of itself, one of the highest enjoyments. The ignorant man passes through the world, dead to all pleasures save those of the senses. He sees no more of the beauties of existence than if he were blind. To the man whose mental eyes have never been touched with the divine breath, the world is all empty—at best a mere gallery of pictures ; while, to the intelligent, 'earth fills her lap with splendours.'

"I regard it as discreditable to this country that, while so much has been done to draw forth the resources of its soil, so little has been done to develop the character of its people. What signifies to me the richness of our territory, if it do not produce good and wise men? What matters it that our cotton or woollen fabrics are improved, if our citizens are deteriorated? What are the perfectness and multiplicity of our productive powers, if our people are miserable, depraved, and ignorant? What though the resources of our soil, our mines, and our seas, be developed, if the intellect of our people be allowed to remain uncultivated? It is there that the true seeds of prosperity and progress lie hid. There lie the truest riches of a state—the knowledge, virtue, and character of the nation.

"It may be—nay, it will inevitably happen—that

education will teach those who suffer how to remove
the causes of their sufferings ; and it may also make
them dissatisfied with an inferiority of social privilege.
This, however, is one of the necessary conditions of
human progress. If man be degraded, he must be
dissatisfied—discontented, if you will—with that condition of degradation, before he can make the necessary effort to rise out of it. It is the opprobrium of
some of the most wretched and suffering classes in
our land, that they are *contented* with their condition.
Theirs is the satisfaction of the blind who have never
known light.

"What is the great idea that has seized the mind
of this age? It is the grand idea of *man*—of the
importance of man as man ; that every human being
has a great mission to perform—has noble faculties
to cultivate, great rights to assert, a vast destiny to
accomplish. And the idea has also seized hold of the
public mind, that every human being should have the
means and the opportunity of education—and of
exercising freely all the powers, faculties, and affec-
tions of his god-like nature.

"What signifies it that our machines and our
fabrics are improved and multiplied, if our men are
not bettered in condition? What matters it how
much steam power we employ, if it keep man more
than ever yoked to the car of toil? Man, I insist, has
a *right* to leisure—for the improvement of his mind
as well as the preservation of his health ;—leisure to
think, leisure to read, leisure to enjoy ; and the true,
the benevolent, the humane, the Christian, application of James Watt's stupendous discovery of the
steam-engine would be — to abridge, instead of
increasing, the toil of the labouring classes, and
enable them to employ the time, thus set free, in the
cultivation and enjoyment of the highest faculties of
their nature. This would be the true improvement
of James Watt's splendid gift to man."

The enthusiasm with which these lectures were
received, and the rousing effect which they produced
on many of the young men who listened to them (of
which I afterwards frequently heard), induced me to

believe that a book written in the same spirit might
be of some use; and I proceeded to carry the idea
into effect. I was asked to deliver the lecture before
the Mechanics Institution at Woodhouse, and before
the young men connected with the Roman Catholic
Church at Leeds. For I may mention that I had
sympathy with all classes and sections of the community; and I believe I had friends amongst them all.
I have often had Roman Catholics, Dissenters, High
Churchmen, and Socialists, meeting together in
the most friendly manner at my house. And I, on
my part, was willing to help them all in every good
work.

I went on enlarging my lecture, and delivered it
at Thirsk and elsewhere. I kept adding to the
examples, and entered into correspondence with men
of influence and action. Some of my best illustrations were obtained in this way; and I endeavoured
to work them up into a sort of continuous narrative.
Then I arrived at the title by which my assemblage
of facts became afterwards known—*Self-Help*; but
the book so-called was not published for many
years after the date of its first delivery as a lecture.
In the meantime, another change in my destiny
occurred.

I hope the reader does not think that I was too
fond of making changes. I could not help it. I
tried to make a living by physic, but failed. I tried
newspaper editing; and, though it kept me, I found
that it would not maintain a wife and family. I tried
book-writing, and failed there too, so far as income
was concerned. Another change was, therefore,
necessary. Dr Mackintosh told me at Edinburgh
that "a rolling stone gathers no moss." However
this may be, I certainly gathered nothing by resting

and not rolling. I thought rolling was worth a trial. Change might do something for me. Idiots never change; but sensible people change for the better. Hence I changed, and now changed again; and my last change was certainly a successful one.

England was now at the commencement of the railway epoch. Since the opening of the Liverpool and Manchester line in 1830, the extension of railways had proceeded very slowly. The line connecting Liverpool with London was only opened in September 1838, on the completion of the London and Birmingham railway. I heard of the event during my first visit to London, after returning from Germany. Railways were gradually being extended in the manufacturing districts. In June 1839, the line from Manchester to Leeds was opened. In June 1840, I was invited to attend the opening of the North Midland Railway from Leeds to Derby. At the junction of the York and North Midland line, a train from York was waiting, containing George Hudson, George Stephenson, and some of the magnates of the North. I afterwards dined with the railway assemblage in the Music Hall at Leeds.

I often had the privilege of seeing and hearing George Stephenson after that event. He was a great favourite at Leeds, and was frequently invited to attend the soirees of the Mechanics Institute. He was a man of handsome presence—white-haired, blue-eyed, and ruddy—a wholesome, genial man. His addresses were very impressive. His very word "PERSEVERE!" had something inspiring in it. His advice was always most weighty, coming as it did from the fulness of his own experience.

Down to the year 1844, the extension of railways

had been comparatively moderate. But with the increase of traffic on the railways already made, and with the consequent increase of dividends, the shares rapidly rose in value, and many new lines were projected. Among the Railway Acts granted in 1845, were the Leeds, Dewsbury, and Manchester Railway (afterwards amalgamated with the London and North-Western Railway), and the Leeds and Thirsk Railway (afterwards amalgamated with the North-Eastern Railway). These two companies had offices in the same building. Railway service was so new, and the increase of new companies had recently been so rapid, that persons of experience were difficult to be had. Mr Fenton* was the secretary and assistant engineer (under Mr Grainger of Edinburgh) of the Leeds and Thirsk Railway; and as his assistant secretary, a Mr Easton, who was a man of experience, was about to leave him, he was in a great dilemma for some person to assist him in the office work. He told me of his difficulty, and said, "If you are not otherwise employed, and could come into the Leeds and Thirsk office to assist me, I should feel greatly obliged."

I considered the matter, and thought, "Shall I make this further change? Shall I leave finally the profession of medicine, in which, in course of time, I might succeed; or the profession of literature, in which I had to a certain extent failed, and where there was little probability of continual success?"

To succeed in medicine requires a great deal of time and experience; as well as, perhaps, family interest. It used to be said of doctors, that they

* Afterwards manager for the Low Moor Iron Company.

rarely got bread enough to eat, until they had not
teeth to eat it. Medical men are, to a certain extent,
the slaves of the public. While persons in other professions spend their evenings in peace, doctors are
obliged to work by night as well as by day—sometimes by night more than by day. If they do not go
to the patient who sends for them instantly, they are
denounced. They are sent for at meal times, or
when in church, or at night while in bed. Dr Lewins,
of Haddington, used to tell this story. A ploughman, after he had done his work, took the plough-
horse, and rode into the town "for the doctor."
"What's the matter?" cried the doctor (who had
been in bed) from the window. "My wife's got a
sair hoast" (or cough). "But what makes you come
at this time of night?" "I thought," said the
ploughman, "that I would be sure to find you at
hame!" Just so. Then a great deal of the work
done for the public is gratuitous. In the case of
those practising amongst the poor—which is the
case with nearly all young men—they think themselves very well off if they get one-half of the amount
of the bills they render, or at most three-fourths.
They are regarded as friends and even angels by
people when they are ill; but when the debt has
been incurred they are regarded as something very
much the reverse. They often get neither money
nor thanks. People often doubt whether they
have received value for their money. In the case
of the butcher, or baker, or tailor, it is different.
There was nothing, therefore, to detain me in this
profession.

Then, with regard to literature—in the case of
newspaper editing, the weekly quota of work must be
done. The editor must write, whether well or ill,

whether he has subjects worthy of discussion or not, he must thresh his straw, though threshed so often before; a veritable task of Sisyphus, requiring much brain work, or at least brain worry, and a good deal of mental endurance. Book-writing again is, after all, but a lottery. You may succeed, if you can find a proper subject, and give enough thought and investigation to its development, which, of course, requires time and leisure. Then, suppose you have finished your book, you must wait for the results of the "half profits" system. If your bookseller fails, as was the case with the principal seller of my *History of Ireland*, all your time and labour go for nothing. The results are absolutely fruitless. This is even more unsatisfactory than the practice of medicine.

Such being the case, and having now a wife and family to support, I accepted the advice of my friend Mr Fenton, and applied for the position of assistant secretary to the Leeds and Thirsk Railway. The mayor, Mr Luckock, backed my application; and having many friends and acquaintances at the Board — amongst others, Mr Henry Cowper Marshall, the chairman, Mr Baines, senior, of the *Leeds Mercury*, and others—I was elected to that office at the end of 1845; and shortly after, on the retirement of Mr Fenton to accept a more remunerative office, I was appointed full secretary. I was now free from the turmoil of politics. I could call my evenings my own, and spend them with my family, in quiet reading and quiet thinking. Though not extraordinarily well paid, I was to a certain extent independent, as my wants were few. My work was not arduous. It was regular and systematic—some might say humdrum; yet it was full of interest.

The object of the Leeds and Thirsk Railway was to connect the manufacturing districts of the West Riding more directly with the towns and villages in Wharfedale, with Harrogate and Knaresboro' Ripon, and the coal and iron districts of the North-West of England. The line, when first granted, effected a junction with the Great North of England (now the North-Eastern) Railway at Thirsk, and shortened the distance to the north by about twenty-three miles. From Leeds, it passed over the river Aire; then due northward through the Bramley Fall sandstone, and by a tunnel of about two miles long, under the Bramhope Ridge; then across the Wharfe, by a long viaduct to Pannal, Harrogate, and Knaresboro', and Ripon, to the junction with the main northern line near Thirsk. The first sod of the railway was cut in October 1845; the foundation stone of the Wharfedale railroad was laid by Mr H. C. Marshall, in March 1846; the first stone of the Bramhope Tunnel was laid by Mr Bray, the contractor, in the following July; and the whole of the work was soon in full progress.

My business — for it was a regular plodding business — consisted in attending the meetings of the Board and taking down the minutes, in arranging the calls upon the shares in compliance with the Act of Parliament, managing the finances, the correspondence, and the various business connected with a large railway company, under the directions of the Board. It was steady, routine work, requiring application, judgment, power of organisation, and trustworthiness. In none of these, I hope, was I found deficient; though the employment was not, on the whole, of a character to bring with it any fame or special reputation.

It is not necessary for me to go through the history of this railway, with which I was connected for so many years. I may mention, however, that the principal difficulty connected with it was an engineering one. When the contractor started with the Bramhope Tunnel, he began to cut into it at both ends, and sunk eight shafts down through the ridge, from south to north, to the level of the tunnel. Engines were erected over them, to pump the water out. When the water was reached, it rushed out like a flood, drove the men out of the shafts and drowned the works. The water came from an immense distance, under the sandstone rock, from as far as Ilkley, about eight or nine miles westward, where the wells were seriously affected. More powerful engines were erected, and still the water could not be pumped away sufficiently quick to enable the workmen to proceed with the quarrying of the tunnel.

George Hudson, who then reigned supreme as Railway King in the North, and who feared the competition of the new line, declared that the Bramhope Tunnel would never be made, that there were no pumps in existence that would pump the water out of the shafts, and that the company would be bankrupt long before the tunnel could be finished. Not so fast! The Leeds and Thirsk Company did not become bankrupt, but King Hudson did before the tunnel was finished. The once omnipotent man fell from his high estate, and was hounded to death by his own toadies and sycophants.

It was a fact, however, that the company could not find engines powerful enough to pump the water out of the shafts at the north end of the tunnel. The consequence was, that the pumping engines were stopped, and the men quarried along the drift-way, until they eventually reached the bottom of the shaft, where the water was most voluminous, and then, through the channel thus given, it flowed away in a sort of torrent at the north end, without any further necessity for pumping. This work was very tedious, and greatly protracted the opening of the railway. The directors nevertheless pushed forward the undertaking, and took measures, by raising new capital and obtaining fresh Acts of Parliament, to extend the line northward to Northallerton, Yarm, Middlesborough, Stockton, and Hartlepool. This rendered it necessary for me to be often in London, during the Parliamentary season, to give evidence before the committees, and to take the other steps with the directors and solicitor, for the progress of the undertaking.

I did not entirely leave my connection with literature. I think it was in December 1846, that a large meeting of the Manchester Unity of Odd-fellows took place in the Music Hall, at which Mr William Beckett, M.P., and Dr Hook made speeches, as well as Mr Robert Baker, Factory Commissioner, and myself. Mr Alexander Sherriffs was in the chair. He was then stationmaster at Marsh Lane, Leeds. By virtue of his ability, he was promoted step by step to be general manager of the York and North Midland Railway Company. At the end of his life, he became Member for Worcester, and was director of several companies of considerable commercial importance. The attention of Mr Edward Baines, senior, was attracted to the question by the proceedings at the above meeting. He asked me confidentially if I would furnish a series of articles on the Benefit Societies of the working-classes for the *Leeds Mercury;* and I had much pleasure in complying with his request. The proceedings of the Oddfellows were at that time little known, and I believe the articles in the *Mercury* proved of service. Mr Baines afterwards appeared publicly at a meeting in support of the institution. I was afterwards induced to undertake the editing of the quarterly *Oddfellows Magazine,* published at Leeds; in which I inserted many articles upon "Health," "The Improvement and Education of Women," "Suggestions for the Improvement of the Rates of Contribution," "Building Societies," "Life Assurance," "The Friendly Societies Bill," "Individual Improvement and Social Advancement," "The Condition of Benefit Societies," "Provide," "Laws of Mortality and Sickness," "The True Principles of Benevolent Societies," "The Widows' and Orphans' Fund," and other similar subjects.

When William Howitt and John Saunders, with great intentions, started the *People's Journal* in 1845, the former asked me to contribute articles, and in the first year I sent three, on "Benefit Societies and Education." During the second year (1846) I sent four, on "Factory Women," "Popular Amusement and Recreation," and two brief biographies (Vincent and Cobden). In the third year, I sent two more on the subject of Factory Women, and the measures being then taken for the improvement of their moral and social condition. This useful and interesting publication having been brought to an end by a quarrel between the proprietors, William Howitt started a weekly journal of his own, to which I transferred my small services.

To the first volume of *Howitt's Journal* I contributed an article on "A Scheme of Free Libraries," which, I believe, had the effect of starting a system of itinerant libraries for Yorkshire, principally through the active instrumentality of Mr Hole, in connection with the Leeds Mechanics Institute. The system was taken from that established by Samuel Brown in Haddington many years before, to which I was so greatly indebted when a youth. I also published two brief biographies in the same volume. To the second volume, I contributed three more memoirs of distinguished persons; and to the third, four more; and then the publication broke down, amidst a storm of angry communications and replies from the proprietors of the two ruined journals— Howitt and Saunders. It was altogether a most unhappy termination of an originally prosperous enterprise.

In the midst of Mr Howitt's labours upon his journal, he called upon me with Miss Margaret Gillies, an old friend; and spent the night at my house while I lived at Woodhouse Cliffe, near Leeds. The two had been at Hargate Hill, near Barnsley, for the purpose of seeing Ebenezer Elliott—the one for the purpose of making some memoranda for an article, and the other for the purpose of making a drawing of the "Corn-law Rhymer," both of which appeared in *Howitt's Journal* of 3rd April 1847. They told me that Elliott was ill and suffering; but that he would be glad to see me, in memory of old times, if I could ever run over and see him at his country house. I could not find time then; but about two years later, when the late William Bridges Adams, the engineer, who supplied our railway with some rolling stock, told me that he was going over to see Elliott, and invited me to accompany him, I determined to run over to Hargate Hill and visit the suffering and venerable poet.

It was on a Saturday afternoon, towards the end of October, that we were put down at Darfield Station on the North Midland Railway, and proceeded to walk up the hill towards Great Houghton Common. It was one of the last lovely days of autumn, when the faint breath of summer was still lingering among the woods and fields, as if too loath to depart from the earth she had gladdened. The foliage of the hedges and coppice was tinted in russet, purple, and brown, with just enough of green to give that perfect autumnal tint so lovely and pictorial. The beech-nuts were dropping from the trees and crackled underfoot, while a rich damp smell arose from the decaying leaves by the roadside.

After a short walk up the old Roman road leading into the famous Watling Street, in some places commanding beautiful views over the undulating country, we reached the village of Old Houghton, at the south end of which stands the famous Old Hall, an interesting remnant of middle-age antiquity. It was once the seat of the owner of the adjoining lands, a stern Presbyterian, but was now reduced to the condition of a public-house—"To what base uses may we come, Horatio!" Its fantastic gable ends, projecting windows, quaint doorway, diamond "quarrels," and its great size looming up in the twilight, with the well-known repute which the house bears of being "haunted," made one regard it with a strange awe-like feeling. It seemed not like a thing of this everyday world. Indeed, the place breathes the atmosphere of the olden time, which is not even dispelled by the inscription outside of "licensed to be drunk on the premises."

As it was open to the public, we entered, and then we observed a number of village labourers, ploughmen, and delvers, sitting in a boxed-off corner of the old squire's hall, drinking their Saturday night's quota of beer, amidst clouds of tobacco smoke; whilst the landlady, seated at a tap in a corner of the apartment, was dealing out potations to all comers and purchasers. A huge black deer's head and antlers projected from the wall near the door—evidently part of the antique furniture of the place; and we had a glimpse of a fine broad stone staircase winding up one of the deep bays of the Hall, evidently leading to the state apartments above. After this brief glance we proceeded up the hill to the more inviting house of the poet.

We reached it in the dusk of the autumn evening. There was just light enough to enable us to perceive that it was situated on a pleasant height near the hill-top, and commanded an extensive prospect of the undulating and finely-wooded country towards the south; while to the north there stretched away an extensive tract of moorland, covered with gorse bushes. The house we approached consisted of a simple, gable-ended, old English farm cottage, surrounded by a nicely kept garden and grass plot, with some of the late monthly roses still in bloom.

We were cordially welcomed by the poet, his wife, and two interesting daughters. Elliott looked the invalid that he was; for he was suffering from the fatal disease that soon after carried him off. He was pale and thin, and his hair was almost white. Age and suffering had deeply marked his features since I last saw him in his office at Sheffield. An anxious expression of features indicated the acute pain which

K

he constantly carried about with him. And yet he conversed cheerfully, and his manner was as flatteringly kind as ever.

After we had dismissed the subject of his health, the conversation ranged upon general topics; his countenance brightened up; he forgot himself and his anxieties, and seemed to become a new man. Notwithstanding his physical weakness—and he lay on an American rocking-chair propped up with pillows— his heart beat as warm and true as ever to the cause of human fellowship and universal good. The Bread Tax, which he had so often denounced, had now been repealed. He went over the old battle struggles of his life; displayed the same zeal, and held the same strong faith in the cause about which he had rhymed, long before it had seized possession of the public mind. He mentioned, what I had not before known, that the Sheffield Anti-Corn-Law Association was the first to start the system of operations afterwards adopted by the League, and that they were the first to employ Paulton as a public lecturer. But to Cobden he gave the praise of having popularised the cause, and knocked it into the public mind by dint of sheer hard work and strong practical common-sense; and to Cobden he still looked as the great leader of the day —the most advanced and influential man of his time. He was severe upon the Socialists. "What is a Communist?" he asked. "One who has yearnings for equal division of unequal earnings. Idler or bungler, he is willing to fork out his penny and pocket your shilling."

The patriotic struggle in Hungary enlisted his warmest sympathies; and he regarded Kossuth as "cast in the mould of the great heroes of antiquity." Of the Russian Czar he spoke as "that tremendous

villain Nicholas," and he believed him to be so
infatuated with his success in Hungary, that he would
not know where to stop, but would rush blindly to
his ruin.

The conversation passed on towards his occupations in this remote country spot, whither he had
retired from the busy throng of men, and the
engrossing pursuits and anxieties of business. Here,
he said, he had given himself up to meditation; nor
had he been idle with his pen, for he had a volume
of prose and poetry nearly ready for publication.
Strange to say, he spoke of his prose as the better
part of his writings, and, as he himself thought, much
superior to his poetry. But he is not the first instance
of a writer who has been in error as to the comparative
value of his works. On that question the world, and
especially posterity, will pronounce the true verdict.
His wife, he said, had been his best critic. The two
seemed very affectionate. She familiarly addressed
him as "Ebb" or "Ebby." This sounded very oddly
in my ears.

He spoke with great interest of the beautiful
scenery of the neighbourhood, which had been a
source to him, during his healthy period, of immense
joy and delight. He said we must go and see the
two great old oaks about a mile to the north, near
the old Roman road, under the shadow of which the
Wapentake, or muster of Weapon men, assembled
in former times. In the hollow of one of these oaks,
in more recent days, Nevison the highwayman used
to take shelter. Then he spoke of the fine wooded
country which stretched towards the south—Went-
worth, Wharncliffe, Conisborough, and the fine
scenery of the Dearne and the Don; and of the
many traditions which still lingered about the neigh-

bourhood, which, he said, some Walter Scott, could he gather them up before they died away, might make glow again with life and beauty.

"Did you see," he asked, "that curious Old Hall on your way up?"

"Yes."

"Well," he said, "that terrible despot, Lord Strafford, married his third wife from that very house, and afterwards lived in it for some time. No wonder the country folks say it is haunted; for if it be true that unquiet, perturbed spirits have power to wander on the earth, after the body to which they were before bound is dead, then *his* could never endure the rest of the grave. After his death, the Old Hall became the property of Sir William Rhodes, a stout Presbyterian and Parliamentarian. When the great civil war broke out, Rhodes took the field with his tenantry on the side of the Parliament, and the first encounter with the Royalists took place only a few miles north of Old Houghton. While Rhodes was at Tadcaster with Sir Thomas Fairfax, Captain Grey (an ancestor of the present Earl Grey), at the head of a body of 300 Royalist horse, attacked the Old Hall; and as there were only some thirty farm-servants left to defend it, the place was taken and set on fire. Everything that could burn was destroyed. But Oliver Cromwell eventually rode down the Cavaliers with his ploughmen at Marston Moor; and then Rhodes took possession of the Old Hall, and repaired it. You would see the little chapel at its west end: that was added, and a godly Presbyterian divine was appointed to minister in it; and a road was made from thence to Driffield, to enable the people of that place to reach it by a short and convenient route."

"I forget how it happened," he continued, "but I believe it was by marriage, that the estate fell into the possession, in these later days, of Monckton Milnes, the father of the poet, to whom it now belongs. As Monk Frystone was preferred for a family residence, the Old Hall was allowed to fall to decay; the fine old furniture and tapestry were removed to the new house at Monk Frystone; and the Old Hall is now used as a public-house."

And then the conversation turned upon young Monckton Milnes, his fine poetry, and his beautiful *Life of Keats:* on Keats, of whom Elliott spoke in enthusiastic terms as "the great resurrectionized Greek": on Carlyle, whom he admired as one of the greatest of living poets, though not writing in rhyme: on the Howitts, and their fine country books: on Longfellow, whose *Evangeline*, then just published, he longed to read. Of Southey he spoke in terms of much affection. "Southey," he said, "does not like my politics: he thinks me rabid; but he admires my poetry. I have two sons in the Church; he has gone out of his way to recommend their promotion, and secure livings for them. I am much indebted to him for his kindness and goodness. Besides, I admire his poetry and his prose, especially his *Life of Nelson*, which will perhaps live longer than all that he has written." And thus the evening stole on with delightful converse in the midst of that quiet, happy family—the listeners recking not that the lips of the eloquent speaker would soon be moist with the dews of death.

On my return home, I sent Ebenezer Elliott a copy of Longfellow's *Evangeline*, a shilling edition, which had just been published in England, and I received from him the following letter:—

"Hargate Hill, near Barnsley,
"*3rd November* 1849.

"My dear Sir,—
          "If ever you can spare a little time,
bring Mrs Smiles with you. I think we could keep
you 'wick,' as we Yorkshire folks say, for a few days.
We have always a stranger's bed, slept in every other
night, and it will hold two; and though we can't go
to market as you can, we are seldom without bacon
and eggs. You would be quite a godsend — not
that I want for society here, but it is of the wrong
sort.
    "How truly good you are! But I know not how
to repay you for *Evangeline*—unless I send you a
shilling, and that, I suppose, would affront you.
    "Longfellow is indeed a poet, and he has done
what I deemed an impossibility; he has written
English hexameters, giving our mighty lyre a new
string! When Tennyson dies, he should read
Evangeline to Homer.—I am, yours very truly,
                          "Ebenezer Elliott.

    "My wife and daughters send their best respects
to you and your lady, and it is perhaps well that the
latter does not hear what they say of *you*.
    "*N.B.*—They are discovering that you are a
Scotsman."

    But it was not to be. Poor Elliott died in less
than a month from the date of his letter to me—that
is, on the 1st of December 1849. The sadly pained
look of his face prepared me for the event. I knew
that his disease was fatal, and perhaps he knew it
himself. Yet he kept up his own spirits, and the
spirits of those about him, in a wonderful way. Only
a fortnight before his death, his beloved daughter
was married. He was supported from his bed to
the window, to see the return of the party from
church. The fatigue was almost more than he could
bear. "My child," he said to his daughter Fanny,

" I feel so weak that an infant might fell me with a primrose." Hearing a Robin Redbreast singing beneath his chamber window, he had strength enough left to dictate to his daughter the following sweet little poem, to the air of " 'Tis time this heart should be unmoved " :—

> " Thy notes, sweet Robin, soft as dew,
>   Heard soon or late, are dear to me ;
> To music I could bid adieu,
>   But not to thee.

> " When from my eyes this life-full throng
>   Has past away, no more to be ;
> Then, autumn's primrose, Robin's song,
>   Return to me."

These were his last lines.

There was a mixture of fierceness and yet of tenderness in Elliott's poetical writings. When he felt himself the champion of an oppressed class, he wrote with a welding heat, and threw out thoughts full of burning passion, "like white hot bolts of steel." Such verses sprang out of a truly noble wrath ; but better thoughts came to him in quieter times, and then he overflowed with sympathy for his fellow-men. While denouncing his opponents so hotly in political strife, he had all the while a deep well of tenderness in his heart. He used to say that he was descended from some famous Elliott, a border reiver from beyond the Tweed ; and perhaps some of the ancient bitterness still clung to him. Nevertheless, he was fearless, honest, sincere, and persevering—a fine specimen of that determined, sturdy character, which has made the North of England the hive of the world's industry. Although, like Burns, he wrote an epitaph for his own tombstone, I think that the

following lines, written nine months before his
death, describe his best and truest character more
fittingly.

"LET ME REST.

" He does well who does his best :
　Is he weary? let him rest :
　Brothers ! I have done my best,
　I am weary—let me rest.
　After toiling oft in vain,
　Baffled, yet to struggle fain ;
　After toiling long, to gain
　Little good with mickle pain,—
　Let me rest—But lay me low,
　Where the hedgeside roses blow ;
　Where the little daises grow,
　When the winds a-maying go ;
　Where the footpath rustics plod ;
　Where the breeze-bow'd poplars nod ;
　Where the old woods worship God ;
　Where His pencil paints the sod ;
　Where the wedded throstle sings ;
　Where the young bird tries his wings ;
　Where the wailing plover swings
　Near the runlet's rushy springs !
　Where, at times, the tempest's roar,
　Shaking distant sea and shore,
　Still will rave old Barnesdale o'er
　To be heard by me no more !
　There, beneath the breezy west,
　Tir'd and thankful, let me rest,
　Like a child, that sleepeth best
　On its gentle mother's breast."

There is a feature in Elliott's history worthy of
notice. His life proved, what has been a disputed
point, that the cultivation of poetic and literary
tastes is perfectly compatible with success in trade
and commerce. It is a favourite dogma of some,
that he who courts the muses or indulges in composition must necessarily be unfitted for the practical
business of life; and that to succeed in trade or
business, a man must live altogether for it, and

never rise above the consideration of its petty
details. This is, in my opinion, a false and grovel-
ling notion, and at variance with actual experience.
In this matter I speak for myself, and merely use
the experience of Ebenezer Elliott in confirmation of
my views.

Generally speaking, you will find the successful
literary man a person of industry, application,
steadiness, and sobriety. He must be a hard worker.
He must sedulously apply himself. He must
economise time, and coin it into sterling thought, if
not into sterling money. His habits tell upon his
character, and mould it into consistency. If he is in
business, he must needs be diligent; and his intelligence will give him resources, which to the ignorant
man are denied. It may not have been so in the
last century, when the literary man was a *rara avis*,
a world's wonder, who was fêted and lionised until
he became irretrievably spoilt; but now, when all
men are readers, and a host of men have become
writers, the literary man is no longer a novelty;
he drags quietly along in the social team, engages
in business, economises, and succeeds, just as
other men do, and often to much better purpose
than the illiterate and uncultivated. Some of the
most successful men in business at the present day,
are men who wield the pen in the intervals of their
daily occupations,* some for self-culture, others for
pleasure, others because they have something cheerful
or instructive to communicate to their fellow-men.
Shall we say that they are less usefully employed
than if they had been sitting at a concert hearing a
symphony, in a theatre seeing a play, at the club

* I have furnished many illustrations of this statement in
Character, pp. 111-122.

playing whist, sleeping over a newspaper, or, after a dinner, cracking filberts over the wine, and perhaps riddling their "friends" with the sparrow-hail of next-door-neighbour scandal?

Ebenezer Elliott not only attended sedulously to his business, but improved his mind and cultivated his literary taste during the hours of leisure. He had more difficulties to encounter than most men. He was originally a dull boy, though sensitive. He was unable to learn anything, and was regarded as unconquerably stupid. He used to regard his companion, John Ross, who did his sums for him, with intense admiration. His brother Giles was very clever, and could learn anything; but he was ruined by praise, and did nothing. Giles was put into an office, in which his father was clerk, to write out invoices and post the ledger; while Ebenezer was sent into the foundry to do hard and dirty work. The positions of the two boys became completely reversed in their subsequent lives. The character of Ebenezer was formed amid the rough surroundings of the forge and the foundry, but, stimulated by the desire of excelling, he was indefatigable in study. He went into the steel and bar-iron trade at Sheffield, and by attention to his business, he realised enough for a competency, and eventually retired upon it. At the same time he gained a reputation as a poet, equal to that of the best of his time; though I do not think his merits are sufficiently esteemed. There is no complete collection of his works; nor has any complete memoir of him yet been written. I have often thought that a Life of Ebenezer Elliott, if properly composed, might prove a thrilling and inspiring book for young men. He himself once wrote the commencement of his autobiography, but

was stopped by the recollection of some terrible
crisis in his life. He could not get over it, and laid
down his pen in despair. I hope it may yet be
possible for a life of this good man and true poet to
be published. It might be equal to that of Benjamin
Franklin, and much better than that of William
Hutton. Elliott was, on the whole, one of the
most interesting and remarkable men of modern
times.

During the same year in which Elliott died (1849),
I was requested to give evidence before a select committee of the House of Commons, on the Establishment of Free Public Libraries. I happened to be in
London on the business of the Railway Company,
and was very glad to give such information as I
possessed. Mr Ewart was in the chair; Mr Disraeli,
Mr Monckton Milnes, Lord Elcho, and others, were
on the committee. I related briefly what I knew of
the want of libraries in Leeds and the West Riding
of Yorkshire; of the libraries in connection with
Mechanics Institutes; of the Mutual Improvement
Societies established by the working-classes and the
difficulties they had in purchasing books of reference;
of the want of elementary instruction in the first
place; and the want of opportunities afterwards
for those who have learnt to read. Mr Monckton
Milnes put a curious question: "Have you found
the literary habits of artisans very much affected by
the circumstances of good or bad trade?" "Yes;
but not to so large an extent as might be supposed.
During a period of great depression, two or three
years ago, several mechanics institutions were formed
in villages in the West Riding, because the working
people had time to spare; but as soon as the mills
began running full time again, the institutions were

dropped. The people had simply employed in self-improvement the time that was liberated during the scarcity of employment in the mills." I also gave some evidence as to the uses of the system of Itinerating Libraries which had been established in Haddingtonshire; and afterwards sent in a letter giving a tabular view of the libraries in connection with the Yorkshire Union of Mechanics Institutes, which was published with the minutes of evidence and the report of the proceedings.

In the following year, a permissive Act was passed for the purpose of promoting Public Libraries, and for establishing and extending Public Museums of Art and Science in Municipal Boroughs, in the interest of the instruction and recreation of the people. I took the opportunity of publishing a letter in the *Leeds Mercury* of 9th November 1850, calling attention to these important powers, and urging their adoption in Leeds. I concluded as follows :—

" I know that the cost will be objected to. I only speak of the extreme desirableness of our having a Town Hall, with a Public Library, and accommodation for a Public Museum. What was the cost of our gaol? What of our pauper training schools? We have built these irrespective of the question of cost. Are we to have it said of us that we lack spirit to get up any public buildings, excepting they be for the purposes of accommodating criminals and paupers? Do we not owe something to ourselves and to those who are neither criminals nor paupers? Is not the founding of a Public Library as creditable, as necessary, and as beneficial, a work as the erection of a gaol? I conclude by expressing my conviction that the borough of Leeds would do itself lasting honour by taking the lead in providing a Public Library under the provisions of the Public Libraries and Museums Act of 1850."

Years passed before the Free Library Act was passed; and now it is doing good public service. My words may have been like seed cast into the ground, to bring forth fruit after many days.

CHAPTER XI

I CONTINUED to work regularly at the Railway Company's Office. There was much to do; "calls" to be made and looked after; money to be borrowed on loan and debenture to meet the heavy charges for constructing the line; and a good deal of correspondence to be conducted. New Acts had also to be applied for, which led me to be often in London to give evidence during the Parliamentary session.

The line, as originally laid out, ended at a junction with the Great North of England Railway, near Thirsk. But this was no sufficient terminus. It was found necessary to carry the line further, and to bring it into connection with the important seaport towns of the North. It was then determined to apply for Acts to enable the line to be extended to Stockton, Hartlepool, and perhaps Sunderland and Newcastle-upon-Tyne; as well as to make junctions with the Stockton and Darlington Railway, near Stockton and Middlesborough, and also with the York and Newcastle Railway at Ferryhill, in the county of Durham.

In 1848, Acts were applied for and obtained, to extend the railway to Stockton-on-Tees, and to a junction with the Stockton and Hartlepool Railway, by which an access could be obtained to the thriving new port of West Hartlepool. The name of the Company was altered from "Leeds and Thirsk" to "Leeds Northern." New shares were got out and taken up with difficulty. Preference shares were created, and taken up with greater ease. In the meantime the works were pushed forward. The first locomotive passed through the Bramhope Tunnel on the 31st of May 1849; and the directors opened the line to Thirsk on the 9th of July following.

In the meantime, a large block of land had been purchased in Wellington Street for the purposes of the new station in Leeds. Several other companies desired to have station accommodation in the town, more especially the London and North-Western Company, which had absorbed the Leeds, Dewsbury, and Huddersfield Railway; the Great Northern, which had obtained access to Leeds; and the Leeds and Manchester Company, which desired to have station accommodation of its own. The necessary land was purchased under the powers of the Leeds and Thirsk Act; and the four companies arranged to have the land divided and the necessary station works erected under the control of a special Board or Committee, the members of which were appointed by the four companies concerned. At their first meeting they appointed me secretary of the "Leeds Central Station," and this, of course, led to new work.

The new Board contained some very interesting personages—intimately connected with the early history of railways in England. Among these the most important was Henry Booth, the first secretary of the Liverpool and Manchester Railway, the inventor of the coupling screw and of several other useful contrivances connected with railway working.

Booth was a man of remarkable shrewdness and ability; he had a considerable literary turn, and had the germ of the mechanician in him from his earliest years. He might have made a fortune by his coupling screw had he patented it; but he threw this useful invention open to the world. It was, moreover, his suggestion of the multi-tubular boiler, which enabled George Stephenson's Rocket to win the prize at Rainhill, when the amount of the prize was equally divided between Booth and Stephenson. This important invention also was not patented, so that Mr Booth was a man who deserved the gratitude of the entire railway world.

Mr Cubitt was the engineer who represented the Great Northern Company, and Mr Hawkshaw the Leeds and Manchester Company — both very interesting men. It was a treat to observe the quickness with which they saw the points of a case, and the rapidity with which they did their work—brushing away everything that was immaterial and subsidiary—all that could be done by subordinates, who were required diligently to report progress.

Mr Beckett Denison, one of the members for the West Riding, was almost invariably present at the meetings of the Board, and when there he was always appointed to preside. He made an excellent chairman. He kept the discussions closely to the point, allowed no gossip to interfere, saw that the heads of the minutes taken were accurate; and when the business was despatched, which was done quickly but perfectly, he was as cheerful and gossipy as the rest. It was like a fresh breeze of air to get Beckett Denison to appear amongst us. He was a fine, tall, jolly man—full of fun; and yet an excellent man of business.

I remained the secretary of this Board (the Leeds Central Station) until the completion of the arrangements, which was after I left the company's service. It is not necessary to go into the details of a railway secretary's work. One day is like another, as with all routine business. My evenings were all my own. I could do with them what I thought pleasant, profitable, and useful. I have said that I used to write some articles for *The People's* and afterwards for *Howitt's Journal.* Both these publications died, amidst strife, in 1848; and in the course of the following year I entered into another arrangement, which gave me a good deal of literary employment during my leisure hours.

In the summer of 1849, my friend Miss Cushman was invited to spend a few days or weeks at my house; and she asked beforehand "if she might bring a friend with her." "By all means," was my reply. She accordingly brought her friend; and she turned out to be Miss Eliza Cook, the well-known popular poetess. In the course of this visit, Miss Cook told me the reason of her desire to see me. It was because she intended to start a weekly periodical, and she asked me if I would help her with some useful articles—such as I had been accustomed to write for other papers. I agreed, and sent her an article weekly, on such subjects as "The Preservation of Health," "The Practice of Temperance," "Providing against the Evil Day," "Emigration," "Young Men's Mutual Improvement Societies," "Industrial Schools for Young Women," and a few biographic sketches.

Among the latter, I gave, in the fifth number of *Eliza Cook's Journal,* an outline of the life of George Stephenson. I obtained my information principally

L

from my friend and fellow-official, John Bourne,
engineer of the Leeds Northern Railway. Like every
Newcastle man, he was a great admirer of the manly
character and inborn genius of the father of railway
engineering. He had worked under him and with
him, on several of the coal lines of the north; and had
a great store of anecdotes of his early life, and the
difficulties he had surmounted in his efforts after
knowledge. Some of them were traditional, and had
gathered, in the course of re-telling, accretions
which were more or less fictitious—something like
the "Three Black Crows." For instance, the story
of his being at first a "trapper" in the coal pit, was
not well founded. The story, also, of his having first
made love to the mistress and then (being rejected)
to her servant, was only a fiction of the imagination.
I did not know at the time that these stories were
apocryphal, and I gave circulation to Mr Bourne's
narrative. The article was copied into the newspapers, in town and country, and no doubt helped
the circulation of Miss Cook's journal in many
ways.

The idea occurred to me, that the life of George
Stephenson was one well worth writing out fully—
not only because of the striking character of the man,
but because of the wonderful impulse which he had
given to civilisation by the development of the railway locomotive. There must be many men still
living, who could give information about his early
life, his growth, his education, his history, and his
great achievements. If the opportunity were allowed
to pass, a great deal of good example as well as of
interesting history, might be utterly lost to future
students of the times amidst which we lived. I
determined to call upon Robert Stephenson at his

offices in London, during one of the many visits which I then paid to the Metropolis.

I was received by Mr Stephenson very kindly. In answer to my inquiries, he said that there had been some talk of writing the life of his father, but that nothing had been done. Indeed, he had given up the hope of seeing it undertaken. Besides, he doubted whether the subject possessed much interest; and he did not think the theme likely to attract the attention of literary men of eminence.

"If people get a railroad," he said, "it is all that they want: they do not care how or by whom it is made. Look at the *Life of Telford*, a very interesting man: it has been published lately, and has fallen still-born from the press."

I replied that I thought the *Life of Telford* had been very badly done, and, as a biography, contained very little of human interest. If I decided to write the life of his father, I would endeavour to treat of his character as a Man as well as an Engineer.

"Well," he said, "I think you are right. But I thought it better to warn you against losing your time, your labour, and your money. If, however, you decide to write the Life, let me know, and I shall be very glad to help you."

This was all that I could hope for at that time. I took advantage of the next Easter holidays, and went down to Newcastle to look over the ground. Mr Stephenson furnished me with a letter to Mr Budden, his business manager at the Forth Street works. I saw him, and he gave me some information. I went to George Stephenson's birthplace at Wylam, and had an interview with Jonathan Foster, who told me all about "Puffing Billy" and the old colliery engines. After a few days' inquiry, I found the results I was able to collect were very meagre. The information I wanted existed only in the memories of individuals, from whom it had to be gathered by intercourse, and by slow degrees. Thus I came to the conclusion that the preparation of a satisfactory Life of George Stephenson, from authentic sources, required an actual residence for some period in the districts where he had lived; and as the pursuits in which I was then engaged rendered this altogether out of the question, I abandoned the project—but it turned out that this was only for a time.

To return to my contributions to Eliza Cook. During the first year of her journal, I furnished only one article a week. But as the publication went on, the editress seemed to like my articles more and more. In the second volume, I contributed an article entitled "Drinking," which excited a good deal of interest amongst the temperance people. A deputation waited on Miss Cook, and presented her with a handsomely-bound copy of Peter Burne's *Teetotaller's Companion, or, A Plea for Temperance*, "in acknowledgement of her efforts to promote the benefit of society, and particularly for the excellent article on 'Drinking' in No. 39 of her valuable journal." Miss Cook kindly sent me the present, with this inscription : "As this volume is due to my esteemed friend Dr Smiles rather than to myself, I have sincere pleasure in presenting it to him, with the earnest hope that his benevolence and talent may ever produce, as they do now, good to man and honour to God."

Miss Cook asked me to increase my contributions, and I proceeded accordingly. I wrote stories, noveletes, reviews, travels, articles on domestic life, on young women, on boys and young men, on benefit societies, on savings banks, on popular education, on temperance, and a large number of brief biographies. Miss Cook was not satisfied. Like Oliver, she still "asked for more"; until in the fourth and fifth volumes of her journal, I must have contributed at least one half of the articles in each number. I turned all my holiday journeys to account. I contributed my "Walk up the Rhine," my visits to Bolton Abbey (that charming resort of Yorkshire people); and, in 1851, after making a journey to Ireland during my annual fortnight's holiday, I communicated the results to the journal in my "Autumn Trip through Munster." This continued for several years, until the middle of 1854, when, the journal getting into new hands in consequence of the illness of Miss Cook, I ceased my contributions, and an end came to that source of employment for my leisure hours.

The only question in which I continued to take a public interest was that of Education. Men were still calling out for the extension of political privileges, although there was every reason to fear that the bulk of grown men were grossly uneducated, even in the first rudiments of learning. More than half the women married at the parish church could not write their own names. Matters were still worse at Bradford, and other towns in the West Riding. Lancashire was even worse than Yorkshire. Agitations were got up to remedy this state of things.

Among others, Dr Hook, the vicar of Leeds, published a pamphlet recommending a system of national education, in which religion should be excluded from the school teaching (but be taught, as in Holland, by special religious teachers), and that the schools should be supported by local rates, and superintended by committees chosen by the justices of the peace. This was considered by many an exceedingly liberal view at the time. The Doctor urged that churchmen and dissenters should merge their differences, in order, at least, to ensure an efficient school education for the rising generation of children; "for although," he said, " I would not confound moral training with what I consider to be religious education, yet such training may be used as the handmaid of religion, and for want of it, thousands of our fellow-creatures are relapsing into barbarism, and becoming worse than heathen."

On the other hand, the dissenters were at that time opposed to anything in the shape of help by Act of Parliament. They would not have State help; they would not have help from local rates and local management. They insisted that education, as well as religion, should be conferred by voluntary efforts only. But voluntaryism was doing next to nothing for education. The only flourishing schools at that time were the schools established by the Church and by Wesleyan congregations, and these were aided by direct subventions from the State. According to the returns published in the minutes of the Committee of Council on Education for 1850, thirty-seven schools (principally built and supported by members of the Church) were receiving about £2280 in Annual Educational Grants; whereas there was only one school belonging to the dissenters in Leeds supported on the purely voluntary principle.

In April 1850 some persons—for the most part belonging to the working class—interested in the progress of Education, and anxious to do away with this unsatisfactory state of things, desired me to attend a public meeting in the Court House, to support a resolution in favour of the Bill then before the House of Commons, "to promote the secular education of the people of England and Wales." I consented to do so. I also formed part of a deputation to wait upon Dr Hook, and to ask him to attend the meeting. The Doctor received us very kindly; but he said, "I have published my views on the subject, and my appearance on the occasion might possibly be hurtful to the cause. Nevertheless, I wish you every success."

The meeting was held in the Court House on the 11th of April 1850. My old friend, Mr Hamer Stansfeld, presided, and made an excellent speech. In the course of his remarks he said, "It is lamentable to find the point of view from which this educational struggle is regarded by some—that religion is the bar to the progress of education. It is not religion that is to blame, but sectarianism — principles almost opposite in their nature. It is the intent and purpose of Christianity to draw us together and teach us to love one another. It is, alas, the tendency of sectarianism to produce the very opposite results. I would myself that the pure spirit of the Christian religion were interwoven with every thought and word and deed of man, and consequently should prefer the combination of unsectarian religion with education; but should the working-classes prefer a secular scheme, and that the religious part should be left to the care and attention of the parents and the minister of religion, and to the action of the voluntary principle, I would trust them. Educate them upon their own terms—educate them at their own price— educate, educate, educate—and rest assured that, if

once an educated people, they will be all the more
likely to be a religious people."

I followed Mr Stansfeld, and moved the first
resolution. I believe I made the longest speech
of the evening — I say nothing of its value. I
was followed by Mr William Brook and others;
and the resolutions were carried with immense
applause.

It must, however, be added that the Voluntaries,
or Anti-State Educationists, did not put in an appearance at this meeting. They made a requisition to
the mayor to summon another public meeting in the
Cloth Hall Yard, for the purpose of petitioning
Parliament against the measure then before the
House of Commons. The meeting was held accordingly on the 16th of April; and there the pitched
battle was fought. The resolution against the Bill
was moved by Alderman Carbutt, and supported
by the Rev. Mr Williams, Mr Edward Baines,
and others. Mr Hamer Stansfeld moved, and I
seconded, an amendment in favour of the Bill: this
was ably supported by Mr Councillor Barker, and
after much vigorous speaking the amendment was
declared to be carried.

This, however, was only the beginning of the
agitation. In the following year, two schemes were
started at Manchester—one the National Public
School Association, of which Mr Cobden was among
the principal advocates, and the other the Rev. Mr
Richson's plan. The leading system of both was
that the public schools were to be maintained by local
rates, and subject to responsible local management.
I entered again into communication with Mr Cobden,
and received from him the following letter, which will
explain his views on the subject :—

"EXHIBITION BUILDING, KENSINGTON ROAD,
"LONDON, 10th *October* 1851.

"MY DEAR SIR,—

"It appears to me that the education question, in its practical shape, is being fought out now in the wards and congregations of Manchester. The 'National' and the 'Manchester and Salford Plan' are those under discussion; and it appears to me that the prevailing form of opinion is in favour of the latter. If so, a private Bill will be applied for, applicable to Manchester only, and will, I have no doubt, be obtained; and in that case it will probably become a model for other places. I do not disguise from myself that the 'Manchester and Salford Plan' will be to a great extent a new endowment of all religions.

"As a Churchman, I could not, of course, pretend that it violates my conscience. But I thought that it would be differently viewed by Dissenters; and in justice to them I made an effort to carry the Secular System. But it seems to me that the latter scheme has been met by the more influential part of the Dissenters with more opposition than the Manchester and Salford Plan; and I therefore consider that for the present it is hopeless to contend against the Church and Dissent.

"So strongly am I impressed with the necessity of some progress being made in the education of the people, that I do not feel myself justified in opposing any plan having that object in view; and therefore, unless the majority of the people of Manchester oppose the local scheme, I shall certainly not do so. If it be carried, I have no doubt Leeds will soon apply for a similar Act.

"I think the course pursued by the Dissenters is most unfortunate for the cause of education, and most unwise with regard to the interests of 'Voluntaryism'; but the latter is their own affair. At one thing I am greatly surprised—that they should so little understand the tendency of public opinion as to dream for a moment that they can prevent *any* and *every* scheme of public education from being adopted. But, as I grow older, I expect less wisdom or consistency from public bodies.—Believe me, in haste, your truly, R. COBDEN."

The agitation went on for some time. Mr Edward Baines (afterwards Sir Edward), the great leader of the "Voluntaries," delivered a lecture in the Stock Exchange Hall of Leeds, urging the adequacy of voluntary effort to educate the rising generation. In fairness to the Public School Association, whose views I advocated, Mr Baines generously permitted me to answer his lecture in the columns of the *Leeds Mercury*, of which he was editor. My answer was afterwards published and circulated gratuitously by the National Public School Association at Manchester. Mr Cobden again wrote to me from Midhurst, Sussex, and said :—

"I beg to thank you for taking up the cudgels for *common sense* and *common prudence*. What an extraordinary spectacle it is to see our friend Baines fighting against *both !* How any man, honest as he undoubtedly is, with eyes open, and walking in the paths of active life, can endeavour to reconcile us to the present state of the education of the masses, passes my comprehension."

And again :—

"Many thanks for your favour and papers. The facts contained in your letter respecting the failures of Voluntaryism (*in*voluntaryism would be better) in Leeds, ought to silence our good friend of *The Mercury*. But his sound and acute intellect is evidently under the influence of monomania upon the education question. It is only this that can account for the fallacious way in which he persists in arguing against a *centralised government* scheme, when everybody but himself knows that what we all want is a *parochial* or municipal plan, which he is doing his utmost to prevent us from obtaining.

"In a later article, almost entirely devoted to this argument, he uses the word 'Government' or 'State' about thirty times. How is it possible ever to come to an end in a controversy when one of the disputants thus persists in starting from fallacious premises? The quotation from Justice Coleridge is the true answer to Mr Baines's school statistics.

"The fact is the children of the poor do not learn enough to enable them in after life to read with ease or pleasure. The schools are often mere pretences for education—sometimes, indeed, put up to prevent somebody else from educating the people. There is too much truth in the remark made by Archbishop Whately at Manchester—that some people join in the education movement for the purpose of thwarting it. If we were half as anxious for the education of the people as we pretend, don't you think we should manage to get over the sectarian impediments that are now allowed to impede us?

"I observe what you say about starting a newspaper in London.* If I were bent upon a speculation in Cockney journalism, I would reserve myself till the compulsory stamp is abolished, which must be ere long. It is too gross a proof of the hypocrisy of our advocacy of education to put fetters on the press and taxes upon the raw materials of its manufacture. When the stamp is off, we shall have papers of all sizes and prices; and the largest circulation will be the London penny and halfpenny *dailies*. These will not take the place of the *Times*, which is now the cheapest paper in the world—talent, size, and cost of production, taken into consideration; but they will supply the wants of those who do not require so expensive and elaborate an article as the *Times*.

"Have you seen the article against the removal of the stamp in the *Edinburgh Review*? It argues that the newspaper proprietors and the public are gainers by the present system of compelling each copy of the paper to be stamped, but giving in return the privilege of retransmission for any number of turns by post. Now, I meet this argument, put

* As the amalgamation of the Railway Company with which I was connected, with two other adjacent companies, was under consideration—which would probably put an end to my services as a railway secretary—I at one time contemplated such an event,

forth by the old-established journals, with this proposal. I will allow all existing newspapers to retain their present privilege of retransmission, provided they continue to stamp their whole impression; allowing all papers hereafter established the option of stamping or not, but giving them the privilege of sending their stamped copies once only, with the same stamp, through the post. How long would the old proprietors continue to argue that the present system is most advantagous for the press and the public?

"The *Reviewer*, who is the conductor of an old established *Free Trade* (in corn) paper, lays great stress on the fact that people retransmit the 5d. papers through the post several times, and continue to read them three or four days after publication. That is—not being able to buy a paper at first hand, they take it second hand. It is about the last article which in America could be sold at any price on such conditions. Poor people, in the village where I am writing (Dunford, Midhurst), are glad to take my tea leaves the day after I have used them; but what a strange argument it would be, if I were to use that fact as a reason why the duty should not be taken off tea!"

Two years after the above meeting held in the Cloth Hall Yard, when the amendment was carried in favour of local rates and local administration, another meeting was called to petition against the Bill then before Parliament, for the promotion of education in cities and boroughs in England. It was held on the 13th of June 1853. I was in London on parliamentary business at the time, but I was afterwards informed that the notice of the meeting had been given in the dissenting chapels, and that the Voluntaries mustered very strongly at the public meeting held in the Coloured Cloth Hall Yard. Mr James Garth Marshall moved the resolution in favour of National Education; an amendment against the

Bill was proposed by Mr Alderman Carbutt, and, being put to the meeting, was declared to be carried. Thus the resolution carried at the first public meeting was negatived by that carried at the second public meeting held two years later.

I may here give a further communication received from Mr Cobden. I believe the first part of the letter refers to some articles which I was solicited to write for a Glasgow newspaper, called (I think) *The Constitutional*, in which I recommended the adoption of some method of local legislation, by which much expense might be saved, and the time of the Imperial Parliament greatly economised. The idea of bringing numbers of witnesses from the remotest parts of the empire, on some Gas Bill, or Drainage Bill, or Water Bill, or Railway Bill, seemed to me absurd, and I cited many reasons for the adoption of my proposed measure. Hence Mr Cobden's reference to it.

"MIDHURST, 17th *November* 1853.

" MY DEAR SIR,—
            " I agree with you in the tendency of both your articles.

" As respects local legislation, I think it would be a great step in your direction if we had general Acts passed, applicable to the current wants of towns or districts, the provisions of which might be applied voluntarily by the majority of the locality, in the way in which the Municipal Corporation Act can be applied to a town. But I would make it more easy than by a reference to the Privy Council: and here your idea of local legislatures might be brought to bear. For instance, why should not we have a general lighting, watering, improving, educating, etc., Act?—each containing provisions applicable to *any* locality? But the truth is, our governing class is at heart (notwithstanding great professions) not fond of increasing the power of local self-government.

"As respects your other article on Strikes, I think what is generally wanted is a more thorough recognition of *the rights of individuals.* Depend on it, there is a spice of despotism at the bottom of all this intervention by combined bodies in the concerns of individuals—and you know how abjectly subservient the working-classes are to the dictation of a trades-union junta. I think we shall not get right till there is a revolt against all such organisations, whether on one side or another, in the interest of *liberty*—PERSONAL LIBERTY. The much greater respect felt between both classes and individuals for one another in these social questions in America, arises from the far higher respect felt for the personal liberty of Man, *as such*, than we, with all our boasting, really feel. The vices of a hard, overbearing regime, natural to our aristocratic form of government, enter into all the relations of life, both social and political, and no class is free from the taint. We are an overbearing people, to other nations and to ourselves.

"By the way, apropos of our old question, which lies at the bottom of all others, I observe that our friend Baines, in his last week's paper, has a letter to prove how much progress we are making in schooling, and he gives some statistics to show that we have, during the last eighteen or twenty years, increased our schools to the extent of 7000; and he takes credit to the *voluntary system* for all this. But this is just the time during which our wretchedly imperfect government system has been at work, and in which we have made Government Grants to the extent of a million or a million and a half sterling for building schools, which would go a great way towards erecting all the school-houses named. But many of these schools, so far from giving education, are really little better than pretences for *not* educating the people.— Yours very truly,

"R. COBDEN."

In this position the educational question continued for many years; and there is little doubt that the agitation in Lancashire and Yorkshire ripened the opinions of many leading men on the subject. At last, when Household Suffrage in towns was granted by the Conservative Government of Lord Derby in 1867, and it was found that there must be a measure of National Education, in order to enable the new constituencies properly to use their powers, the prejudices of the Dissenters in favour of voluntary education were suddenly swept to one side by public opinion; and Mr Forster, member for Bradford, by a rare union of tact, wisdom, and common sense, introduced and carried his measure for the long-wished-for education of the English people. It embodied nearly all that the National Public School Association had so fruitlessly demanded years before; and on the whole, it has till now worked fairly well. In course of time, its defects, to which all things human are liable, will doubtless be remedied.

It is curious to see how public bodies can so summarily "jump Jim Crow." Some forty years ago, the English Dissenters insisted that public education could only be obtained as the result of voluntary effort. Then, when it became manifest that voluntary education was giving an advantage to the Established Church (whose members were more liberal with their money), they repudiated voluntaryism, in regard to the education of the young; and at last they have become the most vehement advocates of State- and Rate-supported education in the country. The Dissenters now ardently support Board Schools, while Churchmen have assumed the position (which Dissenters have abandoned) of Voluntary Educationists!

During the last three years that I lived in Leeds, I remained quietly within my shell. I took no part in public meetings of any sort. I was occupied in pushing forward the amalgamation of the Leeds Northern Company with the York, Newcastle, and Berwick, and the York and North Midland Companies. The first-named company had extended its lines into Durham, thus linking itself to the Stockton and Darlington Railway, the Clarence Railway, the Stockton and Hartlepool Railway, and the York, Newcastle, and Berwick Railway. Steps were taken to extend the line from Ferryhill on the Clarence line, by Durham, Chester-le-Street, and along the Team Valley, to Newcastle-upon-Tyne. The line was surveyed, the plans were deposited, the public along the valley generally supported the project; and there seemed every reason to believe that the Act would be carried, but unfortunately, the line, as first laid out, came too near the Durham Observatory. The working of the heavy locomotives so near would cause some aberration of the instruments, and the directors of the Observatory resolved to oppose the measure. To get rid of their opposition, an agreement was entered into to the effect that if the Act were granted, the line as laid out would not be made, but a deviation through the city of Durham would be applied for in a future session of Parliament. This proved fatal to the Bill. The agreement was read before the committee of the House of Commons, and there was an end of the application.

In the next session of Parliament, however, supported by the locality, new plans were prepared, avoiding the Observatory, and proposing to supply a much more convenient station in the High Street of Durham. The directors of the York, Newcastle, and Berwick Company, seeing the probability of a new and rival line being established in the heart of this

important district, wisely resolved to bring the competition to an end, by entering into an arrangement
for the amalgamation, not only of the Leeds Northern
Railway, but of the York and North Midland Railway, which extended to Hull, Doncaster, Normanton,
and Leeds. Conferences of directors accordingly
took place. Offers were made, discussed, altered, and
improved; and at last were laid before the shareholders of the respective companies. These negotiations extended over many months, and even years;
and finally, when everything was settled, it was my
lot to draw up the report for the proprietors of my
company, urging the necessity of their giving assent
to the amalgamation.

I felt, when signing the final report, as if it
were driving the last nail into my own coffin. But
it was the best thing to be done for all parties—
for the public as well as for the shareholders; and I
did the work to the best of my power. Eventually,
the shareholders of all the companies agreed to the
amalgamation, on a certain clearly understood division of the net profits. The final resolutions were
carried; the Leeds Northern Railway came to an
end; and I prepared to go over to Newcastle with
the books, to have the shares registered in the books
of the amalgamated company.

CHAPTER XII

I WENT over to Newcastle in the summer of 1854. I took with me the books, reports, minutes, and correspondence, to place them in the archives of the amalgamated company. There was still a good deal of work to be done, as was likely to be the case with so large a concern; and I was told that if I would write a letter, there was likely to be an opening made for me, into which I could fit nicely. As I had been of some use in pushing on the amalgamation, and had worked hard for its completion, some of the directors thought that I might still be retained in the service of the company.

There was not, perhaps, much room in the offices of the Central Station at Newcastle; so I was put into a waiting-room alongside the secretary's office, lit by a skylight; and there I worked among my papers and correspondence. It was rather fruitless and monotonous work. There was little special business to do. I never saw the Board, and only once attended a committee meeting of the directors. Mr Bourne introduced me to some of his friends at Newcastle; but I was comparatively alone in the place, and away from my family, who were still at Leeds; as well as from my acquaintances in that neighbourhood. As the central offices were only to be temporarily at Newcastle, and as it was proposed to remove them to York, I waited to see what the result might be as regarded myself. I took lodgings in the Elswick Road, and even went so far as to go to York and look after a house there, in the event of my being removed to that city.

Meanwhile, in order to occupy my evenings, I proceeded to make some inquiry about the early history of George Stephenson, of whom I had published a brief account some five years before, in a London journal. It was fine summer weather; the days were long and fair; and the places to be visited were all within easy reach of Newcastle. After my work at the office, I could leave the station, and spend a few hours on making inquiries, then home by the late train about ten o'clock. On Saturday afternoons, when the office work ended at two, there was still more time for my investigations.

I went first to Wylam, Stephenson's birthplace. I found the cottage at High Street House—the red-tiled, rubble house, in which the great engineer had been born. I entered, and asked the old woman if this was the place. "Aye," she said, "Geordie was born here, in this very room." Everybody knew him as "Geordie." I asked if there was any old person in the neighbourhood who knew old Robert Stephenson, his father. "Yes," she answered, "there's auld Kit Heppell, wha kennt him verra weel." After looking over the place, and observing the colliery waggon road which still lay in front of the door, I went to the village of Wylam, past the old pumping engines and disused locomotives, and found Kit Heppel. He was an old man, but had still plenty of life in him. "Yes, he knew Old Bob,

Geordie's fayther. He wur like a pair o' deals nailed thegether, and a bit o' flesh i' th' inside—as queer as Dick's hatband: went thrice aboot, an' wudn't tie. His wife Mabel wur a delicat' boddie, and varry flighty. I kennt them verra weel: they wur an honest family, but sair hadden doon i' th' world." Then he told me of the small earnings of Old Bob, and the difficulty he had in bringing up his family of six children ; of his love for birds and animals, and the stories he told to the children by his engine-fire ; and of his having left Wylam when the coal was "worked oot," and gone to live at Dewley Burn, near Throckley Colliery.

On another evening, I went to Ovingham, to ascertain whether George Stephenson's birth had been registered there. The village of Ovingham is situated further up the Tyne. Thomas Bewick, the reviver of the art of wood-engraving, was born near it, at Cherryburn, a single house on the south side of the river. The stream here pours over a gravelly, shallow bed, and ripples past willowy islands, while little villages peep out from amidst the thick foliage. The scene is perfectly rural, and entirely free from the smoke of coal engines. Not far off is the fine old ruin of Prudhoe Castle, protected by a deep fosse, formerly crossed by a drawbridge. Ovingham is on the north side of the Tyne, and the river is crossed by means of a ferryboat—

> "O, where is the boatman, my bonny hinney ?
> O, where is the boatman ? bring him to me—
> To ferry me over the Tyne to my honey,
> And I will remember the boatman and thee."

I was ferried across; but found no record in the register of the birth of George Stephenson. I observed the tombstones of the Carrs (to whose family George Stephenson's mother belonged) underneath the central window at the east end of the church, as well as the tombstone of Thomas Bewick, under the western gable. Although my expedition was fruitless, I enjoyed the beautiful evening, and the lovely scenery.

I afterwards went to Heddon-on-the-Wall, to inspect the register there; but no record of George Stephenson's birth could be found. The probability was, that it was not registered, as in former times registrations were very imperfectly conducted. Most of the places in the line of road from east to west, have the name of "wall" attached to them—being in the direction of the old Roman road. They begin at Walsend, or at the end of the wall, below Newcastle; and extend westward through Walbottle, Heddon-on-the-Wall, Wall Houses, Wall, Walwick, Walton, and so on, as far westward as Bowness on the Solway, where the Roman wall ended. At Heddon-on-the-Wall, the vallum passed through the centre of the village.

I followed up my search by degrees. On another fine evening, I left the train at Ryton Station, was ferried across the Tyne, and made my way to Dewley Burn, where old Robert Stephenson lived for a time with his family, and where his son George first began to work for his daily bread. Near the house where he lived, are to be seen the burn and the clay-pits where he used to make his dirt-pies with his companion Bill Thirlwall, and afterwards his model clay engines, using the hemlocks for imaginary steam-pipes. It was curious to find how interested the people were in communicating everything they knew about "Geordie." Colliers, brakesmen, enginemen, and others—all who had known him intimately, or

had worked with him, or had even heard traditions
of him, were equally willing to help. There was no
jealousy about him. He was one of themselves, and
they were proud of him. He had toiled amongst
them with his hands, worked his way up perseveringly from one position to another, and after he had
been lifted by his genius to the highest position, they
were prouder of him than ever. What Robert Nicoll
said of Robert Burns might be applied to him—

> " Before the proudest of the earth
>   We stand, with an uplifted brow ;
> Like us, thou wast a toiling man—
>   And we are noble now."

On another occasion, I crossed the fields to
Callerton Pits—the fields where George, when a boy,
had pulled turnips at twopence the day, "and many
a cold finger," he said, "I had." The pits are now
all closed, but I saw the place where George had first
driven the gin-horse at an increased wage of eight-
pence. A collier who remembered him, described
him as "a grit growing lad, with bare legs and feet."
And he described, with great gusto, Geordie's fight
with Ned Nelson, the bully of Black Callerton.

Another visit was made to Newburn on the
Tyne, where George was first taken on as assistant fireman, and afterwards promoted to be full fireman. When his wages were raised to twelve shillings
a week, he declared himself to be "a made man for
life"! There he learnt to read and cast-up accounts,
and fairly entered upon the work of self-education.
A brief interruption occurred. He fell in love with
Fanny Henderson, and married her at the parish
church. I found her marriage duly registered, and
took a tracing of it. Both the signatures were
written in the hand of the bridegroom, who had

evidently brushed them over with his sleeve before they were dry. After the marriage, the couple rode off to Willington Quay, George's young wife riding on a pillion behind him, and holding on by his waist.

I next went to Willington Quay, fifteen miles down the Tyne, to see the house where the newly wedded pair had taken up their abode. It was standing then, though it has since been removed to give place to the Stephenson Memorial Schools. But it would have been better to keep the birthplace of Robert Stephenson as it stood. It was at Willington that George took charge of the engine at the Ballast Hill, and in his spare hours worked at self improvement. William Fairbairn (afterwards Sir William) told me that he had known George Stephenson well while living by the quayside—that he often visited him at his fireside, and admired the neatness, cleanness, and tidiness of his wife and her household arrangements. Fairbairn used to take charge of George's engine to enable him to earn a few extra shillings in the evening by heaving ballast out of the ships' holds. He said he also remembered George's taking to clock-cleaning and shoe-making, and that there was scarcely anything to which he was not willing to put his hand. William Coe informed me that he had bought a pair of shoes, of George Stephenson's make, for 7s. 6d., and they were not only cheap, but excellent.

My next visit was to Edward Pease, father of all the Peases, at Darlington. I wrote to him and requested an interview on any Saturday afternoon— that being my holiday, and the only day on which I could conveniently leave Newcastle. He kindly granted my request, and mentioned a day on which I could meet him. I went out one Saturday afternoon, and saw the fine old man. It was a pleasure to meet such a cheerful, beneficent gentleman. He was eighty-eight when I saw him, and he was as bright and hopeful and as communicative as ever. "Aye!" he said, "and you are inquiring about the beginning of the railway? It is truly a wonderful story!" And then he told me of how the project of the line from Darlington to Stockton was started—how the canal was first proposed, and Brindley, and Whitworth, and Dodd, and Rennie, suggested their schemes—how Stockton waited for Darlington, and Darlington waited for Stockton, and yet nothing was done. Then in 1810 a railway was proposed, but the committee went to sleep. Canals and railways— railways and canals; still no progress. And yet the coal owners were very anxious to get their coals to York as well as to the sea. "I got my friends," said Mr Pease, "to subscribe for shares in a railway in 1818, but we were defeated in three successive sessions by the Duke of Cleveland. Still we persevered. I wrote letters, which were published in a York news- paper, showing the uses of a railway worked by horses. We thought nothing of the locomotive at that time. At last we got our Act. But Mr Lambton, afterwards the Earl of Durham, had a proviso inserted requiring us to charge only a half- penny per ton per mile for all coal intended for shipment at Stockton. This was to prevent our line being used in competition against his coal shipped at Sunderland. Although we thought it might be ruinous, it actually proved our safety." *

Then he went on to speak of the first interview he had had with George Stephenson and Nicholas

* It was thought that this low rate would ruin the venture. See *Life of George Stephenson*, Centenary Edition, p. 70.—ED.

Wood. The two strangers from Killingworth called
upon him one day, and Nicholas introduced his companion as the engine-wright at Killingworth, who
knew a good deal about railways and locomotives.
"The Locomotive" was a new word for Mr Pease,
but eventually he was to become very familiar with
it. He told the strangers that their whole calculations
had been based on the employment of *horse* power.
But Stephenson told him that the locomotive would
eventually supersede the use of horse power upon
railroads. "I have been using the engine," he said,
since 1814, to draw coals from the pit to the loading
station on the Tyne; and I am certain that it is the
power best suited to your wants. But come over to
Killingworth," he concluded, "and see my locomotive
at work."

After a long conversation the strangers left, to
walk home through Durham to Newcastle. Mr
Pease was much impressed by the interview. He
took the opportunity soon after of going over to
Killingworth, where he inquired for "George
Stephenson, Esquire, Engineer." No one knew of
such a person. At length, after much conversation
among the old women and neighbours, one of them
asked if it was not "Geordie the engine-wright" that
he wanted. "No doubt," he answered, "it is the
engineer who works the locomotive." Then George
Stephenson was found, and proceeded to show off
before Mr Pease the qualities of his wonderful
engine. The result of the interview, first in Mr
Pease's house at Darlington, and afterwards on the
waggon way at Killingworth, was that George was
appointed the engineer of the Stockton and Darlington
Railway, and that it was eventually determined to
use the locomotive on trial for working the railway

when made. Not only so, but Mr Pease was so strongly satisfied with the importance of the new invention, that when Stephenson proposed to establish a manufactory in Newcastle for the building of locomotive engines, he joined with him in the adventure, and became a partner in the undertaking, which eventually proved exceedingly prosperous.

After much interesting conversation with Mr Pease, and a walk with him through the rapidly improving town, I remained to dine with him and his daughter: and left for Newcastle, freighted with valuable information, by a late train. But I need not give the particulars here, as I have related them elsewhere.

I thought, now that I had made so fair a beginning with the early life of George Stephenson, that I would like to inform Robert Stephenson of my progress. I had seen him on the subject in March 1851. Three years and a half had passed, and still nothing appeared to be done. Would he believe that I intended to do nothing more in the matter? In answer to my letter, he wrote as follows:—

"DOVER, 26th September 1854.

"DEAR SIR,—

"I am glad to hear that you have not given up the idea of writing a memoir of my late father; and now that I have more leisure, it will afford me pleasure to assist you in many points which are only known to myself, especially in reference to the phases which the locomotive engine put on at different periods of his active and remarkable life—a life which spreads over a period comprising probably one of the most interesting pages in the history of civilisation.

"I am about to visit Newcastle, when I shall make a point of giving you my views respecting the form which the memoir, in my opinion, ought to take, and

respecting the mechanical portions I shall feel it my
duty to assist.

"I hope by the end of the week to be in Newcastle.—Yours very truly,

"ROBERT STEPHENSON."

This was more satisfactory than when I had last
seen Mr Stephenson. He had then warned me
against undertaking the memoir, because he did not
think it would be interesting, and might only cause
me loss of labour and money. Now, he seemed to be
of a different opinion, and wrote in a manner entirely
confirmatory of my views as to the interest of the
subject. I afterwards found that the field was clear,
and that no one intended to write anything on the
subject of George Stephenson's life. But I was
aware that I had only made a beginning of the
subject, and that a great deal more remained to be
done.

Mr Stephenson arrived in Newcastle by the
beginning of October. I dined with him occasionally
at the Queen's Head, in Grey Street, where he put up.
He took me over the engineering establishment in
Forth Street, and told me something of its history.
Since the germ of it had been started by his father,
assisted by Edward Pease, it had grown to an
immense affair, employing about a thousand men
and boys, and paying in wages over £1000 a
week.

But I derived the most interest and information
from a visit to Killingworth and the neighbourhood,
made in his company. One fine Sunday afternoon in
October, he drove me over in an open carriage, by the
road which he had so often gone over in his boyhood.
"I know every foot of this road," he said. "I used to

come over it every day on my cuddy to attend Bruce's school in Newcastle." We went over the Town Moor, and, on arriving at the village of Gosforth, went up the Benton Grange Road. Arriving at Long Benton, he said, " Do you see that red-tiled house, with the outside stair?—that is the place where Rutter kept his school, and where I learnt my A B C." On reaching the ochre quarry, he observed, " There is where my father erected his first pumping-engine, which cleared the place of water in a week." Not far off, he pointed to the High Pit, where he had "sent them to the bottom," * to the delight of the pitman.

We then walked along the waggon way to Killingworth, and, reaching a little clay-floored cottage by the roadside, he said, "There is where my grandfather lived! He was quite blind in his old age, and my father kept him in comfort. I remember well, how I used to ride into his cottage on my cuddy, and he would examine the creature, feel him all over, and pronounce him to be a 'real blood' donkey." Then he told me of the trick he played to the swearing bully, Straker—how he, with another boy, attacked him on a dark night, and made him "stand and deliver!"

We reached Glebe Farm, once inhabited by John Wigham. "There," he said, "was the scene of some of my best education in boyhood; for Wigham was a superior man, and I then thought him a very clever fellow. But now we are at Killingworth! This was my father's cottage, and see, there is the dial over it, still numbering the hours while the sun shines. Many a sore head I had while making the necessary

* After clearing the pit of water. See *Lives of the Engineers*, 20th impression, p. 43.—ED.

calculations to adapt the dial face to the latitude of Killingworth."

We went into the cottage, and he pointed out the arrangements. "There's where the tame blackie* used to sit. There is still the old oven, in which my father put in the pitman's watch, and made it go, simply by melting the oil." And thus the afternoon wore away, and a number of recollections were told in a homely, pleasant, and kindly manner. Robert Stephenson had nothing of the snob in him. He was not ashamed of his father having been a working man ; on the contrary, he was proud of his having worked his way up from a low condition by dint of his inherent genius, perseverance, and industry. I spent the evening with him, and made many notes, which I afterwards duly recorded.

During my stay at Newcastle, I called upon Thomas Hindmarsh, the brother of George Stephenson's second wife. I wished to know something of the accuracy of the story which I had heard from Mr Bourne, about George having first courted Miss Hindmarsh, and then, because he was refused, having made love to Fanny Henderson, her servant. He told me the story was "all nonsense." Fanny had never been their servant ; and besides, George, after remaining a widower for fourteen years, had been introduced to his sister by himself, at his earnest solicitation. Thus I was able to correct this portion of the personal history.

I was desirous of obtaining some information from Nicholas Wood, who knew George Stephenson well, and had not only been his master, but his fellow-worker during many years. I saw Mr Wood several times at his office on Quayside and at other places.

* Blackbird.—ED.

He said he would be glad to help me; but although I made many applications, I never obtained any information. I used to think that he was a little jealous of his former servant's reputation.

One day, hanging about the station, I met George Hudson the deposed "Railway King." He had been to the Board for the purpose of imploring their mercy. I had some conversation with the poor fellow. He was almost in tears, and said the directors were disposed to be very hard on him, and wished to wrench from him the last farthing he possessed. He referred to his property at Whitby, which the North-Eastern Company wished to obtain. I believe they eventually got it, and towards the end of his life, Hudson was maintained principally by a subscription raised amongst a few of his friends. The man was perhaps more foolish than reckless. Had he been utterly unprincipled, and acted with sufficient cunning, he might have become as rich as Crœsus. But he was nothing like so clever as he was represented to be by the toadies who surrounded and influenced him, and he ended his days in comparative poverty.

Before I left Newcastle I had the pleasure of running down to Darlington again one Saturday afternoon, for the purpose of having an interview with John Dixon, the engineer of the Stockton and Darlington Railway. When a young man, he had been employed with Robert Stephenson in "taking the sights" on that line, while George Stephenson was laying it out afresh. He was afterwards employed on Chat Moss as assistant engineer for the Liverpool and Manchester Railway, and had a great deal of interesting information to communicate. Indeed, he was of the greatest possible use to me—

not only by what he related as to the beginnings of the Stockton and Darlington line, but as to the means taken to lay out the railway over Chat Moss— supposed to be an almost impossible proceeding before George Stephenson took the work in hand. Mr Dixon afterwards wrote out for me, in full detail, an account of his proceedings on Chat Moss, and the means taken by the leading engineer to master and conquer his difficulties.

On 6th October I was awakened about midnight by two tremendous explosions. I went to sleep again, but next morning I was informed that the town had almost been "blewn up." It was at first thought that the explosions had occurred through design, but it was ascertained that they were merely the result of accident. A warehouse at Gateshead, full of sulphur and saltpetre, took fire, and a great mass of water running into it, the water was vaporised, and, uniting with the combustible materials, formed a tremendously explosive mixture. Such, at all events, was the explanation given at the time of the terrific explosion. However this may be, the windows of every house in the neighbourhood were shattered into a thousand atoms, and the mass of burning stuff was shot across the Tyne upon ships and ware- houses, which at once burst into flame. A large number of persons were killed and injured, and about half a million's worth of property was lost. Next morning, when I went down to see the place, it looked as if it had been subjected to a bombard- ment. The whole shore, on both sides of the river, seemed to be a mass of ruins.

But I was myself personally the subject of another explosion. I was now waiting the result of my removal to Newcastle. To use the words of

Bacon, I had "given hostages to fortune" in the shape of five sons and daughters; and I had no wish to change. I had been nine years with the Company; and the concern had become so large that I thought some room might be made for me. I should have been willing to take any reasonable position, with a moderate salary. But none was offered. Places were found for all the old officers, excepting myself. Mr Duncan Maclaren of Edinburgh was "determined to have his man in." My friends, who were few in number, were not so determined as Duncan. Accordingly he "had his man in"—a very proper person, from his "own romantic town" —and I prepared to look about me for another position, and I was certainly not to blame for *this* change.

As the Scottish proverb has it, "As ae door steeks, anither opens." The South-Eastern Railway Company happened at this time to advertise for a secretary. I had no end of strong recommendations, especially from Leeds, where I was well known—from Mr Henry Cowper Marshall, my former chairman, Mr William Beckett, banker, Sir George Goodman, member for Leeds, and other gentlemen. Besides, I had the advantage of being known to experienced men of railway reputation, possessed of more than local fame, such as Henry Booth, of Liverpool, John (afterwards Sir John) Hawkshaw, of Manchester, Sir William Cubitt, of London, and many other distinguished gentlemen. I did not know a single person at the Board of the South-Eastern Company, and therefore I suppose these recommendations had their proper effect. A large number of applications were made for the position. Out of the applicants, four were selected to meet the Board, of whom I was one. After a satisfactory interview, I returned to Newcastle, and on the morning of the 11th of November 1854 (after a wonderful shower of meteors the evening before), I received a letter from Captain Barlow, the general manager of the South-Eastern Railway, informing me that I had been appointed to the vacant office.

I then sent in my resignation to the North-Eastern directors, and received a minute of the Board "expressing their entire satisfaction at the manner in which Mr Smiles had always discharged his duties, and more especially when engaged in forwarding the arrangement between the three companies, arising out of the union of their interests," and so on. This was the net result; though it was better than nothing. I shook hands pleasantly with everybody when parting, and took leave of my old friend, John Bourne, the engineer, with much regret. I went up to London at once, and my wife, family, and household goods followed me a month later. Before I had settled down in my place, I received the following letter from Robert Stephenson :—

"24 GREAT GEORGE STREET, WESTMINSTER,
"29th November 1854.

"MY DEAR SIR,—
"I am very glad to hear of your success, and I trust sincerely it may be permanent; for I fear you will find the South-Eastern a very difficult concern to keep in train satisfactorily. More of this when I have the pleasure of seeing you.

"I am delighted that you saw Dixon before leaving the North; no man knew my father better. I will not fail to send a missive to Nicholas Wood, which I have no doubt he will respond to. I had little or no hope in your succeeding in appointments with him.—Yours faithfully,
"ROBERT STEPHENSON."

N

Such was the position of affairs when I entered on my office. I began to doubt whether I could ever find time enough to write out the Life of George Stephenson, and a history of the new branch of national enterprise. For, after all, I had only made a beginning.

Samuel Bowles

"That may be," he said, "but they do not give 'the proceedings.'" He appealed to the solicitor, who constantly sat at the Board. The solicitor referred to the Act, which said ' minutes and proceedings." I had therefore to amend my ways, and insert not only what was determined upon, but what was proposed and discussed. All this was, of course, with a view to future proceedings, when an appeal came to be made to the shareholders.

The majority of the Board, not having a good speaker, determined to introduce a new man for the purpose of meeting Macgregor and Forster. They found him in an able gentleman, who, however, was without a qualification. The majority gave him the qualification, and elected him to a vacant seat. He soon proved his power as a speaker, by walking into Macgregor. The latter had sent to the Register Office, and ascertained the nature of his qualification. He then rose, pounced upon the new man like a vulture, and tore him to pieces. It was exciting and amusing, but it was not business. I had never seen such a thing before. In former times, I had seen men of active habits meet round a table for the purpose of getting through their work, and pass their minutes without rising from their seats. But here were men who rose to their feet, and made elaborate and cutting speeches, without getting through any work at all. It seemed to me a fruitless waste of time.

But all this was preliminary to an appeal to the shareholders, who were to elect a batch of new directors in the following month of March. Everything gave way to this business. Those who were in wished to remain in, and many who were out desired to become members of the Board. The

number of candidates was great; some with only
the bare qualification, and nearly all without any
railway experience. Deputations went down to
Manchester and Liverpool, where the principal part
of the stock in the company was held, to address
meetings of shareholders. The printers were set to
work, and large numbers of proxies, and conflicting
statements, were issued. At last, the half-yearly
meeting was held; and a very uproarious affair it
was. The result was, that Mr Macgregor, finding
that he had no chance, gracefully retired, together
with his former deputy chairman; that Mr Forster,
with his batch of candidates, was rejected; and that
some four or five new directors were added to the
Board. I had no difficulty in getting on pleasantly
with the new men. After a short interregnum, the
Honourable James Byng was made chairman; and
I maintained a pleasant and agreeable intercourse
with that gentleman during the twelve years that I
remained with the company. He was an honest
and honourable man, and, in the midst of considerable difficulties, always did the best that he
could for the advantage of the constituents he
represented.

There was, however, a great obstacle to the
prosperity of the company, in the establishment of a
rival line within the district that should have been
fully served by the South-Eastern Company. In
1853, the East Kent Company had obtained an Act
for giving railway accommodation to the important district between Chatham and Canterbury.
That accommodation should certainly have been
supplied by the company which already had possession of the county. But some feelings of personal
pride seem to have stood in the way; and the new

line got into the hands of scheming contractors. It was of no use pointing out that the new line should be constructed and worked by the existing company. I was informed that the requisite capital could never be obtained, and that the new line would never be made. I could only point to the experience I had gained through the Leeds and Thirsk Railway, which had established itself in the face of equally great difficulties, but had been wisely absorbed by the North-Eastern Railway in its more extensive arrangements. The new line pointed to Dover in the one direction, and to London in the other; my impression from the first was, that the line would be made and extended in both directions. And, sure enough, in 1855, an Act was obtained to extend the line to Dover.

Meanwhile, my new Board began its operations. A great deal had to be done to improve matters. The poor South-Eastern seems to have been regarded as a great milch cow, affording sustenance to everybody instead of to the proprietors. The number of "dead heads" (as they are called in America) passing along the railway was enormous. Everybody who wanted an advantage, expected it from the railway.

The Emperor of the French had just made his visit to England with the Empress, and been received at Dover by the South-Eastern magnates with great ceremony, and returned to France with great *éclat*, when an event occurred which threw us into consternation. It originated in the same desire for having a tug at the great milch cow. Railway companies have neither souls nor bodies, but they have purses; and when it was found (as afterwards appeared) that a person high up in the Passenger Department was

in collusion with a guard and a common thief to rob
the company of the gold carried on the line for the
London bullionists, it must be admitted that things
had been allowed to go a great deal too far, and that
a clearance of some of the incapables (to say the least
of them) must soon be made.

On the 19th of May the news reached London from
Paris, that three large boxes, containing bullion to the
value of £14,000, had been robbed on their journey
between the two places, and that the weight of the
bullion bars had been replaced with shot! This was
frightful news. The Board was summoned to consider
the matter. A reward for the apprehension of the
thieves was offered. The police detectives were set
to work: and reports came in as to the circumstances
connected with the affair.

It appeared that the boxes containing the bullion
had been received at the London Station at twenty
minutes to eight, on the evening of the 15th of May;
that they had been weighed, and the record kept;
that they had gone down to Folkestone by the late
train, and had remained there all night; that they
had been carried over by the *Lord Warden* steamer
to Boulogne on the following day, and been given over
by the company's agent to the agent of the Messa-
geries Générales; and that they had been finally
carried on to Paris by the North of France
Railway.

The first idea was, that the robbery had been
committed by foreigners on the French railway.
Representations to this effect were made to the
Central Commissioner of Police at Boulogne, and an
inquiry was instituted. It appeared that the weights
of the boxes had varied at London and Boulogne;
that there was nothing to show that this "audacious

robbery " had been committed at Boulogne ; and the commissioner pointed to the fact that the cases containing the bullion had remained at Folkestone from 11 o'clock at night until 10 o'clock the next morning—inferentially pointing to that place as the probable scene of the robbery. A further report came from Paris, to the effect that all investigations had failed to discover any clue which might lead to detection of the thieves.

And here the matter rested for some time. Meanwhile, I was requested by Mr Tester, the assistant-superintendent in the passenger manager's office, to furnish him with a certificate of character on his leaving the company's service, to assume the position of General Manager of the Royal Swedish Railway. I did not know Mr Tester, but was informed by his chief that he had been a faithful servant, and that I might give him the certificate of character which he requested. Who Mr Tester was, will be ascertained in a future part of this narrative.

It was necessary, as I have said, to make many changes, for the management was loose. First, a new engineer was appointed ; then a new storekeeper ; then a law clerk, stationed in the office, to be constantly at hand, instead of having professional solicitors attending the Board ; then a surveyor to look after the company's rents ; and, finally, a new general manager and a goods manager. I had great pleasure in acting with these gentlemen. They were active, able, and honest. The law clerk and general manager were long my esteemed friends ; and I worked with them cordially for the benefit of the company.

Mr Rees, the new law clerk, was a man of great ability. He was then young, and comparatively inexperienced, though he has since obtained great consideration as a first-rate Parliamentary agent. He thought it strange that we should have been able to find no traces of the gold robbery; not even a hint of where it had been done. Mr Rees's father was a well-known solicitor, who at one time had been able to effect a discovery in a similar case. The two, father and son, went down to Folkestone, where the gold had lain during the night before its supposed transport to Boulogne. The bullion chests had then lain all night in an office of which the door was always open, and not in the strong-room appointed for the purpose. There could be no doubt, so they thought, that things had been so arranged by design, and that the station-master was in the secret. Old Mr Rees fixed his penetrating eye upon the station-master, who, he thought, quailed before his glance, as much as to say, "Ah! you have found me out, have you?" Hints were dropped, but nothing was done. There was no evidence whatever, nor any symptom of evidence.

Many months passed, until, towards the end of 1856—after the lapse of more than a year—a young woman called at my office, and gave her name as Fanny Kay. She said she had come to give some information as to the gold robbery. There had been a great many hints before this time, and I did not expect much. But, as I was much occupied by correspondence, I took the woman into Mr Rees's office, introduced her to the law clerk, and left her there. I afterwards asked, "Is there any probability of your finding out this affair?" "Well," he replied, "everything is confidential as yet. But if what this woman says be right, we have all been wrong." The next time I saw Mr Rees, he told me that he had been at

Portland Prison, and discovered the whole secret. Here is a very brief account of the transaction. It was the result of Mr Rees's personal examination of a person called Edward Agar, then undergoing penal servitude at Portland.

"The robbery," said Agar, "was first proposed to me by Pearse. I knew him about seven years ago. He was then in the service of the company as ticket-printer. Laward and Burgess, first and second guards, were also to be in it. I went down to Folkestone several times to see how it could be done; but I was afraid to have anything to do with it. I went abroad, first to Paris, then to Jamaica and the United States.

"When I returned from the latter country, towards the end of 1853, I met Pearse by accident just by Covent Garden Market. He was then a clerk in the betting office of Clipson, King Street. I went there occasionally and made several bets. I went to Evans' and other places with Pearse. He again brought up the subject of the gold robbery. He said there had been an alteration in the conduct of the railway, and he thought he could now get the keys of the bullion boxes. I said if he could get the keys, it might be done, but not otherwise. We went down to Folkestone and remained there about a fortnight, watching the arrival of the trains and the management of the bullion boxes. One of the keys was kept in the booking office of the station, the other was kept in a cupboard at the harbour-master's office. Pearse proposed that I should get in at night and obtain the keys. I declined, and said that if the keys could not be got in any other way, I would have nothing to do with it.

"I made the acquaintance of the station clerks, and went with them and played billiards at nights, and a few games at cards. I asked them about the bullion, but I got no information from them. I then went over to Boulogne, to see how the gold was dealt with there. I remained there nearly a week. I then returned to London. During all this time I was in communication with Burgess the guard.

"Previous to my going to Boulogne, Pearse told me that he thought he could get an impression of one of the keys (No. 1), for the other (No. 2) had been lost. I asked how he could get it. He said, from Tester, in the superintendent's office at London Bridge. I said I should like to see the key myself. Pearse saw Tester, who agreed to see me. We all met at a public-house at the corner of Tooley Street. Tester produced two keys, both of one lock (No. 1). I then took the impression of it in wax. I returned the keys to Tester, who took them away. Pearse had told Tester what the keys were wanted for. Tester was to have his share with the rest—Burgess, Pearse, and myself.

"It then became a question how to get at key No. 2. Pearse proposed to send a money parcel down to Folkestone, and that I should be there to receive it, and see where they brought the key from. I consented. I left about £500 with Pearse, and it was sent down in the bullion chest. I went to the office on the day after it arrived, and the clerk brought out the keys from his cupboard, and unlocked the chest, taking out and giving me the parcel, and requiring a receipt. After returning to London, I went down to Folkestone with Pearse; and towards evening, just before the Boulogne boat arrived, as we knew that the clerks generally left the office to attend to the passengers and baggage, we thought that would be our opportunity. We watched the clerks go out, and immediately went into the office, and found the cupboard door with the key in it. We opened it, found the bullion key, and took an impression of it in wax. We returned the same evening to London.

"I got the keys made by a scale-beam forger in Church Street, Shoreditch. I gave him the size, and then myself filed them down to match the impressions. I met Burgess a great many times, and went down with him to Dover to try the keys in the bullion box. One of the locks was not used, but I got both keys to fit. We then watched for an opportunity to effect the robbery.

"We bought a quantity of shot at the Shot Tower by Hungerford Bridge, 28 lbs., and put it into bags, so as to pack readily into the boxes. We carried them in carpet bags many times, in a four-wheeled cab, to St Thomas Street, while I went to Burgess on the platform of London Bridge Station, to ascertain if the proper quantity of gold was going down. This went on for about a fortnight. One night I observed Burgess just by the exit gate at the Dover part of the platform. He raised his cap and wiped his face—the signal that the gold was there. I went back to St Thomas Street, got into the cab, and told the man to drive round to the station. A porter came and took the bags. I told the man to enter the luggage and wait till I came from the booking office, where I took two 2nd class tickets. Burgess put the two bags into the van behind the door. The bullion safe was then brought up and placed in the van.

"Tester used to meet us every night to give us information as to the gold going down. The reason why we did not go at once was that we wanted sovereigns if we could get them, and we had determined not to go for less than £12,000—the amount which we could carry, and had shot for. Tester met us as usual at 8 o'clock. He walked up to the station and we met on the platform, but we took no notice of each other. I had been up more than once to see Tester in his office.

"I got into Burgess's van. Pearse got into a 1st class carriage, Tester into another. As soon as the train had started, at 8.30 P.M., I opened one of the safes with the key. I then opened the box containing the long bars of Australian gold. I took one of the bars out and put it into a black leather enamelled bag made expressly for Tester. By this time we had arrived at Redhill. Tester came up, and Burgess— as had been previously arranged—placed the bag upon the platform. Tester took it up, and ran across to meet the up train, then about due, by which he returned to London. This was done to relieve us of part of the weight.

"Pearse got into the van at Redhill. We then took the gold out of the boxes, and replaced it with shot. He fastened down the boxes with the same nails and bands as were previously used, and sealed them up as before. We remained in the van for some time after locking up the safe. We got out at Folkestone upper station, and took our seats in a 1st class carriage for Dover. The empty boxes went down to Folkestone Harbour. On getting out at Dover, we went to Burgess's van, and each of us took away one carpet bag. We carried them to a coffee-house in the neighbourhood, where we had supper, and shortly after returned to London by the up mail train, of which Burgess was guard. Burgess had provided us previously with two Ostend tickets.

"On reaching London early in the morning, we took a cab on the incline, and told the man to drive us to the Great Western Station. On the road, we told him we had made a mistake, and asked him to drive to Euston. He drove us to a coffee-house in Drummond Street, where we slept for an hour ; then to Pearse's house, Kilburn : then by another cab to my house at Cambridge Villas, Shepherd's Bush. There we broke up and melted the gold. Pearse bought some fire bricks and a crucible, as well as an iron ingot. In the meantime, Pearse sold 100 ounces of the gold, a piece cut off one of the large Australian bars. We went on melting, and then took the whole to Pearse's house.

"The proceeds of the sale of gold, to the extent of over £2000, was divided between Pearse, Burgess, and Tester. I was to have mine later, as the others said they wanted money. Burgess had £700, and Tester £700, both in notes. Several sums borrowed by Burgess and Tester were repaid to me. I may add, that on the morning after the robbery I met Tester by appointment at the railway stairs leading down to the Borough Market by St Saviour's Church. He then gave me the gold bar he had brought up from Redhill in the small black bag. When I was arrested, all the rest of the gold was with Pearse at his Kilburn villa as well as the coupons of Spielmans. Pearse told me he should dig a hole in the pantry under the steps of the front entrance, in which to conceal it."

Such was the confession of Agar to Mr Rees at Portland, with a great deal more evidence implicating other parties, which need not be mentioned here.

Agar had been apprehended, tried, and convicted for a crime of which he was probably not guilty. He left his wife and child at Pearse's, and trusted to their being maintained out of the proceeds of the gold robbery. But Pearse and his wife quarrelled with Fanny Kay, and turned her out of doors. Then it was that she called upon me, and that I handed her over to Mr Rees; after which he went down to Portland to collect the above evidence.

Steps were taken to apprehend Pearse and Burgess, the latter still acting as a guard. Tester was expected home from Sweden on a visit to his friends at Deal. He also was secured. The whole of the prisoners were brought before Baron Martin at the Central Criminal Court on the 13th January 1857. The evidence above given was confirmed by Agar in full detail. I was present in the court. Agar was a smallish, thin man, with a keen bright eye; he gave his evidence with great clearness. Baron Martin said of him, that if he had given his attention to some legitimate business or profession, he might have reached distinction. Of the other prisoners—especially Tester and Burgess, who had so dishonestly abused their trust—the Judge spoke with contempt; and Pearse was but a common thief, who, finding that he could do nothing without superior skill, called in Agar—as the ordinary medical practitioners, in a difficult case, would call in an experienced surgeon or physician.

The punishment given to Pearse was too small. He was only convicted of larceny, and sentenced to two years' imprisonment, with hard labour, three of the months to be passed in solitary confinement. Burgess the guard, and Tester the manager of the Royal Swedish Railway, were sentenced to fourteen years' transportation. Agar was sent back to endure his penal servitude at Portland.

Such was the end of the Gold Robbery!

But what had become of my long-contemplated Life of George Stephenson? I fear that, in the midst of all my occupations, I had omitted further attention to it. I had very little leisure, and my time, even my evenings, were entirely occupied with railway work. I had seen Robert Stephenson from time to time; and in the course of 1855 I had occasion to write to him professionally, requesting him, at the instance of the directors, to advise with them as to an improvement in the Shakespeare Cliff tunnel, near Dover, which had recently been the cause of a fatal accident to a private in the Grenadier Guards. To this letter, I received the following reply :—

"NEWCASTLE-ON-TYNE, 4th October 1855.

"MY DEAR SIR,—
        "By this post you will receive a reply to your official communication, declining to go into the matter, as I have decided (and I have acted on the decision for the last two years) to withdraw myself entirely from all new professional engagements. This I have done chiefly on account of my health not being very good.

"With regard to the notes upon my father's early steps with the Locomotive Engine, they have been done some time, and I hope shortly to see you on this subject; but I shall be engaged for ten days or a fortnight out of London mainly. Since you undertook your new situation, you have frequently passed through my mind, and I began to feel that your new engagements would be far too numerous to admit of your giving the Biography any attention.

"Moreover, I felt that if your Board found that you were not giving your whole time to their business, it might cause dissatisfaction. I was aware, also, that you had had a struggle with a section of the Board, when you obtained the appointment. When you succeeded, I knew that you would have many serious difficulties to contend with.   A divided Board, a reduced income, increasing expenses, and, as a necessary consequence, discontented shareholders. None of these contribute to a secretary's comfort, and as I take rather a gloomy view of the future prospects of the South-Eastern, I fear your troubles are not at an end.

"I intend leaving England for a cruise in some southern clime in about three weeks, but I will make a point of seeing you for an hour or two, before that time.

"Brunel or Hawkshaw would either of them be good men to confer with Ashcroft on the tunnels, and from what I have heard, the matter will not brook delay.—Yours faithfully,

"ROBERT STEPHENSON."

This was wise advice, and I resolved to follow it, until I had sufficient leisure time at my disposal.

CHAPTER XIV

A SUCCESSFUL AUTHOR AT LAST!

THE work at the office was by no means uninteresting. Though some of it was monotonous, it was pleasant and agreeable. I had always plenty to do, what with correspondence, minutes, and reports; and active work is always attended with happiness. So, at least, I have found in the course of my life.

I endeavoured, so far as I could, to clear off the work of every day, so as to begin every morning with a *carte blanche* as it were—free and unfettered. Sometimes this was difficult, especially when we were approaching the half-yearly meetings. But still I managed to get through the day's work; and when there were arrears to dispose of, I took a bag of correspondence home with me, to settle and arrange it there. In this way, I often sat up until a late hour, perhaps until two or three in the morning.

When an arrangement was made to have only one Board meeting in the fortnight, so as to suit the convenience of the Liverpool and Manchester directors, it became still more difficult to get through the work satisfactorily. All the correspondence had to be gone through and attended to in the course of the

O

day.   Besides, there were the minutes of four committee meetings held on Wednesdays, to be written out and made ready for confirmation at the fortnightly board on the following day. Sometimes I found it difficult to accomplish this work; and sitting long at my desk, either at the office or at home, often gave me a splitting headache. Indeed, I began to think that there might be some difficulty in carrying on the work further.

Then it was that the idea of dictating the minutes, and the answers to the greater part of the correspondence, occurred to me. I had made the acquaintance of Mr (afterwards Sir Arthur) Helps, secretary of the Privy Council. He told me that he had found an immense advantage in dictating, not only his letters, but his books. It saved time, and enabled him to clear away his correspondence. He said that he used, while riding home by railway from London to Kew, to turn over in his mind the subject of his forthcoming works (such as his *Companions of my Solitude* and *Friends in Council*), that he would prepare the thoughts and sentences, and retain them complete in his mind; and that then, on reaching home, he would dictate them to his daughter, who had in this way written out nearly the whole of his books.

I acted upon the suggestion, and inserted an advertisement in the *Times* for a short-hand writer. I had many applications for the position, and at length selected a clever reporter. I found some difficulty at first, in communicating my ideas to another for the purpose of being set down in black and white. But practice soon made perfect; and at length I was enabled to get through all my work in the shortest possible time. By dictation, I dis-

burthened my mind at once. The matter was written
out in long hand and submitted for my approval.
The letters were sent off at once, and the minutes
were copied out and ready for submission and
approval on the following morning. By this means
I was enabled to get through my work with pleasure
and dispatch.

There was one thing, however, that I could never
accomplish. I could never dictate anything that
was to appear in print. I must see the sentences
before me, coming out, as it were, at my fingers' ends;
and shape, and prune, and modify them, for purposes
of publication. Sir Arthur Helps was able to do this;
but he must have had a better memory for words and
consecutive sentences than I had. Composition was
often very difficult in my case; and I made many
erasures and alterations before I was fully satisfied
with my productions. My brain was at work, as well
as my fingers; and the excitement of the one had its
correlation in the activity of the others.

At the same time, the dictation of minutes and of
ordinary business letters proved of immense advantage. My health was restored; I could clear away
my work for the day; and I went home with my
mind clear and unfagged. I recovered my evening's
leisure, and could spend it in amusement, recreation,
or the pleasure of social converse. The question
then occurred, what was I to do with the leisure time
thus set at liberty? My object always was—for,
indeed, it had become a habit—to turn my spare
minutes to some useful account. There was that
old Life of George Stephenson that had been hanging
over my head for so many years. Could I not
proceed with it now? And was it right to write out
the contemplated book?

I know that there are many people who think that a man of business who devotes his leisure to writing a book is in a measure lost. He ought to devote his whole time either to business or literature; and literary men are not considered business men. Had I proposed to spend my evenings at the theatre, or at concerts, or at the club, no one would have complained; but to spend it in writing a book, with my name on the title-page, was a very different matter. What has a railway secretary, who is paid for his work as such, to do with writing books? And yet I thought that, provided I did the work of the railway company thoroughly—and I believe that I did—I was at liberty to do with the leisure of my evenings what I thought proper, provided the result was not at variance with my other duties. The reader will observe that I am arguing for my own liberty in the matter.

There was one thing in which I was very particular—the regularity of my attendance at the office. I was always there first—with one exception; and that was my good assistant, Robert Hudson—a most good, conscientious, and devoted man—the backbone of the Secretariat, during the many years that he remained with the company. But I was always before the bulk of the clerks, and the example had, no doubt, its influence. I was so regular in passing the window of my neighbour, Wilson of Blackheath, on my way to the station, that he declared that he could set his clock by my movements.

I made up my mind, then, to proceed with my Life of Stephenson. But before I proceed to describe the history of this book, I may mention that, on arriving in London towards the end of 1854, I sent the MS. of *Self-Help* to Messrs Routledge & Co.

Mr Walker, of Leeds, had offered to publish the book on half-profits, but I preferred to have a London publisher. The circumstances of the times were, however, opposed to the publication of new books. The Crimean War was raging, and people were satisfied with the perusal of their newspapers. The Messrs Routledge accordingly declined to publish the book. Their reply was as follows :—

"LONDON, FARRINGDON STREET,
"*25th February* 1855.

"SIR,—

"We regret having detained your MS. so long. We were in hopes that we should have been able to publish it; but trade still continues so dull that we find it will be quite impossible. We shall be happy to give you the MS. at any time; and are, Sir, your obedient servants,

"GEORGE ROUTLEDGE & Co."

So far as I can recollect, I did not place my name on the title-page of the proposed work. Indeed, my name was not worth anything at all, for my two previous works—one in 1838 and the other in 1844 —had been failures, and were forgotten. I went to Messrs Routledge for the MS., laid it to one side for future uses, and then proceeded with my proposed Life of George Stephenson.

I again communicated with Robert Stephenson. I learned from him that no one had yet proposed to write the Life; and that if I did not proceed with it, the probability was that it never would be done. I was still under the same impression as before, that there were materials in the subject for an original and striking memoir. I told him my ideas of the way in which the Life should be treated. First, there was the early history, on which I had already obtained a large amount of information. Then there was the history of the locomotive, which, Robert Stephenson told me, he had written out in full detail. There was next the invention of railways, starting into full life under the eyes of the present generation, and producing the most extraordinary results upon the action and framework of society. Then there was the supersession of the old methods of travelling by means of the locomotive, the development of railway enterprise up to the period of speculation and gambling, the extension of railways to foreign countries, and some account of the principal persons connected with the advance of this great revolution in our commercial interests. The task was not very easy, but I thought that it might be satisfactorily accomplished. If it were not done now, the probability was, that, owing to the death of the principal persons connected with the development of railways, it never would be done. To all this Mr Stephenson agreed, and he promised me throughout his hearty co-operation.

I was still anxious for the information which Mr Nicholas Wood of Newcastle had promised me many years before. He had been present at the first trial of the "Geordy" Lamp in the Killingworth pit, and knew a great deal of the early history of the locomotive. Though he had been George Stephenson's master, I believed that jealousy would not prevent his helping me to a certain extent. I asked Robert Stephenson's assistance, and he wrote to me, saying, "Nicholas Wood has never replied to my letter: I shall fire another shot with a heavier charge." But no information came. Then I wrote to Mr Bourne, engineer of the North-Eastern Railway, asking for his assistance. Mr Bourne saw Mr Wood, on which

the latter said, "Well, if you will put in for me that
bit siding at Penshaw, I will give you all the information that Mr Smiles wants." On inquiry, Mr Bourne
found that to put in the "bit siding at Penshaw,"
would cost more than £3000. He asked me if the
information was worth that money, on which I
replied, that it was not worth 3000 farthings.
I told Robert Stephenson of the result of my
application.

"Ah," he said, "it is Nick all over. His motto
is, 'Nothing for nothing for nobody'!"

The truth is that I could do very well without the
information asked for. The report and evidence respecting the "Geordy" Safety Lamps had been published; and besides, Mr Wood had written out his
account of the early history of the locomotive in his
Practical Treatise on Railroads. Strange to say, long
before any controversy arose about the blast-pipe,
Nicholas Wood had (though not believing in its virtue)
given all the credit to Stephenson; but after it had
been found that the steam-blast was the life blood of
the locomotive, and that Timothy Hackworth claimed
its invention, Mr Wood withdrew that part of the
treatise from his book, thereby seriously injuring the
authenticity of his history. But Robert Stephenson
handed me the first edition of the work, published
in 1825, long before the steam-blast had become a
matter of controversy.

I had already obtained all the requisite information from Edward Pease as to the projection and
construction of the Stockton and Darlington Railway. And now I wished to get access to the best
information relative to the Liverpool and Manchester
Railway—the opening of which marks the era of a
great change in all popular ideas respecting loco-

motion. Fortunately, the men were still alive—Mr
Gooch, Mr Dixon, Mr Swanwick, and Mr Henry
Booth—who had taken part in that undertaking;
and they gave me all the information that I desired.
Through the influence of Robert Stephenson, also,
I obtained many valuable facts from Sir Joshua
Walmsley, Mr T. Sopwith, Mr Charles Parker, Mr
Vaughan of Snibston, Mr Binns of Claycross, and
many more. Mr Stephenson himself, of course,
supplied the principal information in the book, especially as to the history of the locomotive. Little or
no information was derived from books or reports,
but nearly all from personal inquiry and intercourse.

I proceeded at home quietly to work up the subject
from my old notes. I wrote in the evenings, mostly
after six; sometimes alternating my occupation with
a walk on Blackheath, preparing a sentence or laying
out a subject, and returning home to commit the
results to paper. I had no library then, but used to
write with my children playing about me; I had no
difficulty in concentrating my attention upon the
subject in hand. While I had been a newspaper
editor, I used to write with the clang of the steam-
engine and printing-press in my ears; and afterwards, at the railway office, I worked amidst constant interruptions and inquiries, which I was
always ready to answer.

I did not attempt to write in any particular sort
of "style." I first endeavoured thoroughly to understand the subject, and then the sentences flowed from
my pen without conscious effort. If I wrote quickly
and expressively, it was because I had been vigor-
ously active during my walk. I think Southey was
right when he said to Ebenezer Elliott, "My rule of
writing is, to express myself, 1st, as perspicuously as

possible; 2nd, as concisely as possible; and 3rd, as impressively as possible." This is the way to be felt, and understood, and remembered. The writer who relies upon "style" dances in fetters. Sydney Smith said truthfully, "Every style is good that is not tiresome." Another thing—a man must himself understand before he begins to write: this is the most infallible mode of being understood by others.

After a long and protracted period—long, because of the numerous interviews with friends of Stephenson, and also because of the few intermittent hours I could give to writing out the results of the interviews in the leisure of my evenings—I at length got the manuscript into shape, and went up to Robert Stephenson's house in Gloucester Square, to read some portions of it over to him and his friend Mr Sopwith. I sought out some of the most interesting parts—his father's early life, and the history of the Safety Lamp. I read on and on; and when I looked up, Sopwith was drowsy, and Robert Stephenson was profoundly asleep! Gracious goodness! was this to be the result of my labours with the public? But it is true, my audience had dined; and dined well. When I stopped, Stephenson suddenly looked up, and said, "Oh! I hear you very well. Go on, if you please."

I went on a little further, and this time my audience kept wide awake.

"Well," said Stephenson finally, "who is to be your publisher?"

"I intend," I answered, "to try Mr Murray first, as I consider him to be at the top of the publishing business."

"If a few hundred pounds would be of use," he

rejoined, "for illustrations and such like, let me know."

"I don't think that will be at all necessary," I answered, "as I have no doubt I can get the book published, without expense to anybody."

Stephenson afterwards said to me that he was surprised at my answer, and that he saw I must have some confidence in the success of the book.

Having finished the MS. towards the end of 1856, I called upon Mr Murray, and found him willing to publish the book on half-profits. He suggested, however, that the MS. should be placed in the hands of an experienced author for revision and correction. I afterwards found that Mr (afterwards Sir John) Milton was my reviser.* His fee was £30. He cut out a good many anecdotes, which I took an early opportunity of restoring; as I think that personal anecdotes, when characteristic, greatly enliven the pages of a biography.

The book was ready for publication in June 1857. On the 26th of May, at the anniversary of the Civil Engineers Institution, I presented to the secretary the first bound copy of the volume, which was looked over by some of the members. A few days later, I received the following letter from Robert Stephenson :—

"34 GLOUCESTER SQUARE, 8*th June* 1857.

"MY DEAR SIR,—

"Now that your work is advertised, I believe you will get a good deal of correspondence of my father's. I enclose you a little batch from Thomas Gooch, who was associated with my father in the execution of the Manchester and Leeds Rail-

* Mr, afterwards Sir J. Milton, sometime clerk and chief-clerk in the War Office, occasionally acted as literary adviser to the late Mr John Murray.—ED.

way. I have no doubt more will come to hand; but
you will perceive that much of the correspondence
could scarcely with propriety be published at this
time—the allusions to the men of the Great Western
to wit!

"Those who have perused the volume you left at
the Institution, not beyond two or three, like the tone
and feeling of the Biography very much indeed.
They like both the head and the heart that produced
it.—Yours very faithfully,

"ROBERT STEPHENSON."

Copies of the "Life" were as usual sent out to the
press. How would the critics receive the volume?
I remember a clever description, by the late W. S.
Landor, in his *Imaginary Conversations*, of the manner
in which the critics receive a new book. "Some
slowly rise, like carp in a pond when food is thrown
among them; some snatch suddenly at a morsel and
swallow it; others touch it gently with their barbe,
pass deliberately by, and leave it; others wriggle and
rub against it more disdainfully; others, in sober
truth, know not what to make of it, swim round and
round it, eye it on the sunny side, eye it on the
shady; approach it, question it, shoulder it, flap it
with their tails, turn it over, look askance at it, take
a peashell or a worm instead of it, and plunge again
their contented heads into the comfortable mud:
after some seasons the same food will suit their
stomachs better."

I must say that, on the whole, the critics received
my new book very favourably. The *Spectator*, indeed,
said, "little was left for Mr Smiles to do, but to fill
in the details." But what is a Biography without
the details? The details are everything. To take
a much more important case. Most people knew
something of the lives of Johnson and Scott; but

merit was certainly due to Boswell and Lockhart for filling in the details. The *Athenæum* was cordial; the usually staid *Economist* was enthusiastic; the *Saturday Review* was full of praise. These and other reviews appeared in print shortly after the appearance of the book; and favourable notices were re-echoed from the provinces. In the course of the following month, Mr Murray informed me that the Life had been so well received, that he had very few copies remaining of the 1000 composing the first edition, and that he must send the book to press again as soon as possible. Another edition of 1500 copies was accordingly printed and sold; and in the following September, a further edition of 2000 copies, in which many amendments and additions were made, was disposed of.*

Then came the reviews in the Monthlies and the Quarterlies, as well as two long consecutive articles in the *Times* of 9th and 16th September: all of which had the effect of sending off the book. Indeed, on several occasions, the type of one edition had only been half distributed, when another edition was called for. It had also the honour of being reprinted in America—without my knowledge or consent. This is usually the case with all English books that succeed. Failures are, of course, never stolen. I was once complaining to an American lady of the unsatisfactory state of the copyright law between England and America. "Oh!" she exclaimed, "you ought to be satisfied with the fame you achieve by the in-

---

* Since the above passage was written, I have read the *Life of George Eliot*, and observe that she was an admirer of the book. "*The Life of George Stephenson,*" she wrote to a friend, "has been a real profit and pleasure. . . . He is one of my great heroes: has he not a dear old face?"

creased circulation of your works." "Well, madam,"
I answered, "I do not know what it may be in
America, but in England, fame is considered a very
hungry diet."

The result of the publication was, that in the
course of little more than a year, five editions of the
8vo *Life of George Stephenson*, amounting in all to
7500 copies, were printed. In 1859, a reduced and
cheaper copy of the work was published; and afterwards a larger and handsomer edition, to range with
the *Lives of the Engineers.* At the time at which I
write these lines, some 60,000 copies of the book
have been printed in England—the last being the
Centenary Edition at 2s. 6d.

Behold me at last, at the advanced age of forty-
five, a successful author! People wondered how a
person so utterly unknown in the literary world
should have been able to write a successful book,
especially on the topic of a railway engineer. But
they did not know the long training I had had for
the work, and the difficulties I had overcome—the
encounter with which, indeed, had educated me—nor
the reading, thinking, observation, and perseverance,
which are about the sole conditions for success in
anything.

When I found that I could succeed in writing a
respectable book, I took from the drawer, where it
had lain so long, my rejected MS. on *Self-Help*, and
thought of rewriting it and offering it to the public.
I took some pains with it, and had it ready for the
printer in July 1859. I intended at first to publish it
without my name on the title-page; but Mr Murray
warned me against doing so. "You ought to
recollect," he said, "that success is a lottery in
literature, and you abandon your vantage-ground by

publishing anonymously." I therefore eventually agreed to give my name on the title-page.

My object in writing out *Self-Help*, and delivering it at first in the form of lectures, and afterwards re-writing and publishing it in the form of a book, was principally to illustrate and enforce the power of George Stephenson's great word—PERSEVERANCE. I had been greatly attracted when a boy by Mr Craik's *Pursuit of Knowledge under Difficulties*. I had read it often, and knew its many striking passages almost by heart. It occurred to me, that a similar treatise, dealing not so much with literary achievements and the acquisition of knowledge, as with the ordinary business and pursuits of common life, illustrated by examples of conduct and character drawn from reading, observation, and experience, might be equally useful to the rising generation. It seemed to me that the most important results in daily life are to be obtained, not through the exercise of extraordinary powers, such as genius and intellect, but through the energetic use of simple means and ordinary qualities, with which nearly all human individuals have been more or less endowed. Such was my object, and I think that, on the whole, I hit my mark.

Mr Murray was willing to incur the risk of print-ing the book on the half-profit system. But, looking to the publication of *George Stephenson*, I thought I might myself incur the risk. Accordingly, the work was published on the usual commission. Then arose the question as to the number to be printed of the first edition. I thought the book might succeed, but I was not particularly sanguine. Mr Murray, however, said, "I think, *with* your name on the title-page, you may venture to commence

with the printing of 3000 copies." Even that
was a large number of an untried book. It was
offered at Mr Murray's annual sale in November,
and the whole edition was sold off. "In fact,"
he said, "the work has followed the hint of its
own title." Orders for 3000 more were given to the
printer, though the specimen copies had not yet been
sent out to the press for review. When the reviews
appeared, they were favourable. The book went, as
Mr Cooke said, "like hot rolls"; and yet, by the 2nd
of March following, the copies had not yet been sent
to the country papers. Indeed, the book was received
with more applause than the *Life of Stephenson*.
During the first year 20,000 copies were printed, and
15,000 the second. Since then, the book has continued in demand. Up to the present time, I think
that about 160,000 have been printed.*

When the book was announced, Messrs Ticknor
& Fields, the American publishers, were so well satisfied with the results of their publication of the *Life of
George Stephenson*—which was undertaken without
my knowledge or consent—that they offered £25 for a
set of the advance sheets of *Self-Help*. Mr Murray
said, "It is not much to give, but it is something
saved out of the fire." Mr Cooke, his partner, also
said, "We think you would do well to accept the £25
as *generally* they offer only £5 or £10 for such a
work." The proposal was accordingly accepted. It
appeared that shortly after the publication of the
book in America, it was largely purchased for the
School Libraries in Ohio and other States of the
Union; so that Ticknor & Fields must have done
well by their spirited and generous arrangement.

* At the beginning of 1905 the number printed was close on
258,000.—ED.

But they could not retain the monopoly in America. Other publishers reissued the book. I have seen three editions, but I am told there are many more.

The *Atlantic Monthly*, then published by Ticknor & Fields, contained an article on International Copyright in October 1867, from which it appeared that the practice then was, that if an American publisher issued a reprint of a foreign work, he by that fact acquired an exclusive right to the republication of all subsequent works by the same author (p. 441). This was the "courtesy of the trade" in America. It shortly meant this: "If I steal from an English author once, I have the right of stealing everything that he publishes in any future year." Not only so, but "all and several of these rights may be bought and sold, like any other kind of property." The same article contained a statement that Messrs Ticknor & Fields, "on principle, and as an essential part of their system, send to foreign authors a share of the proceeds of these works, and this they have habitually done for twenty-five years." I can only say that in my own case, they published the *Life of George Stephenson*, and afterwards *Industrial Biography*, without my knowledge or consent, and that they did not send me the value of a brass farthing for the privilege of publishing either of those works.

I was, however, sufficiently satisfied with the results of my publication at home. It would be considered absurdly eulogistic were I to detail the many marks of sympathy and gratitude which I have received from all classes of the community, at home and abroad. I hope I shall be excused for mentioning a few curious instances. One gentleman

at Dundee, who named his son after me, assures me
that he is indebted to me for what he is to-day: he
says my words have often cheered and spurred him
on in the battle of life. Another, at Hastings, says,
"*Self-Help* has been of extraordinary service to me.
I have repeatedly gained hope and courage from its
aphorisms and brave sentences; and with them I
have tried to encourage others." A third, a lady at
Birmingham, writes to thank me for my lessons,
which have so cheered and encouraged her son, who
is now far away, an emigrant at Waimato, New
Zealand. "Smiles's *Self-Help*," he writes, "has
been the cause of an entire alteration in my life, and
I thank God I have read it. I am now devoted to
study and hard work, and I mean to rise, both as
regards my moral and intellectual life. I only wish
I could see the man who wrote the book, and *thank*
him from my heart." The lady who wrote the letter
adds, "You may, perhaps, imagine with what feelings
his mother read this passage; for when my son went
out, he was thoughtless, and we were *anxious* about
him. 'Out of the abundance of the heart' etc., is
my only excuse. Thank God!"

A working man at Exeter was not less grateful.
He thanks me for what I have done for the benefit of
his class. He says my books "have instructed and
helped him greatly," and he "wishes that every working man would read them through and through, and
ponder them well." Another correspondent, resident
in the same city, says that "since perusing the book,
he had experienced an entire revolution in his habits,
and is grateful to the author as the primary cause.
Instead of regarding life as a weary course, which
has to be got over as a task, I now view it in the
light of a trust of which I must make the most;

and, acting accordingly, I am beginning to feel a satisfaction that I never felt before."

One night I met at a friend's house a gentleman who said he "desired to shake me by the hand, and to thank me for all I had done for him." "How is that?" I asked. "When a young man," he said, "I was on the slide downward. I was careless, thoughtless, and pleasure-seeking. Your *Self-Help* came in the nick of time. I read it, and pondered over it, until it seized entire hold of me. I endeavoured to put its lessons into practice. I became sober, punctual, attentive, and began to be trusted. I was promoted, and eventually rose to be a partner in my firm. I am now a prosperous man, and have to thank you for it all." This was certainly a most encouraging testimony to the results of my small literary efforts.

I knew a widow lady who was encouraged to persevere in art, from the instances of perseverance which she found related in *Self-Help* and two other young ladies who were encouraged to write for their living and the support of their relations—all of whom are now recognised and famous. A young surgeon at Blackheath tells me that my little book, first placed in his hands by his father, "gave fresh energy and hopeful enthusiasm to his career." He thanks me cordially "for being one of the chief causes in giving an inclination to my mind, which, I hope, will bear good fruit, as well as more ennobling views of life and its duties."

This is surely eulogy enough. But I cannot refrain from adding another instance. At first, I did not know what to make of it. Many years after the book had been published, I received a letter from Dublin from a person I had never heard of,

beginning "My dear Sir." He apologised for
addressing me in so familiar a manner; but it all
arose from "dear old *Self-Help*," which had become
his most familiar friend and adviser. His story was
as follows :—

Eleven years before the date of his letter, he had
seen an announcement of the book. That, he
thought, is the volume for me; besides, the *Free-
man's Journal* had praised it. He saved a shilling,
for he was then only a boy; but when he went to the
bookseller, he found the price of the book was beyond
his means. The bookseller showed it to him : "Little
did I think," he says, "of the fruit that was concealed
therein." Nevertheless, he was only put off for a
little. He saved again, and in three weeks he was
able to buy the book, "though pence were then of
far greater importance to me than pounds now
are."

"Now," he adds, "comes the strange part of my
story. Such was the influence worked upon me by
your description of what has been done and what
could be done by continued industry and determined
perseverance, that you made me believe it possible to
do things that I and thousands more had regarded as
impossible. Such, however, was its effect. I had
already served seven years to the Wine and Spirit
trade, which I every year regarded with greater
dislike. I now wished to change my occupation, and
embrace some less equivocal calling. After a time, I
embarked all my earnings and savings in the
druggist and chemist business; and as Smiles had
been my guide, I determined to take you into my
concern as a sleeping partner. Hence you will see
your name, in conjunction with my own, at the top
of my letters and shop-bills. My friends were very
much opposed to my undertaking, and did everything
to deter me from entering upon it, believing that
I should have succeeded very well in the spirit trade,
which was my own proper business. They did not

know who my partner was, but supposed he must be a man of capital and experience. I had, of course, many difficulties to encounter; but after years of struggle and labour I made my way. Not to trouble you with too many details, I may say that I became prosperous. Your name smiled upon me. Many of my customers addressed me by your name as well as by my own, and I answered to the one equally with the other. Indeed, I scarcely knew which was which. After three years I opened another branch in a different part of the city. That too succeeded. So that you will see I have many reasons to believe in dear old *Self-Help;* and I long much to shake by the hand so good a guide and friend as the writer of the book."

I had not yet seen my correspondent; but in the course of a short time I had the pleasure of making his acquaintance. He was all that I could have expected of him—active, enterprising, and intelligent. He was still young, and desirous of distinguishing himself in another walk of life. He had saved enough money to enable him to enter at Trinity College as a student. First he thought of embracing Law; eventually he determined upon devoting himself to the Church. After disposing of his business, he went to Stonyhurst College in Lancashire; then he went to Rome, where he remained for three years; now he is at Oxford, preparing himself for ordination in the Roman Catholic Church. Knowing well the vicious tendency of drinking habits, he intends to devote the rest of his life to promoting the cause of temperance. I still treasure as a gift from him, a present on which is inscribed, "To Samuel Smiles, Esq., as a small token of esteem."

Self-Help was translated into most foreign languages. The first I heard of it was from a Dutch clergyman, who was in England attending the marriage of a niece of my friend, Mr Eborall.

He said to me, "We know your name very well in
Holland." "How is that?" I asked. "From your
book *Help u Zelfen:* it is one of the most popular
books in the country." He afterwards sent me a
copy; and there it was, complete, in Dutch. The
next translation, I think, was made at Hamburg, in
Germany; but it was badly done, and another
translation came out at Colberg a few years later.
Denmark and Sweden followed; then France; then
Buenos Ayres, in Portuguese. Translations were
also made at Prague into the Czech language, and at
Wagram into the Croatian. I was informed by Mr
Ralston that Russia has several translations, though
I have not seen them. There are two in Spain, and
the last that I have heard of is in Turkish.

The translation made into Italian was a great
success. The book, I was told, had been more successful than any published in that country. When I
was in Italy (of which more hereafter), in 1879, more
than 40,000 copies had been published. The late Dr
Max Schlesinger told me that, while in Egypt some
years ago, he had visited one of the Khedive's palaces,
then being fitted up by an Italian architect. On looking
at the inscriptions and mottoes written on the walls,
and on the magnificent furniture of the house, Dr
Schlesinger asked what they were. The Italian
informed him that they were texts from the Koran.
"But they are not all from the Koran," he added;
"indeed, they are principally from Smeelis." "From
whom?" "Oh! you are an Englishman: you ought
to know Smeelis! They are from his *Self-Help:*
they are much better than the texts from the Koran!"
Dr Schlesinger told me this anecdote with much gusto
on his return to London.

I cannot tell the number of Eastern languages

into which *Self-Help* has been translated. In 1874, Mr Murray wrote to me, "Two days ago, I gave leave for a translation of *Self-Help* into Arabic, for the use of the people of Mount Lebanon!" Translations were made into several of the languages of India, more especially into Tamil, Marati, Gujarati, Hindustani, and Canarese. When Professor K. Nakamura, the Japanese, was in England in 1868, he heard a good deal about *Self-Help*, and took a copy of the work home with him. He translated it while on shipboard, and published it on arriving at Shidz'oka shortly afterwards. He entitled it, *European Decision of Character Book*—there being no equivalent for *Self-Help* in the Japanese language. In a letter which I received from Professor Nakamura, through the hands of the Honourable G. Takeda, delegate to the International Exhibition in 1873, he said, "Will you allow me to thank you with a sincere mind for your literary work, which has had a good result in our little island of Japan." He then proceeded to give me an account of the manner in which he was induced to make the translation, and now, he adds, "I am glad to see the results, for almost all the high class of our fellow-countrymen know what *Self-Help* is."

The translated book, a copy of which was handed to me by the Honourable G. Takeda, was a remarkable document. It had become expanded into a book of about 2000 pages, and read from the end backwards. The characters reminded one of an entymological collection. They stood apart, like insects in a case at the British Museum; but, on closer scrutiny, they seemed to represent, not the lower creatures, but familiar objects, such as houses, windows, fireplaces, and various domestic utensils, involved in fantastic flourishes capable of no European explanation. On looking at the book and its characters, it does not afford matter for surprise that the Japanese should be contemplating the abandonment of their own language, and a resort to straightforward, condensed, and sensible English!

CHAPTER XV

LITERATURE occupied a very small portion of my thoughts, and a still smaller portion of my working faculties. It was, of course, a great pleasure to me occasionally to withdraw myself from the daily fatigue of office duties, and take refuge in quiet thinking and reflective study. But I had comparatively little unbroken leisure. When I had done my day's work, and read up the news of the day, there was little time left for other purposes. For months together, I did not set down a word for the printer. There was only enough time left for rest, and recreation, and sleep.

Our company was usually at war with the adjoining companies. On one side there was the Brighton, and on the other the East Kent. They had always to be watched, as they in turn watched us. The Board met only once a fortnight. It was scarcely to be expected that gentlemen who gave only an intermittent attention to the affairs of a large company, could take so much interest in it as the working staff, of whom I was one. It was the subject of our daily business and of our constant thoughts. Mr Eborall, the general manager, a most worthy and excellent man, was in constant communication with me; and consulted me about everything in connection with the company's affairs.

One of the most trying affairs we had to consider, was the extension of the East Kent line in and through the district which we had heretofore exclusively occupied. It was a short-sighted policy on the part of the previous directors, not to have fully occupied the ground between Chatham and Canterbury, and made a railway for the accommodation of the public in North Kent. But the mischief had been initiated in 1853, before our connection with the company. A line was granted by Parliament, and the works were in course of construction. Overtures were made for the amalgamation of the concerns; but no serious proposal was ever submitted for consideration. Our directors were under the impression that the line would never be completed; and were rather disposed to laugh the new undertaking to scorn.

The rival line was not only made, but new extensions were obtained—eastwards towards Dover and Margate, and westwards towards London. "They would never be made; they could never be finished!" No doubt they ruined many people, shareholders as well as contractors; but they were made, and they were finished. What Oxenstiern said to his son was very true, "Go forth, my son, and see with how little wisdom the world is governed!" the same might be said of some railway directions.

There was one gentleman at our Board, who held the dogma of "closing the capital account." A very good dogma, provided the work to be done is only of strictly limited amount. Suppose, for instance, the Liverpool and Manchester directors had proposed to "close the capital account" when they had completed their line from Liverpool to Manchester! It would have been equivalent to "shutting up shop"! But instead of this, the company went on adding to their accommodation, until they had as many miles of station siding laid down in and around Liverpool alone, as they had laid down between Liverpool and Manchester! That line of thirty miles became expanded and connected with other lines, until at length it formed part of a network of railways, the property of one company, of over fourteen hundred miles in extent, representing a capital invested in railway works and plant, of over fifty millions sterling.

"Closing the capital account" meant this—"We shall give no further railway accommodation"—and that in the case of a City, the largest, without exception, in the world—a City of about four millions of people, and with a constantly increasing population— a City containing more than the entire population of Scotland, Sweden, Holland, or Portugal. The railway traffic of London is necessarily of immense magnitude, arising from the circumstance that it is not only the great distributive centre of the traffic of Great Britain, but that it contains an aggregate of some four millions of people, who are in a great measure dependent upon railways for their daily trade and their daily food, as well as, in a great many cases, for their daily journey to and from a suburban residence.

The new company, therefore, had no difficulty in getting their Acts passed by Parliament for giving greater accommodation to the county of Kent. Parliament also entertained the idea of giving the public the benefit of unrestricted railway competition. This, however, proved to be a mistake. "When combination is possible," said Robert Stephenson, "competition is impossible." At all events, shareholders, when investing their money, look for some profit or other from their undertaking. They do not invest merely from philanthropic motives. Even when they lay down a duplicate line, say between London and Dover, almost parallel with the line already made, they can reckon, at least, on sharing the traffic. And in the long-run they do. The public gets a double service, but it gets no reduction of rates.

This has been the case with the railway competition through Kent. There is scarcely a town that is not served by two railways instead of one; but, instead of having lower fares, the fares are necessarily kept up in order to pay the duplicate working expenses, and a moderate share of profit to those who have invested their money in constructing the duplicate railways. Parliament, in its wisdom, does not seem to have provided for the contingency of the new company combining with the old one, and thus rendering "unrestricted railway competition" impossible.

In an article which I wrote for the *Quarterly Review* in 1868 (after my connection with railways had ceased) I used the following words, which are strictly true :—

" Private companies have had to contend, at great cost, for the privilege of constructing and working the national highways ; but, once obtained, the privilege has proved of comparatively small advantage to them, for they have always been open to attack. One of the favourite ideas of English statesmen— but without a particle of statesmanship in it—has been that it is for the benefit of the public that there should be free competition between railway companies ;

and with that view duplicate lines—whether got up by schemers, contractors, or bona-fide companies—have been authorised and constructed in all directions. Thus, veering about, our legislators have granted powers enabling the competing companies to amalgamate, or to enter into combinations for the purpose of preventing competition, by which the benefits originally promised have been entirely nullified. There has thus been a great waste of capital in Parliamentary contests, and in the construction of unnecessarily expensive lines of railway; and while some of the companies have been reduced to bankruptcy, and all have been more or less impoverished, the result to the public is that they have to pay more for travelling by railway in England than in any other country in Europe." *

To return to the position of the South-Eastern Railway. The directors had admitted, when before Parliament, the desirableness of obtaining access to a terminal station at the West End of London; and in 1857, they pledged themselves to call their proprietors together, and "recommend them to promote or concur in the prosecution in next session, of such a scheme as will effectually supply access to the West End of London, and so complete the system of railway accommodation for Kent and the Continent." Nothing was, however, done to redeem this pledge. But it occurred to me, as well as to others of the

---

* *Quarterly Review*, No. 250. In this article I endeavoured to give the results of much railway experience. I contrasted the results of railways in Belgium with those in England, and recognised the enlightened policy adopted by King Leopold and his ministers. I quote the words of the leading railway managers (p. 322) as to the utter uselessness, as well as the manifest injury, of unrestricted competition. I advocate (what many people will not agree with) the combination of all the Irish railways, into one company, either to be worked by the State, or by one joint-stock concern, as by far the most conducive to public interest and advantage. The late Sir Rowland Hill was also in favour of this view.

staff, that we ought to do something to keep faith, not only with Parliament, but with the shareholders.

The general manager ordered a return to be made of the directions taken by the passengers leaving the London Bridge Station. From this, it appeared that a very large proportion—more than three-fifths—were for places west of Temple Bar, and especially in the neighbourhood of Charing Cross. The result of the inquiry was, that Charing Cross was found to be the most convenient site for a West End terminus. It formed the centre of a series of important thoroughfares ramifying in all directions —to Westminster and the Houses of Parliament; to Regent Street, Pall Mall, Piccadilly, and the West End squares; as well as to St Martin's Lane, leading to Oxford Street on the north, and to the Strand, in the east. It was found that, in view of the population to be accommodated, the neighbourhood of important public exhibitions and institutions, and the persons likely to travel upon the railway, a station at Charing Cross would be much more convenient than those at the other proposed alternative sites — at York Road or Battersea (south of the Thames), or at Pimlico (north of the river), where we should be merely alongside of our rivals of the Brighton and Chatham Companies.

After obtaining all the requisite information, and conferring with Mr Rees, the solicitor of the company, and Mr Ryde, the surveyor, I prepared an elaborate report, which I first submitted to Mr Eborall, and, after it had received his sanction, I laid it before the Board in February 1858. The Board would not undertake to make the extension to the West End, notwithstanding their pledge to Parliament. But they had no objections "to promote or concur in the prosecution" of the proposed extension. They were opposed to the construction of new branches, and still desirous of "closing the capital account."

But how was the extension of the line to Charing Cross to be made? By an independent company, supported by the South-Eastern. They gave me permission to take steps to form such a company. Four gentlemen from the outside were induced to join, and, with four South-Eastern directors, a Board was formed, of which the South-Eastern chairman was appointed president. I prepared a prospectus, and issued it to the public. A considerable number of shares were applied for, and in the long run the South-Eastern company subscribed for the remainder.

Many years before, the London and South-Western Company had obtained an Act extending their line from Waterloo Station to the south end of London Bridge. The line passed through a very inferior description of house property, of comparatively inconsiderable value. This Act had been allowed to lapse, through the effluxion of time. The London and South-Western directors were waited on, for the purpose of ascertaining whether they would now concur in the renewed application to Parliament, as the extension of their line to the City would be not less valuable than the extension of the South-Eastern to the West End. But they declined, and it was necessary that we should proceed to Parliament alone.

Mr Ryde laid out the new line of railway; and Mr Rees, the solicitor, assisted in the promotion

of the Bill through Parliament. Both worked with
great ability and energy. Mr Eborall, the general
manager, gave his cordial assistance, as he saw
that the new line would eventually give his company the command in a great measure of the
West End traffic. We had the advantage, also,
of securing the assistance of Mr (now Sir John)
Hawkshaw, as our leading parliamentary engineer.
Mr Toogood was appointed the parliamentary agent.

It was originally intended that the West End
station should be on the spot occupied by Northumberland House. The Duke of Northumberland's
solicitors were seen; and though they were at first
agreeable, the duke afterwards withdrew his assent.
As his opposition would most probably have been
fatal to the Bill, the site was subsequently changed
to Hungerford Market; and as the old suspension
bridge at Hungerford was not a paying property,
we were able to buy the whole affair at a comparatively moderate price. Curiously enough, the
chairman of the Hungerford market and bridge was
a director of the South-Eastern Company; and he
was enabled to perform a little manipulation with the
depreciated shares of the former company, very much
to his own advantage. From an unwilling abettor
of the Charing Cross line, he thenceforward became
a cordial supporter. Thus the whole body were
pulled, like sheep through a hedge, onwards towards
Charing Cross.

The Bill went before Parliament in 1859, and was
strongly opposed, principally by the Brighton Railway
Company and the trustees of St Thomas's Hospital.
The former declined to join in the extension, and
probably were opposed to our establishing a West
End station in competition with their Pimlico

terminus. But the chief opposition was from St Thomas's Hospital.*

It happened that the proposed line could not be constructed without passing through a corner of the hospital grounds, though without touching the hospital buildings themselves. The governors were of opinion that the construction of the railway would be fatal to the continued use of the place for medical purposes; and there may have been some reason for their contention. At all events, the parliamentary committee adopted their view. They passed the Bill, with the provision that the railway company should, if called upon, purchase the whole of the hospital grounds and buildings.

The Bill was admirably advocated before the Commons Committee by Mr (afterwards Sir) W. J. Alexander, Bart. The printed document which I had prepared for the South-Eastern Board formed his principal brief; and the facts and figures it contained were publicly stated before the committee, and were never contradicted. The great battle with the hospital trustees was settled in the Commons, and the Bill passed the Lords without any difficulty.

Then came the purchase of the hospital property and buildings. It was certainly a very heavy case— perhaps the largest that had ever come before an arbitrator in London. The price to be paid by the railway company was to be settled by an independent valuer. Such a person was found at Manchester. The arbitrator's court was held, with barristers, solicitors, leading valuers, and numerous witnesses. Evidence was given without limit. The arbitrator shed his

* This hospital was then situated in High Street, Southwark, in a building erected in 1706.—ED.

lustre upon the court for a fortnight. At length, after the leading barristers—including Lloyd, of "Lloyd's bonds"—had delivered their final speeches, the arbitrator retired to prepare his final award.

The arbitrator proved a very Daniel. He at length gave in his award, duly signed and attested. It was that the railway company should pay the sum of £290,000 for the property and buildings of St Thomas's Hospital! It was a very large sum indeed. But how had the sapient arbitrator arrived at this precise amount? The valuers were all in a dilemma. At last, Mr Ryde called in upon me one day, and said, "I have found it out! Yes! here it is!" He showed me the figures of the various valuers. There were nine in all. "Add these up, and divide by nine, and there is the result—£290,000!" Any School Board pupil teacher, or even any unskilled labourer, with a little knowledge of arithmetic, might have done as much. There was scarcely any need to send all the way to Manchester for a second Daniel like this. And yet it is to be feared that this rough-and-ready method of arriving at a valuation is not unknown among city valuers even at the present day.

It is unnecessary to say anything about the superiority of Charing Cross as a West End terminus. When Boswell spoke to Dr Johnson of the quick succession of people passing along Fleet Street, the doctor said, "Why, sir, Fleet Street has a very animated appearance; but I think the full tide of human existence is at Charing Cross!" It is the same now as it was a hundred years ago. Charing Cross is still the centre of the West End. Nothing can be compared with it for situation. It is close to all the great clusters of traffic. Carried on a lofty

Q

viaduct across the Thames, and on a level with the adjacent streets, the Charing Cross Station is brought almost to the very doors of an immense mass of people living, or having to do business, in the western parts of London.

Before the line was made, the bridges across the Thames were overcrowded with 'buses, cabs, and hansoms, carrying passengers to and from the terminus at the south end of London Bridge. After the opening of the line, at the beginning of 1864, the bridges were in a great measure cleared, and a great advantage was thus conferred upon the public. But it was not for a merely philanthropic benefit that the Charing Cross Railway was constructed. The South-Eastern Company itself derived the principal advantage. The new line opened up the whole range of sea coast, along the mouth of the Thames, and round by Dover to Hastings, to an immense new mass of population in the western parts of London ; it also brought the wealthiest travelling class in direct communication with the Continent, by Folkestone and Boulogne, and by Dover and Calais.

Where a large and rapidly increasing city has to be supplied with railway facilities, as I have already said, the capital account cannot be kept "closed." The railway company must enlarge its accommodation according to the increasing demands. When, therefore, it was found that the Brighton Company were secretly negotiating with contractors for the extension of their lines to Tunbridge Wells, in violation of the territorial arrangement existing between the companies, our general manager, Mr Eborall, boldly laid a scheme before the Board, for constructing a direct line between Lewisham and Tunbridge (by Sevenoaks) and a loop line between

Lee and Dartford, thereby cutting off the angle at Redhill, and bringing the line into direct communication with Folkestone and Dover on the one hand, and Tunbridge Wells and Hastings on the other; while a direct connection was made with the whole line of the North Kent communications, as far as Gravesend, Chatham, and Maidstone, and afterwards Victoria on the Medway.

Had the "capital account" been "closed," and the Charing Cross line not been made, in addition to these other important extensions, the South-Eastern Company—to use a favourite phrase—would inevitably have been "smashed up." We should have had no station but at the south end of London Bridge; while the Brighton and the Chatham and Dover Companies would each have possessed both City and West End stations. Away would have gone the bulk of the continental, as well as the Tunbridge Wells and Hastings traffic. Indeed, the Brighton Company insisted, in 1860, on 70 per cent. of the Hastings traffic being granted them in the division of the West End traffic.

Since the opening of the Charing Cross terminus, and the direct line to Tunbridge, the results have proved very different. The capital expended has gone up in amount, yet the shares have gone to a premium, and the dividends have been increased. And in time to come, the public will have no reason to complain of the construction of the Charing Cross railway, and the additional facilities which have been afforded them, not only for access to suburban residences in Kent, but for getting readily to the seaside, and for quick communication between Dover and Folkestone and the continental ports.

All this, however, may prove very tedious to

those whose minds are not interested and steeped—
as mine then was—in the thought of London
traffic and passenger accommodation. There were
many other things requiring attention. I remember
a most important matter—the remodelling of the
rules and regulations upon the line, for the purpose
of avoiding accidents. It was found, on inquiry,
that some of the regulations were slightly con-
tradictory, and that they wanted codifying and
rearrangement. In rendering these rules more intelligible, as well as grammatical, I believe that I
was of some use.

The idea of "an accident" occurring on the line
always set us "in a quake." Nothing can be more
horrifying to a person employed in railway service.
It deprived many of us of our night's rest. My dear
friend Eborall was always of an anxious turn of mind.
He could never get rid of his business. He would
take it home with him; take it to bed with him;
turn it over and over to the loss of his sleep; and
rise up with it in the morning; for it ever burdened
his mind. Sometimes, when a thing had struck him
in the night that he wished to remember, he would
get up, light the gas, and commit it to his memor-
andum book.

But the most careful preliminary arrangements
cannot overcome the infirmities of human nature.
Rules may be perfect; but not men. I remember
one day Eborall rushed into my room, which adjoined
his own, and said, with frightful alarm, "I am off to
Staplehurst by a special engine: I hear there is an
awful accident." It was too true. It appeared that
the "ganger," or superintendent of plate-layers, had
taken up a portion of the line overhanging a rivulet,
for the purpose of repairing it with new beams and

rails. He had looked at his time-book, but mistaken the hour! On the previous day, the tidal train would not have arrived till about two hours later; but now (without his knowing it, through his individual mistake) it was due! He had not even sent his signalman along the line, to protect the road. Up came the train from Folkestone, and dashed into the opening; and eight of the fourteen carriages were thrown into the brook underneath. It is a dreadful thing, even to think of. The event occurred on a fine afternoon in June 1865.

Of course, the company had to bear all the expense involved by the accident. Everything was done for the relief of the sufferers, and the people of the neighbourhood were most kind. Gallimore, the district inspector, and Benge, the foreman platelayer, were found guilty of manslaughter, and were sent to prison. But their punishment could not remedy the awful injury that had been done.

Not long after the accident, a young lady called upon Mr Eborall, and claimed some damage for the injury done to her dress. As it was necessary to ask for references—for it was a practice of certain persons to make a trade of claiming compensation in railway accidents—he desired to know if any person was with her at the time the accident occurred. "Yes!" she said, "my mother, and Mr Charles Dickens." This was the first time we had heard that Charles Dickens was in the train. I believe that he first referred to the fact at the conclusion of his novel of *Edwin Drood*. He died five years later. Although railway collisions sometimes produce permanent injury to the brain, I never heard that he suffered from this cause. He died most probably from too much work, too much reading of his works, and too much unrest.

Shortly after the occurrence of the above event, we were invaded by a number of inventors, all suggesting remedies for railway accidents. The most extraordinary applicant was an old sea captain. He said no accident need occur if his remedy were adopted. What was it? It was to provide two strong anchors and chains, suspended to the last carriage of every train. When an accident seemed likely to occur, the anchors were to be suddenly let go! I need scarcely say what would have been the result of the adoption of this plan. One might as well have run the train against a brick wall. The result would certainly have been the destruction of most of the carriages, and the ripping up of about a hundred yards of the permanent way. It was merely an illustration of the old story of "Nothing like leather!"

CHAPTER XVI

I LED a double life at this time—my life at the office and my life at home. Many men of business do this. After a day's labour they look forward to pleasure— to domestic comfort, to evening enjoyment, to exercise and change of occupation, and to work that is grateful instead of work that is worrying. It was my practice, at the time of which I write, to wind up the day by a game of billiards with one or other of my sons. It was a capital exercise—rather tiring, and not too exciting—before retiring for the night.

A wise man accumulates his force by means of rest. Seeming idleness is not all idleness. It means recuperation. A man enjoys his rest all the better because of work; and he will do his work all the better because of rest. In fact, we must rest in order to work. At the same time, change of occupation is often equivalent to rest. Hence Fénelon said, "Le changement des études est toujours un délassement pour moi." Many brain-workers have recognised the truth of this idea.

I had always plenty of intellectual amusements and occupations to fill up my leisure hours. I had enough work mapped out to fill up many years. If

247

I could not accomplish it, some one else would. No matter: there was always something to look forward to in hope. I even found that the intervals of busy life might be more favourable to effective study than altogether unbroken leisure. I pursued knowledge as a recreation, during the spare hours of an active official career. My mind was active, in my journeys to and from the office, or during my walks on Blackheath or in Greenwich Park; and my thoughts had often become fittingly clothed with words, without a conscious effort, before I sat down to write.

After it had been ascertained that I could write a satisfactory book, I received many proposals from publishers and others to undertake some special work for their house. But I kept free of all such engagements. I desired to use my leisure in my own way, and to be perfectly untrammelled in all that I did. I accepted, however, Mr Murray's invitation to write a few articles for the *Quarterly Review*. Of these, the "Difficulties of Railway Engineering" appeared in January 1858; and the articles on "Iron Bridges," and on "James Watt" in July and October of the same year. Mr Robert Stephenson supplied me with some of the materials for the article on "Iron Bridges."

I had some conversation with Mr Stephenson as to the work which I next thought of writing—*The Lives of the Engineers*. He was a good deal surprised at the general applause with which his father's Life had been received. It was what he had scarcely expected; and yet, no doubt it had arisen mainly through my not overlaying it with too many engineering details, and bringing out, as much as possible, the human and individual character of the

Man. Still, he doubted whether I could rely upon
the same element of success in the lives of departed
engineers, who had died and left scarcely a trace of
their history—left little or nothing behind them but
their works. Still, I thought it possible that some
interesting reminiscences of personal life and character might yet be collected and preserved for the
benefit of others.

On prosecuting the inquiry, I found the subject
to be exceedingly attractive. The events in the lives
of the early engineers were, for the most part, a
succession of individual struggles, sometimes rising
almost to the heroic. In one case, the object of
interest was a London goldsmith, Myddelton—the
first engineer who supplied London with pure water;
in another, he was a retired seaman, Captain Perry—
one of the earliest marsh drainers; or a wheelwright,
like Brindley, the great unlettered giant, who became
the first English canal maker; or an attorney's clerk,
like Smeaton, who built one of the first great light-
houses as a finger-post of the sea, on the Eddystone
Rock; or an instrument-maker, like Watt, who
invented the practical working steam-engine; or a
millwright, like Rennie, the constructor of the noblest
modern bridges; or a working mason, like Telford, who afterwards became a sort of Colossus of
roads.

All these men were strong-minded, resolute, and
ingenious men; impelled to their special pursuits by
the force of their constructive instincts. In most
cases they had to make for themselves a way; for
there was none to point out to them the road,
which, until then, had been untravelled. Indeed,
there was almost a dramatic interest in their noble
efforts, their temporary defeats, and eventually their

triumphs; and their rising up, in spite of manifold obstructions and difficulties, from obscurity to fame.

But how to clothe these biographies with personal interest? This was a matter of much difficulty. But I did what I could. I placed myself in communication with all who were likely to give me information. I spent the few brief holidays I could snatch from my daily labour, in visiting the sites of the great engineering works. I went over the New River as far as Ware in Hertfordshire. This I could do on a summer Saturday afternoon. I went down to Brading Haven in the Isle of Wight, and made a sketch of Myddelton's great embankment; and I afterwards spent an Easter holiday in visiting Myddelton's birthplace at Galch Hill, near Denbigh, North Wales.

By careful inquiry, I was enabled to collect a great deal of new and curious information about Brindley. I visited his works, on my way to and from Wales, together with his last residence at Turnhurst, and his burial-place at New Chapel in the same neighbourhood. I spent the holiday of another year in visiting the birthplace of Telford in Eskdale, north of the Scottish border; and there I found a great deal of new information about that distinguished engineer. The same with Greenock, the birthplace of Watt; and Phantassie, in East Lothian, the birthplace of Rennie. Wherever information was to be had, I endeavoured to obtain it.

I could not read at the British Museum myself, or at the State Paper Office, or at the Corporation Records of the City of London; but I obtained the help of some excellent readers and extractors of evidence. The best of these was Mr W. Walker Wilkins (since dead), to whom I was under great obligations. Mr Martin, editor of *The Statesman's Year-Book*, was also of great use to me. After the death of Mr Wilkins, I wished to have some assistance at the British Museum and at the City Record Office; and observing the advertisements of several ladies in the *Athenæum* as readers, I engaged one of them. I found her of no use; then I engaged another; and after that a third. But I found that the great defect of ladies' help was incompleteness and inaccuracy. They neglected dates and references. They could not even copy correctly. They had no originality, and could not follow up a track of investigation. So that I had to go all over their work again to secure accuracy; and as doing the work twice over was of no use, I finally gave them up. I hope that Girton and Newnham will do something to educate ladies in attention, accuracy, and thoughtfulness.

In the case of both Wilkins and Martin, they could follow out a special line of reference; would consult book after book to obtain the proper authentic information; and copy accurately, with correct references down to the exact page and edition of the book copied from. Martin, though a foreigner (I believe a Russian, as he had the true Sarmatian features), had a true love of English literature, and an extensive knowledge of books.

In writing out the lives of Boulton and Watt, I had the advantage of consulting the whole of the literature of the firm—in the shape of the immense number of letters in the possession of the grandson of Mr Boulton, the present occupant of Tew Park, Oxfordshire. These were kindly sent to my house, and I consulted them at my leisure. I also visited all the scenes described in their story, at Birmingham, at Handsworth, as well as in Scotland, and in Cornwall. While making inquiries on the subject of Dr Roebuck's early connection with James Watt as to the invention of the steam-engine, I bethought me of my former acquaintance with John Arthur Roebuck, and wrote to him on the subject. The following was his answer:—

"19 ASHLEY PLACE,
"12*th January* 1858.

"MY DEAR SIR,—
"I have been absent from home for some time, and only returned last Saturday, so that I have been unable before to-day to answer your letter of the 28th of December last. I pray you to excuse this.

"I am sorry to say that I have no information respecting Dr Roebuck's connection with Watt. We Roebucks were always a race of Ishmaelites, and in our wanderings we have seldom paid much attention to family records. The misfortunes which deprived Dr Roebuck of the material benefits to be derived from the steam-engine, deprived him also of any honour to which he might be entitled from the same source; and this has rendered the subject a sore one to our family. Dr Roebuck's share in the transactions connected with the steam-engine will never be known; for mere family traditions will not pass for history. The last member of Dr Roebuck's family (Mrs Stuart), died in Birmingham, I think in 1836; and she was accustomed to dwell upon the merits of her father, in language that would surprise those who attribute to Watt the exclusive merit of the discoveries and inventions made in connection with the steam-engine. But I, knowing how useless would be any attempt of redistributing that merit, paid little attention to her reclamations.

"Accept, I pray, my thanks for all that you have done, and believe me, very truly yours,
"J. A. ROEBUCK."

I placed my various friends under contribution while writing the lives of Telford and Rennie, and among other letters I received the following from the late Peter Cunningham :—

"25 ARLINGTON STREET, 11*th July* 1860.

"MY DEAR SIR,—

"My father knew Telford, but that was all. Out of his skill as an engineer, I remember this much about him. When a Dumfriesshire lad, he addressed a poem, not without merit, of poetic advice, to Robert Burns; and when he made his will, and his fame as an engineer was fixed, he left £500 to Southey, and £500 to Tom Campbell.

"Of Rennie I recollect this story, which I have often heard my father tell; Rennie having told it to him while sitting to Chantrey, for what proved to be one of that sculptor's finest busts. The great engineer was being carried in a coach and four to his estate, for some engineering purpose. At the fourth change of horses, the near side wheeler cast a shoe. The roads had received no mending from General Wade or Macadam, and it was found necessary to pull up at the nearest forge. The Vulcan of the village was drunk at a distant alehouse. Luckily, the forge was alight, and all that a farrier wants was about. The man who gave us Waterloo Bridge set to in a workmanlike manner. A fresh shoe was forged and was soon shod on the horse's foot. Smack went the whip, and quick the spurs; and the coach again sped off. My lord,* who was familiar and loquacious with Rennie before the forge adventure, became distant and silent towards the end of the journey. My lord could not travel in a coach and four with a man who could blow a bellows in a smithy, strip to the shirt, hammer Nasmyth-like on an anvil, shoe a horse, and make

---

* Presumably a fellow-traveller—his fellow-travellers, according to the version elsewhere adopted, were two "Paisley boddies." See *Lives of the Engineers*, p. 379.—ED.

good for his own advantage what Self-Help alone can do.*

"Would not this be a good motto for that book—

> " ' He either fears his fate too much,
>   Or his deserts are small,
>   Who would not put it to the touch,
>   To gain or lose it all.—
>   ' MARQUIS OF MONTROSE.'

"Sir Walter Scott delighted in these lines, when Self-Help was his only resource.—Ever yours truly,
                        " PETER CUNNINGHAM."

Before the first two volumes of the *Lives of the Engineers* were published, Robert Stephenson died. He never recovered from the results of his visit to Norway in 1859. I was desirous of completing his life, and adding it to that of his father, and wrote to Mr Bidder, one of his executors, to that effect. I was under the impression that the two men, father and son, were so intimately associated in life, that they could not well be treated separately. Mr Bidder, however, took another view. He wished an elaborate Life of Robert Stephenson to be published, and he made applications to several eminent literary men, amongst others, to the late Sir Arthur Helps. He then applied to me, through Mr Manby. I could not undertake to go again over the same ground ; and besides, I was already sufficiently occupied with the work in hand. Mr Bidder eventually succeeded in obtaining the assistance of two eminent gentlemen, and the life was published in two large octavo volumes.

* I give this anecdote as related by Peter Cunningham. But Mr Rennie's son, the late Sir John Rennie, C.E., gave me another version, which I accepted as probably the more authentic.

Nevertheless, I finished a summary of the life of Robert Stephenson, and published it with that of his father. Though Robert was an excellent man, and a famous engineer, he himself admitted that "all that he knew and all that he had done was primarily due to the parent whose memory he cherished and revered." And the son was right in his idea of the powerful originality of his father. In estimating the two men, George Stephenson will always stand the first.

I was also requested to write the Life of Mr Brassey, the eminent contractor; but this I declined for the same reason—that my hands were full. The work was eventually done—and well done—by the late Sir Arthur Helps. After the death of Mr Bidder, I was also solicited to write his life; but I did not see my way to undertake it—nor the life of my good friend Mr Sopwith, who left behind him many manuscript volumes of recollections. Both these biographies still remain to be written. The only engineers I wished to add to my collection were the two Brunels; but, on communicating with Mr Hawes, I found that the family preferred that the memoir of the lad engineer, Isambard Kingdom, should be written by his son; and there I left the matter. I contented myself with writing a review of the lives of the father and son in the *Quarterly Review*, No. 223.

I may briefly state that the two volumes of the *Lives of the Engineers*, when first published, were well received. The *Saturday Review* expressed surprise "that the idea of handling the subject of engineering in this manner should not sooner have been seized. No one but a professed engineer could wade through the minute professional details of a severe history of engineering; and yet the subject is one in which all the world, in this mechanical age, takes a deep interest, and which only required to be presented in a biographical shape to be cordially welcomed." Although each of the four volumes was sold at a guinea, principally because of the large expense incurred in illustrating the work, 6000 copies of the first two volumes were sold within a comparatively short period; and the remaining volumes were also issued in about the same numbers. Since then, the book has been issued in five volumes at a much reduced price.

Mr Gladstone was especially pleased with the book on its first appearance. Shortly after receiving a copy, he sent me the following letter :—

"11 DOWNING STREET, *7th February* 1862.

"DEAR MR SMILES,—
"As 'good wine needs no bush,' much less does any work of yours, which you do me the honour and kindness to present, need any apology. I have begun to read, with great interest, your important work, and I hope to peruse it, although in little fragments, each as a composing draught, at midnight hours. Pray accept my thanks.
"It appears to me that you first have given practical expression to a weighty truth—namely, that the character of our engineers is a most signal and marked expression of British character, and their acts a great pioneer of British history.—I remain very faithfully yours,
"W. E. GLADSTONE."

Mr Gladstone afterwards did me the honour to speak of the work—especially of the life of Brindley —with much commendation, at a public meeting in Manchester; and Sir Stafford Northcote did the same at a public meeting in Exeter. Industry is, indeed, of no party; and men of all classes could well unite in celebrating the triumphs of British Engineering.

Two years after the appearance of the *Lives of the Engineers*, I published what may almost be considered a supplement to them: I mean the Lives of the leading Mechanical Inventors under the title of *Industrial Biography*. In the preface to that book, I endeavoured to vindicate myself against critics, who might think I had treated a vulgar and commonplace subject. History, no doubt, deals with the affairs of courts, the deeds of statesmen, and the exploits of warriors, and takes but little heed of inventors or mechanics, on whose industrial labours civilisation and history of the best sort mainly depends, but without exaggerating the importance of this class of biography, I insisted that it had not yet received its due share of attention. While commemorating the works and honouring the names of those who have striven to elevate man above the material and the mechanical, the labours of the important industrial class, to whom society owes so much of its comfort and well-being, are also entitled to consideration. Without derogating from the biographical claims of those who minister to intellect and taste, those who minister to utility need not be overlooked. Thus, when a Frenchman was praising to Sir John Sinclair the artist who invented ruffles, the baronet shrewdly remarked that some merit was also due to the man who added the shirt.

I had the best possible assistance. The best mechanics then living were ready to help me. The late Mr Penn and Mr Field communicated a great deal of useful information relative to Bramah, Clement,

and Maudslay, and to the introduction of the slide-
lathe, planing-machine, and self-acting tools. The
late Sir William Fairbairn of Manchester sent me
his Autobiography, from which I selected most
important extracts; and Mr Nasmyth gave me
his most interesting recollections, not only as
to Maudslay, his friend and master, but as regards his own masterly invention of the steam-
hammer.

The early part of the book contained much information as to the early use of metals in the history of
civilisation; first of copper and bronze, then of iron,
and lastly of steel. When the book was finished, I
sent an early copy to Mr Gladstone; and though
immersed in work, he yet sent me, out of his
abundant and overflowing knowledge, the following
interesting communication:—

"HAWARDEN, 5th November 1863.

"MY DEAR SIR,—
            "Pray accept my best thanks for your
volume. I need not say that I anticipate from it
much pleasure and advantage. Indeed, it is not all
anticipation, for I have begun. And I would observe
that I know not whence Mr Mushet obtains warrant
enough for his proposition that a knowledge of the
mixture of tin, zinc, and copper, seems to have been
among the earliest discoveries of the metallurgist.
Does he mean—what, indeed, seems to be rather
commonly, but, as I think, rather strangely, assumed
—namely, that mixed metals were used before pure
ones? In Dr or Professor Wilson's books, it seems to
be chiefly shown that a proportion of the utensils
which have been *lumped* together as 'bronze' are
really of copper only. Inquirers have not yet, I
think, made use enough of the one great literary
witness to the usages of a primitive age. Homer
belongs to a period between Stone on the one hand,
and Iron on the other. With him, the use of Iron is

just beginning. And it is, I think, very doubtful whether he knows anything of the mixture of metals, though he was familiar with the idea of fusing them. If his χαλκος means bronze, then it is surely a strange fact that he has no word for Copper, which must have been a very common metal; while he has a word for Tin, which was a very rare one, and of which he often mentions the single, but never the compound use.—Believe me, very faithfully yours,

"W. E. GLADSTONE."

Let me also give another letter from Mr Cobden —the last I received from him. I had occasional opportunities of meeting him in London, though I had never an opportunity of meeting him at his house at Midhurst, to which he kindly invited me. The only occasion on which I saw the place was when I attended the funeral of the great free-trader, about eighteen months later.

"MIDHURST, *8th November* 1863.

" MY DEAR SIR,—
        " Pray accept my thanks for your very interesting volume. It is very gratifying to me to be remembered by one for whom I have always entertained a high respect. I have observed with much interest the direction in which you have employed your pen. The field has been a new one, and peculiarly suited to your powers. I venture the prediction that not only an enduring but an increasing renown will attach to the memoirs of these 'Captains of Industry' whose biographies you have recorded; for it cannot be doubted that each succeeding generation will hold in higher estimation those discoveries in physical science to which mankind must attribute henceforth so largely its progress and improvement. It is not to me—whom George Combe discovered to possess a large bump of 'veneration'—an agreeable thought, but I sometimes suspect that the world will be indebted for its civilisation, and for the amelioration of its international relations, less to those pre-

cepts of religion which every nation disregards when convenient, than to the progress of physical science, whose laws will bind all countries in equal and inevitable subjection. That is, however, a wide question; and I should like to make it the text for a gossip with you on the neighbouring South Downs. Again thanking you for remembering me, believe me, yours very truly,

"R. Cobden."

Some people wondered how I contrived not only to perform the secretarial work of a large company, but to write books requiring a good deal of labour and research. I remember once giving this explanation. It all arises from the frugal use of time; and by the thought that when once passed it can never be recalled. *Pereunt et imputantur*—"The hours perish and are laid to our charge"—as is written on the dial of All Souls, Oxford—a solemn and striking admonition to all men. My method was, to accomplish everything during the hours of business, and allow no arrears to accumulate. I never carried any subject of anxiety, or undone work, home with me. I cleared everything off as it arose. My shorthand writers enabled me to do that. I was thus ready every morning for the first new thing that offered.

When the day's work was over, I went home with a mind comparatively free, and then I was able to sit down in my study with the satisfaction of duty done, ready to take a part in filling up some unoccupied niche in the literature of my country. And if any one devotes an hour a day, or even half-an-hour to this purpose, it is astonishing what a great amount of literary work may be accomplished in the course of a few years. As most of the work that I have done has been done by snatches, and at odd moments, sometimes with long intervals of rest between them, I trust that this circumstance will be taken into account by those who criticise my intermittent performances.

My friend Mr Wills, then editor of *All the Year Round*, was one of those who wondered at the various kinds of work which I got through. He sent me the following letter on the subject :—

"26 WELLINGTON STREET, STRAND,
"10th *November* 1863.

"MY DEAR SMILES,—
        "I am ashamed to have delayed thanking you for your very acceptable present until now. I know that the plea of 'want of time' made to you would not be admitted, for you seem to create time— to have twenty-eight or thirty hours in each of your days; less favoured mortals having only twenty-four. To be able to manage the secretariat of a great railway, and to write books too, can only be accounted for on this theory.—Ever faithfully yours,
        "W. H. WILLS."

My friend Wills did not know the exact truth. The fact is, I was engaged in burning the candle at both ends! I was trying to do too much. I remember an anecdote of George Stephenson, who certainly did not stint himself in work; but he saw in others the evils of which he was not conscious in himself. To a young friend he said, "You are overdoing things. The brain can only stand a certain amount of work. If you try to do too much, nature will beat you. There are only sixteen ounces to be got out of the pound : remember that!"

The advice was no doubt very true, but sanguine people overlook caution and prudence. When I got home at night, I took a good cup of tea to freshen me up. Then I sat down and used my brain for three or four hours. I sometimes worked until a late hour.

My brain became excited, and then I could not sleep. But as I must have a night's rest with a view to the labours of the following day, I began the practice of taking sedatives. I knew it was wrong; and yet I did it. I was trying to get eighteen ounces out of the pound; and I found that it would not do. I might have known it beforehand; for I had written and thought much about health and its normal conditions. The result was that I got hipped, ill, and miserable. The result of taking hyoscyamus to provoke sleep is frightful. It gives one the most depressing views of life; as, in fact, is the case with most sedatives. But I think hyoscyamus is the worst of all in that respect.

Then I was worried; and worry is more hurtful than work. I need not say how it was: but I was not disposed to remain in the position that I then occupied. I had no desire to rely upon literature. I looked upon that as a staff, not as a crutch. Indeed, I had offers which I might have accepted had I wished to confine myself to the pen only. But I did not. Another opportunity offered. Mr Gilpin, M.P., a director of the South-Eastern Company, was also a director of an assurance company, and he communicated to me the offer of a position in the latter company at the same salary as I was then receiving. I consulted my friend Mr Eborall, and he advised me to accept the offer. Hence, on the 30th August 1866, I ceased to be a railway secretary, after twenty-one years' connection with railways.

I parted with my old company on the best of terms. The directors were generous to me on leaving. They conveyed to me, in a Board minute, their cordial thanks for my services, made me a handsome present, including a service of plate, and a pass over the company's lines as long as I lived. The office-staff of the company also made me a present of plate in addition to that given by the directors. Both of these were presented to me with complimentary speeches at the handsome dinner given on the occasion of my final departure.

CHAPTER XVII

My new occupation was of a comparatively easy sort. It required attention, judgment, trustworthiness; and I hope that I did the work allotted to me, thoroughly and faithfully. But there is no need to go into any details about it.

Among other things, I required to travel about the country a good deal. In this occupation I gained change of scene, healthy associations, and increasing knowledge of character. I did not altogether give up the use of my literary faculty. I read a good deal, and made many notes. In course of time, I arranged a perfect storehouse of information relative to race and biography. Some of this I have used, but the bulk of it remains unused.

In the course of my travels, I think I must have visited all the principal towns and cities in Britain. I was asked to deliver lectures at the Philosophical Institution at Edinburgh, at the Glasgow Athenæum, and at Liverpool and Manchester. But I was averse to lecturing, and declined the invitations. I did, however, go to Huddersfield, and deliver an address on Technical Education, in October 1867—long before the subject had become matter of public agitation. The Society of Arts did me the honour of printing my address in their Journal of the 13th December of that year.

When I went to Dublin, I consented to give a lecture on "The Huguenots" before the Young Men's Christian Association. I had an excellent and most sympathising audience; and received many compliments from the distinguished persons who were present, and I afterwards gave the same lecture at Hull. I was induced to prosecute my inquiries into the subject, and at length became greatly interested in it. The Huguenots, banished out of France for conscience' sake about two hundred years ago, were all men of a high standard of character; and their descendants for the most part shared in their distinction.

A man who is ready to give up his fortune and his country for the sake of his religion, will commonly be found a man not only of unusual virtue, but of unusual vigour and determination. Aristocrats who were ready to sacrifice their honours and titles, and owners of broad lands who were ready to surrender their estates rather than give up their religion, must necessarily have been persons of remarkable courage and inflexibility of character. Hence the British officers descended from the Huguenot refugees were among the bravest; the merchants were among the truest and most conscientious; and the mechanics were among the cleverest and most ingenious. They were for the most part marked men, even among themselves; and when they came among us, they generally became leaders.

At the same time, I may say that the history of the Huguenots was the history of a party who were beaten in the battle of life. The usual feeling is in favour of men who have succeeded; and the men

who have failed are generally supposed to have
deserved their failure. Hence the Huguenots have
been neglected. Courtly writers blot them out of
history, as Louis XIV. desired to blot them out of
France. Most of the histories of France published
in England contain little notice of them. I might have
used as the motto of my book the following lines by
Mr Story :—

"I sing the hymn of the conquered, who fell in the Battle of Life,—
　The hymn of the wounded, the beaten, who died overwhelmed in the
　　strife ;
　The hymn of the low and the humble, the weary, the broken in
　　heart,
　Who strove and who failed, acting bravely a silent and desperate
　　part ;
　Whose youth bore no flower on its branches, whose hopes burned in
　　ashes away,
　From whose hands slipped the prize they had grasped at, who stood
　　at the dying of day
　With the wreck of their life all around them, unpitied, unheeded,
　　alone,
　With Death swooping down o'er their failure, and all but their Faith
　　overthrown." *

The Huguenots was published in November 1867,
and was, on the whole, well received. Some 10,000
copies of the book were printed and sold. It was
nothing like so successful as some of my other books,
but it was a source of great pleasure to me to write
it ; and I believe that it led the way to more elaborate
works. In the first editions I invited communications
from the descendants of banished Huguenots. This
led to much pleasant correspondence, and the influx
of a considerable amount of additional material.
Some of my correspondents desired to obtain for me
information regarding their missing ancestry ; while

* W. W. Story—*A Poet's Portfolio.*

others corrected the statements I had made. The latter were very welcome, as they enabled me to correct the genealogical history in all further issues of the work. I will only quote one of these letters—that from Lord Eversley, for eighteen years speaker of the House of Commons — because of its peculiar interest :—

"HECKFIELD PLACE, WINCHFIELD,
"*20th February* 1868.

"SIR,—
        "I have read with great interest your account of the religious persecutions in France, consequent upon the revocation of the Edict of Nantes. But I am anxious to correct an inaccuracy with respect to that branch of the Lefevre Family with which I am connected.

"I cannot find an old pedigree which was in existence some years ago in our family ; but I have been unable to trace any connection between them and Dr Lefevre of Poitou, or the celebrated martyr Isaac Lefevre, who, after suffering great persecution for many years, died in the prisons of France. But I enclose a pedigree, commencing with Peter Lefevre, who was born in 1650, having succeeded to his paternal estates in Normandy, a few years before he was forced to fly with his family to England rather than renounce his faith. When he arrived there, he settled at Canterbury, and embarked in trade with the capital he brought over with him. At his death, his son Isaac was apprenticed to the trade, and afterwards set up for himself as a scarlet dyer near Spitalfields. His brother, as you have correctly stated, entered Marlborough's army as a lieut.-colonel, and afterwards resided at Walthamstow, and was high sheriff, I believe, for Essex. Isaac Lefevre's son John was my maternal grandfather, and owned the property at Old Ford and Bromley, which is at present in my possession.

"The pedigree I send you was made out from some old MSS. in our family, and may be relied upon as authentic ; and I forward it to you, as I have no doubt you will be glad, in the next edition of your work, to make the corrections it suggests.—I remain, Sir, your obedient servant,

"EVERSLEY."

I may also give the following letter from Sir J. R. Lefroy, the member of a family which has given some distinguished men to the army and the bench :—

"9th June 1868.

"MY DEAR SIR,—
"You asked me two or three months ago for some information respecting the descent of the Lefroy family from the Walloon refugees. I happened at the time to be engaged in some family researches, and postponed my reply until I had concluded them. The Irish family of the name is descended from the elder son of Anthony Lefroy, a merchant of Leghorn, who died in 1779; and my family from his second son. Thus Chief-Justice Lefroy and my father were first cousins.

"Anthony Lefroy was the descendant of Anthoine Loffroy of Cambray, who came to England in Elizabeth's reign, probably in 1579, and settled at Canterbury, where his descendants followed the business of silk-dyeing for about one hundred and fifty years—as long, in fact, as that branch of trade flourished in Kent. Although the family is now very numerous, it all died down to my great grandfather, the second Anthony, in the last century; and from him we all come. He was a great antiquary and collector. His museum, when it was sold in 1763, was one of the finest ever collected by a private person : it contained over 6600 coins.

"The tradition is that the family motto, 'Unitare Sperno,' relates to the resistance of our ancestors to the persecutions of Alva, and that a Cap of Liberty which we bear in our arms, is derived from the Beggar's Cap assumed when the party of Egmont took the name of 'Les Gueux.' Anthony Lefroy was a friend of Thomas Hollis, and is frequently mentioned in his Memoirs. Hollis displayed excessive fondness for that emblem, and I have sometimes conjectured that it may have a more modern origin.

We possess, I think, nearly all Hollis's publications presented to Anthony Lefroy.—Believe me faithfully,
                                "J. H. LEFROY."

In the course of preparing *The Huguenots, their Settlements, Churches, and Industries in England and Ireland,* and another subsequent work, *The Huguenots in France after the Revocation of the Edict of Nantes,* I made several journeys through France for the purpose of visiting the places made memorable by these illustrious men. I was now able to extend my holidays to three weeks, instead of a fortnight, which was the extent of my usual holiday while I was connected with the railway company. But a great deal of interest can be crammed into three weeks' or even a fortnight's holiday. Among other places, I went to visit the port of La Rochelle, so celebrated in the early history of the Huguenots.

The town is very little changed since it was besieged and taken by the king's army under Cardinal Richelieu in the year 1628; although the embankment or *digue* has been cleared away. It was by means of this that the Cardinal blockaded the mouth of the port, and starved the inhabitants of La Rochelle into submission to the royal authority. Indeed, the two towers erected at the entrance to the harbour, for the purpose of commanding the approach, while the port was still in possession of the English (in the time of Charles V. of France), are still standing complete, a testimony to the admirable mason work of the English artisans.

After the town was captured by Richelieu, it never regained its former pre-eminence. It is now a sluggish, sleepy place, and seems to belong to an old world, which we have long left behind us. Most of the old houses are standing, though some of them

are riddled by bullets fired during the siege, especially
one of the towers above referred to—the Tour de la
Chaine. The Church of Ste Marguérite, in which
Richelieu celebrated mass after entering the town,
now forms part of the establishment of the Oratorian
Frères Chrétiens. The Huguenot temple was pulled
down, but the street in which it stood is still called
the Rue de la Prêche. The descendants of Guiton,
the heroic governor of the town, still live in the place;
but they are Catholics, like the descendants of the
great Duquesne at Poitiers.

M. Delmas, the Protestant pastor, took me over
the town, and pointed out the most notable places
during the siege—more especially the Bastion de
l'Evangile, where the Duke of Anjou's assault was
repulsed with immense loss. He took me also to his
chapel, and took out a mass of old worm-eaten
papers from his document box; but he said the
principal manuscripts connected with the Rochelle
Protestants were in the Marsh Library at Dublin,
whither they had been carried by Dr Bouherau,
whose father had been pastor of the place. M.
Delmas said that the old Protestant families
almost entirely disappeared after the siege; many
of them emigrated to England, and the others went
into the country—where they either belonged to the
"Church in the Desert," or belonged to no church
whatever — except to the Church not made with
hands.

M. Delmas was not hopeful of the future. "If
they teach fatalism," he said, "from our professors'
chairs, how can we hope to gain adherents? We
cannot even expel materialists or deists without the
consent of the Government. Of course we are divided
—how can it be otherwise? As for the Catholics,

they are for the most part formalists—especially as
regards the men. When they do know anything,
unfortunately they go out into the void of infidelity.
They do not come to us."

As I paced the ramparts of La Rochelle, I
bethought me of the enormous sums raised by taxes
on human industry, apparently for the purpose of
perpetuating hatred between different classes of the
community. The money expended on these unpro-
ductive works would have been much better cast
into the sea. Wherever I went, there were still
armed men to be seen—foot and dragoons—without
any apparent cause for their existence. The thought
occurred, not so much whether Europe is Catholic or
Protestant, but whether it is Christianised—whether
it is civilised?

When I left La Rochelle, I crossed the centre
of France by Poitiers, Gueret, and Montluçon to
Moulins, the scene of Sterne's encounter with Maria.
The inn at which I put up—though the best in the
place—was a very poor one, without any of the
appliances of modern and even healthy comfort; so
I sped off for a few days' rest at Vichy, where the
hotel accommodation is of an unexceptionable character. I then went on to Lyons to join my friend
Mr Milsom, who, though a Londoner, had settled in
that city as a silk merchant. He was about to take
his annual journey of inspection and relief to the
poor Protestant ministers of Dauphiny, and had
invited me to accompany him.

We went by railway to Grenoble, whence we
drove along the valley of the Romanche and the
Drac to Briançon, a fortified frontier town situated
almost on the confines of France. From thence the
journey was performed principally by walking, some-

times at the rate of from twenty-five to thirty miles a day. But, as I have already fully described this journey in *The Country of the Vaudois* annexed to my volume on *The Huguenots in France after the Revocation*, I need not further refer to it here.

I availed myself of the opportunity of another summer holiday in a following year, to visit the mountainous country of the Cevennes, and see the places made memorable by the peasant Camisards, during the war which they carried on against their tyrant monarch during so many years. I also visited the fine southern towns and cities of Nismes, Arles, Montpellier, and Marseilles. But, as I have given the results of my journey elsewhere, I need not repeat them here.

After the appearance of the *Huguenots in England and Ireland*, a French translation of it appeared in the following year. But as the sheets were printed at Strasburg, part of the impression was destroyed during the siege of that city by the German army. When those sheets had been reprinted, the work was published with an introductory preface by M. Athanase Coquerel, *fils*. M. Coquerel, after some complimentary remarks, says of the author of the work: " He is not an author by profession. Occupied day by day in his place of business in London, he has almost unconsciously acquired the habit of consecrating his leisure to literary work free from pretence, and inspired by the serious desire of being useful. Become an author almost without dreaming of it, Mr Smiles has found reputation in this persevering and elevating employment of his hours of liberty. He thus forms one more example, and not the least remarkable, of the self-helping men whose lives he has celebrated, and he has found rich resources in himself by the constant and rational exercise of a firm and persevering will."

M. Coquerel complimented me very much; yet I did not quite become an author without dreaming of it. Indeed, from what I have said, it will be observed that I served a long apprenticeship to literature. It was only by dint of labour that I eventually overcame the difficulties that stood in my way. Success in authorship is not to be achieved without labour, any more than success in art, science, or business.

I remember very well the visit of M. Coquerel to my place of daily occupation. He was a kind, bright, cheerful gentleman—a very Celt. I have forgotten the subject of our conversation, but he refers to it in his preface, and I quote his words:—

"How had he been led to turn from his ordinary studies, to devote himself to the history of French refugees in England because of their religion? Here is his answer to this question addressed to myself: 'In writing out the history of many celebrated inventors and mechanics, I was struck with meeting on my way with so large a number of inventors with French names. Surprised at the fact, I sought for the cause, and there soon accumulated before me so large a number of interesting facts, that instead of devoting a chapter to the subject, I found enough to occupy an entire volume. I then studied from the beginning the history of the Huguenots: before long they inspired me with a vivid interest, which increased when I had been able to examine the Registers of their churches or congregations in England, as contained in the numerous books and documents preserved at Somerset House in the offices of the Registrar-General. Besides these, I obtained a great deal of information from the descendants of the Exiles for Conscience' Sake; and now you have the results of my investigations in the published book.'"

S

The editor thus concludes his preface: " We are amongst those who wish to see become more common, more close, more affectionate, the relations of France and England, not only in the interest of these two great peoples, magnificently gifted and endowed each with a genius that is the complement the one of the other, but for the good of the entire human family. We are happy, indeed, to contribute our part, however feeble it may be, to draw closer bonds so useful. It seems to us that, by their community of religion, by their history, their spirit of inquiry and examination, the French Protestants have in this respect incurred a peculiar responsibility. It is with such sentiments that we are happy to recommend to French readers the present work. To the special esteem which the author deserves, we associate the most cordial sympathy for the conscientious efforts of his translator, a gentleman equally familiar with both languages since his birth. It is with pleasure that he consecrates his pen to a work of filial piety in memory of our persecuted ancestors, and in ardent fraternal goodwill toward our brothers of England, their descendants, or their hosts."

CHAPTER XVIII

THE NORTH FRISIAN ISLANDS

I DISMISSED *The Huguenots* from my thoughts, and took up a new subject in the course of my next holiday tour. I wished to find out something about the beginning of the English people, and of the countries and races from which they had sprung. To travel about with an object of this sort in view, gives a new interest to a journey. I knew where I should find the early home of the English race—or at least of that part of it which is Teutonic; for the Englishman is a mixture of many races—Welsh, French, Dutch, Saxon, Dane, and Norman.

Where did we get our perseverance, our industry, our inventiveness, our constructiveness, our supremacy in commerce, our love of home, and yet our love of the sea, and of wandering over the face of the earth? Had England been peopled by Gauls, and the English race, as it is, been blotted out, I suspect that the whole face of the world would have been different. We might, it is true, have had the steam-engine without James Watt, the locomotive without George Stephenson, and the screw steamer without Pellet Smith; but what of the extensive colonisation of North America and Australasia by a people of constitutional habits, carrying with them certain social, political, and religious ideas, unlike those to be found in any other portion of the civilised world?

I suspect that we owe a great deal of this remarkable power to our ancestors on the further side of the German Ocean, to the Frisians, whose legitimate descendants are the Dutch and the people of the south and south-east coasts of England; to the Angles, and the Saxons, who constitute a large body of the mass of our working people; and to the Danes and Northmen, who gave us that intense love of the ocean which we still retain. To these ancestors, allied in many respects, we owe our complex nationality, our self-dependence, our manifold industry, and our commerce, which whitens every sea and kisses every shore. To them, too, we owe our language, which literally, as well as commercially, is becoming the most important language in the world. Including America, India, and the colonies, it gives the key to the commerce of more than 300,000,000 of people; and it is now spreading, not only in books, but in the language of sailors, all over the globe.

I had already travelled through Holland, and knew something of the Frisians, who form, without doubt, the foundation element of Dutch character and seamanship; but in the summer of 1871, I proposed to make a tour through Schleswig-Holstein, and the North Frisian Islands off the west coast of Denmark, where I believed that I should find the descendants of forefathers of a part of the English people, still living in the greatest simplicity and purity.

A great wedge of the German race has thrust itself into Bremen and Holstein, and thus separated the Frisians of North Holland and East Friesland

from those of West Schleswig and the North Frisian
Islands. But in Hamburg there was a great deal to
remind one of England. There were the old gable-
ended houses in the more ancient parts of the town,
reminding one of the old buildings seen in the Side
at Newcastle, at Wakefield, at Hereford, and at
Canterbury. There were the Fletes, like the Vliets
of Holland, reminding one of the place-names ending
with the termination "fleet" (such as Purfleet, North-
fleet, and the river Fleet itself) on the Thames. The
people, too, are like the people at home—large, fair,
and well-favoured ; very like those we see in Suffolk,
Essex, Warwick, Oxford, and in the Midland
counties.

The country north of Hamburg is wooded and
hedge-rowed, very like England ; with much rich
pasture and corn land all through Holstein. The
high-stepped, thick-thatched roofs cover the cottages
as well as the barns, just as we see in old English
villages. We cross the river Stöer at Wrist (we have
a Stour near Canterbury, and a Stour in Essex), and
pass northward and westward, past Niebuhr's famous
county of Ditmarchen, so celebrated for the independence of the inhabitants. Here we have the town of
Lunden near the Eider, almost as ancient as London
on the Thames. North of this point, along the
coast, the people are all Frisians, speaking their
own language, which is more ancient than the
modern German, and really the foundation of our
own.

Husum, on the west coast of Schleswig, is a little
town situated on the railway to Tonning, from which
part a large quantity of cattle, butter, and field
produce is exported to England. Husum is the
capital of the North Frisian islands. Here the

people come to buy and sell; and steamers start daily on their round of the islands. Looked at from a distance, when the tide is up, the Halligen—as the islands are called—look like a number of great hulls afloat upon the sea. It is only when you are near them, that you see they are dotted over with cattle —the herds of the Halligs.

I went northward to a little cluster of houses called Hattstedt, to see the country near Husum. The farmhouses were scattered all about over the face of the land. Each farmstead had everything under one high thatched roof— house, barn, and crops. They looked roomy, large, clean, and comfortable. Every foot of ground in the country was tilled. Each man seems to have enclosed his piece of land, built his house upon it, made it his *ton* or enclosure, and constituted it his *ham* or home; and there his house became as his castle. These people were all freeholders, tilling their own land. The whole country seemed full of well-being and welldoing. The people are large and fair—warmly clad, well shod, and comfortable looking; and their houses looked the picture of cleanli ness.

From Hattstedt church, which stands on high ground, you see the same high thatch-roofed farmsteadings, spreading far away to the North, as far as the eye can reach. The whole country is covered with them. How different from France, where the country people cluster together in villages, doubtless for the sake of society; whereas here the people seem to be satisfied to live apart, each with his wife, and family, and home. Indeed, the name of "Homestead" is as familiar to the English as to the Frisian.

I went round the churchyard, and found the

names on the monuments were, with a little difference in spelling, for the most part English. There
were Mathiesens, Thomsens, Jansens, Christiansens,
Petersens, Paulsens, Hansens, Carstens, and such
like.

I sailed by the little steamer *Syll* from Husum to
Föhr, one of the North Frisian islands. We passed
along a narrow, shallow, and intricate channel,
marked off by branches of trees stuck into the mud.
We passed many little Halligs — little patches of
land, some the size of only a small farm, banked
round, each with a little farmhouse on it. These
had at one time been united with the mainland; but
heavy storms came from the North Sea, washed
away the intervening soil, and left only these little
banked-up patches of land.

When the industrious Frisians along the coast
found their farms slipping from under them, being
washed away by the incoming ocean, and realised
that there was a land flowing with milk and honey
across the sea, waiting for settlement and tillage,
it is no matter for wonder that they should have
taken to their boats with all their belongings—for
they were all sailors as well as farmers—and made
for the new territory, for Britain, for the country
which afterwards became Angle-land or England.

There they would not have to fight with the sea for
the possession of the land; there, there was enough
of it, and to spare. In fact, there were then the
same inducements to emigrate to the east coast of
England as there now are for the over-populated
nations of Germany, Denmark, Norway, England,
Scotland, and Ireland, to sail over the much wider
Atlantic, and settle upon the eastern shores of
Canada and the American continent.

The skipper of our little steamer, Captain Höck, tells me that he is a native of Flensborg, which is in Angeln (England?), and that he remembers a very old dialect used in his district, which is now almost forgotten. It was not Frisian. Indeed, it was as unlike Frisian as it is unlike German. His idea is that it must have been what is now known as Anglo-Saxon. The nearest tongue that he knows, which resembled it in sound as well as in meaning, is broad Scotch. This was very curious.

Most of the people living in the Halligs are Protestants but on one of the largest islands—Nordstrand, opposite Husum — is a colony of Dutch Roman Catholics, who still get their priests from Holland. They are very industrious, hard-working people.

I observe that the all-pervading language connected with the use of the steamboat has extended here—the same as is used on the Rhine and the Nile; and that "ease her," "stop her," "turn a starn," are the captain's orders to the enginemen below.

After many windings through the shallows of the channel, we drew up at the pier of Wick, in the little island of Föhr. Wick or Wich—a common enough name in England and Scotland—was in old times a little harbour, where the whaling ships, setting out from the North Frisian islands towards the North Pole, used to fit and repair.

I walked out into the country to see the land. It presented the same appearance as the neighbourhood of Husum. There were the same high thatched cottages, independent farm-steadings, and comfortable looking cottages. I observed that the women were handsome and well grown, almost invariably fair. But it was difficult to see their faces; for they wore a heavy black fall, which concealed their features. They were also for the most part dressed in black; and those going to market, had a black cloth placed over their baskets. I was told that these women were the wives of sailors, and that while their husbands were at sea, they dressed in this manner, remained at home, and looked after the crops. They were very substantially dressed, but all seemed to be in mourning. The Frisian married women look very like nuns.

The names of the little collections of houses through which I passed, indicated that Paganism had existed in this little island long before Christianity had been extended hither. Hence there was Boldixum or Baldursheim (after the old god Baldur), Wrixum or Freiasheim (after the pagan Freia, the goddess of marriage), Nieblum or Nebelheim and Odersum or Hödersheim, after others of the old heathen gods.

I went into the churchyard of Nieblum, and there found many of the old English names on the monuments. There was Petersen, Nicholsen, Cramers, Boysen, Jacob, Hansen, Johnsen, Harrold.

In the church I found Mr Magnussen, the artist, engaged in painting a picture of his daughter, in Frisian dress, with the entrance to the church as the background. He had painted a picture for the Crown Prince and Princess of Germany, of the people going to communion in the same church. This is now in the prince's house at Berlin. He afterwards painted a picture of the Princess Louise's marriage, which is now the property of Her Majesty.

Magnussen is a native of Bredstedt, and himself a

Frisian. He is perhaps prouder of that than of being a clever artist. He is at present engaged in making a collection of the carvings done by the sailors while engaged on their whaling voyages. He took me to his cottage to see them. Some of them are very ingenious and curious, though he said that some of the finest he possessed were at his house at Hamburg.

While absent from their wives and sweethearts, the sailors did not forget them, but took with them plenty of wood to carve; and on their return they made presents to their beloved ones—boxes, tops of writing tables, "streik-bords" (or flat narrow boards for stretching cloth on), with many cleverly carved figures of animals, fruit, and flowers upon them. I may also mention that all round the island there are numerous whale-ribs to be seen erected over the entrances to the fields, as well as to the churchyards of the island.

Since the war with Denmark, the North Frisian islands have become subject to Germany. The Frisians do not like this. Captain Höck told me that the Danes tried to make Schleswig and Holstein Danish. They tried for twenty-four years and failed ; but the Germans, he added, have now made them Danish in two years. The taxes are all much higher, and already the people long to be again under Denmark. What they dislike most is the compulsory military service. They are all liable. If a man has six sons of proper age and height, only one of them is exempted. The others must all serve. I was told of three fine young fellows, who all died of disease before Metz, during the siege.

"Free as Freise" was long a saying amongst them. They are so no longer. They do not fear to be sailors, for they take to the water like ducks. But soldiering is not in their way. Besides, they will not be forced. The only chance for them is to emigrate. Accordingly, two years before my visit, several hundreds of families had left Föhr for the United States of America; and many more are arranging to depart.

I left Föhr for the island of Sylt or Syld, which lies a few miles to the north. I do not know the origin of the word. It may be from the old word *Sild*, still preserved in Scotland, and derived from Denmark, meaning the herring, or the young of the herring; or it may be from the ordinary English word *sill*, derived from the Scandinavian, meaning a deposit of sand or mud. Anyhow, the island is silted up all round. As our steamer approached it at a late hour, at the end of the long strip of land on the east we had all to get out into boats, and even the little boats could not get to the shore. As we approached, one boat grounded in the mud, and then the men, leaping into the water, set their broad shoulders to it, and heaved it onward. As they approached the land, they called out, "In she gangs, men." I asked a German young lady who was on board what they said. She said she "had no idea: it was not German." I said my impression was, that it was *broad Scots*.

We landed at the Nösse or Ness on the eastern part of the island near Morsum. Places ending in "ness" are known all round the Scotch and English coasts, from Strandburgh Ness in the Shetlands down to Shoebury Ness on the coast of Essex, and Dungeness on the coast of Kent. The ending of *ness* is also known on the other side of the

Channel, at Blanc Nez and Grisnez between Boulogne and Calais. In all these places we have indications left of the wanderings of the northern seamen.

As I had made no arrangements for getting onward to Westerland, to which I was bound, and as there were no means of communication from the place at which I had landed, I was indebted to these German ladies for a place in their conveyance. The night was at first very dark; but by and by a great conflagration burst out in the east. It seemed to be a fire; it proved to be only the moon, and shining over the sea outside the Ness! We drove, by the beautiful moonlight, through the bare, treeless country for about twelve miles to the village of Westerland, where I had the pleasure of enjoying a sound sleep on a sofa. Next morning, I found a clean pleasant lodging for a few days in the house of one Frau Brügmann.

Julius Rodenberg has written a little work entitled *Stilleben auf Sylt*. It is indeed a *very* still life. There is not a sound to be heard, except of the waves breaking on the beach. There are very few carriages about, and the sound of their wheels is deadened by the sand. One of the pleasures of the morning is to mount the sand dunes on the western part of the island, and look over the silent sea. Not a sail is to be seen, for this part of the coast is out of the track of vessels, except occasionally a steamer running from the mouth of the Skagerrack to Hamburg. And yet Sylt is in the exact latitude of Yorkshire. Right across the sea lies England with its fertile fields. It was always easy to reach that country by sea, for with a sailor people, the sea always offers an easy road.

A little north of Westerland, on the western coast, right opposite England, is an opening through the Red Cliff called Risgap, near Riesenloch. It is quite close to Wenningsted. In front of it, further out to sea, used to be Frisian Haven and Old Wenningsted. Both places are still marked upon the old maps. But Old Wenningsted and Frisian Haven have been washed away by the furious North Sea. Tradition, however, says that it was through Risgap that the ancient Frisians passed down to the sea coast before embarking for the land on the other side of the German Ocean. This was the point of departure for Frisian emigrants to England, just as Liverpool now is for English emigrants to America. The sea coast is now, however, entirely silent; and only the blackened skeletons of ships' ribs show that navigation is practised in the neighbourhood.

But the people still continue sailors as before. The first two men I spoke to in Sylt—my landlord and his son-in-law—answered me in English. "How is it you speak English so well?" I asked. "Oh!" said the landlord, "we are all sailors here." As if English was the proper language of sailors! And so it is. English ships, English steam engines, English screw propellers, English engineers, and English commerce are found all over the world. "Ships, colonies, and commerce" has long been our motto; and wherever trade is done, there the English language must be spoken.

The Frisian language has a closer resemblance to the English than to the German. I experimented a little upon the population. To a boy I said one morning, "Schöne zeit!" He shook his head. I then said "Good weather." He understood me at once. "Ta! ta!" I had some conversation with a matron coming from Finnum, and had no difficulty in making myself understood. She said I must be the Englishman that had come into Sylt. Frau Brügmann, my landlady, must have told of my whereabouts. Indeed, the news of my arrival had spread all over the place. When I went across to Keitum to see the museum of Christian Hansen, and to buy some of his books—for he is the solitary author of the island—he told me that he had heard of the arrival of the Englishman "by Brügmann."

The Frisians are not a little proud of their relationship with the English. They resemble each other very much. The Frisians are for the most part fair or light brown, blue-eyed and soft-voiced; they have oval faces, are well formed in figure, and are generally taller than the people on the mainland. The Frisian faces are so like the English, that Mr Christian Hansen has a portrait of our Charles James Fox, which he has adopted as the true portraiture of Mr Decker, the Strand Inspector at Munkmarsch. He says it is an absolutely faithful likeness. Mr Hansen told me that many of our English words resemble the Frisian far more than they do the German. Woman (fûman), wife (weib), and boy (büy) are still preserved in Frisian. "Thunder" and "light" are Frisian, not "donner" and "blitzen" as in German. "Englishmann" not "Engländer"; "work," not "arbeiten." "Housewife" and "homestead" are Frisian. The Scotch have preserved many of the Frisian verbs. They still "gang to bed," and go to "the Kirk." The Scotch proverbs have also a great resemblance to the Frisian.

Mr Hansen recommended me to go to Wenning-stedt to see a very remarkable neolithic barrow there. I passed over a piece of ground containing several tumuli. One of them had been dug open, and was found so full of small chips that it might have been an ancient small arms manufactory. Mr Hansen had got many of his celts, arrowheads, and ancient flint weapons from this place. I brought several of the arrowheads away with me.

The ancient barrow at Wenningstedt is very curious. I descended by a ladder into a tomb, formed by gigantic stones, just like the Kits Coty chamber in Kent. There is a long open entrance to the level of the ground, as in similar monuments in the west of Europe. It is what is known as a chambered tomb. I asked the girl who showed it me what she called the place, to which she replied, "An under grave." It is still covered by its original mound of earth.

Sylt contains several ancient monuments. There is the Burg—an old fortified camp, surrounded by a mound of earth, and a deep moat outside. A footway runs inside the top of the embankment. Not far off is Tinnum, or Thingum, the place where, at some former time, the Thing or Parliament of the place met, and legislated. The "Thing" still survives in Norway; and the name is preserved at Tain and Dingwall in Scotland, at Dingwall in Devonshire, and at Tynwald Hill in the Isle of Man.

After a few days' loafing about the sandhills near Westerland, and walking by the sands of the sea-shore, I prepared to leave my good friends the Brügmanns. I got up early one morning, and started by six for Munkmarsch. Frau Brügmann insisted on getting up and preparing breakfast for me before setting out; and so everything was ready, and set before me, trig, and clean, and neat. I think that one of the best legacies the English, as well as the Dutch, have inherited from their Frisian ancestors, is their healthful cleanliness. That is a great virtue.

I reached the steam ferry at Munkmarsch in good time, and was taken across the shallow waters to Hoyer on the mainland. We joined the railway at Tondern, and went on to Flensborg. My object in reaching this town was to inspect the remains of a very old warship, which had been dug up from Nydam Bog a few years before. I had found it referred to in Victor Hugo's *Travailleurs de la Mer*. The waiters at the Stadt Hamburg, where I put up, knew nothing of it. I asked for the Hotel de Ville. There was no such place. "The Rathhuis?" No; but there was the Police Office. I went thither, and after many inquiries, I was referred to a yard in the main street (No. 582 Kreisgericht), where I found the famous old warship in a loft, almost touching the roof.

The warship is, after all, only a very long open boat; but it must have been capable of carrying about a hundred men. Judged by the remains of it found, this warship must be about fourteen hundred years old. It is a splendid model of a boat; about 79 feet long, by about 15 feet at the widest part, with nineteen seats for the rowers. The vessel must have breasted the seas like a bird. It was doubtless a warship, for the remnants of bows and arrows were found in it; as well as ashen shafts for spear heads. I afterwards found that this warship and its contents had been completely described in a work published in England; so that I need not further describe it.*

I went by steamer down the Flensborg Fjord to see the neighbourhood. We skirted the northern district of Angeln. The people, as well as the country and the houses, are very like those we see in England. The houses are red tiled and white-washed; the cottages are thatched, but tidy look-ing; the fields are separated by hedges, with occasional clumps of trees, just as we see at home. The fields are green and smiling. The number of sailing boats in the fjord resembled the Thames on a sunny day. Possibly the men who rowed this Flensborg warship, some fourteen hundred years ago, may have been the ancestors of Englishmen, who now navigate the world.

From Flensborg I went northward by rail to Fredericia, crossed the Little Belt; then by rail to Fünen; then by the Great Belt to Middelfart; and after a few hours of railway travelling, I found myself in Copenhagen at 10.30 P.M. I found the museums of this city very wonderful; but they are so well described in "Murray" that I need not detail my visit. I next went by steamer up the Cattegat to Gothenborg, for three days steaming across Lakes Wener and Wetter to the city of Stockholm.

On board the boat, I found several persons whom I knew. As the company was associated together for about three days, we got to know each other a little by conversation. There were two Swedish ladies on board, and I remarked to one of them, that the more I knew of the world, the smaller I found it

---

* *Denmark in the Early Iron Age.* By Conrad Englehart, late Director of the Museum of Northern Antiquities at Flensborg. London: Williams and Norgate.

T

to be; what Alexander von Humboldt had said of it, "El mondo es poco"—the world is a little place— was very true.

"Oh, no!" said the lady, "the world is a very big place. I know next to nothing of it!"

"But I should not wonder," I rejoined, "that although we do not know each other, we may find some mutual friend whom we both know."

"No!" she answered resolutely, "that is impossible."

"Very well," I said, "let us try: have you ever been out of Sweden?"

"Oh yes, I have once been in London."

"Then you know some people there."

"I only know two persons: it is such a very big place."

"Who are the two persons?"

"You cannot know them!"

"Well; tell me their names."

"One is called Burrows."

"Yes," I said, "I know him: he is a little fat man, with a brown wig—a stock and share broker."

"It is perfectly true; I stayed in his house while in London!"

"And who is the other?"

"Oh, you cannot know him."

"What is his name?"

"Forbes."

"Yes, I know him—a dapper, bright, clever, curly-haired man—manager of the London, Chatham, and Dover Railway!"

"I am perfectly surprised," said the lady.

"You observe," said I, "that after all the world is a very little place. But now that you have mentioned two persons, I will mention another. Do you know Tester?"

She looked almost frightened, as if she had thought me the ———. "Ah!" she ejaculated, "that was a frightful story. What has become of him?"

The reason of my happening to know these people was very simple. The lady in question was wife of the manager of the Royal Swedish Railway. Burrows had been employed in London to get the shares of that Company into the market; and being also a shareholder in the South-Eastern Railway, he used to come and speak at our meetings. Mr Forbes had been a railway manager on the Continent, was well known to the lady's husband, and I had often met him in connection with our railway competition. Tester, it may be remembered, was the person in our passenger department, who entered into alliance with Agar and Pearse, to rob us of the gold which we carried for the London bullionists; and who went to Sweden (with my certificate of character in his pocket) to take charge of the railway of which the lady's husband was now manager. Had a fourth name been mentioned, most probably I should have been baffled.

But another illustration of the world being a very little place, occurred in the course of the same year. My youngest son was on his voyage from Auckland in New Zealand, to Honolulu in the Sandwich Islands, when a fellow passenger, observing the name on his portmanteau, said, "A remarkable name! Have you any friends in Scotland?"

"Yes!"

"Have you any in Paisley?"

"Yes, an uncle—James Smiles."

"Strange!" said the gentleman, "he is married to

my sister. And I am introducing myself to you in the middle of the Pacific ocean!"

My three days' voyage ended at Stockholm; and after a visit to ancient and modern Upsala, a railway journey across Sweden and Norway to Christiania, and a voyage to Hull over the seas so often crossed by the Norse Vikings long ages ago, I reached my home at Blackheath after a very delightful holiday trip.

CHAPTER XIX

BEFORE making my holiday journey through the North Frisian islands, I left with the printer the manuscript of my little book on *Character*. I had written it out many years before, and stored it away in my literary cupboard. It was, like my other books, the result of my evenings' leisure. I there endeavoured to illustrate the power and efficiency of individual character. My object was to impress the minds of the rising generation with examples of noble behaviour, taken from the lives of the best men and women who had ever lived.

I also left with the printer the sheets of another book—the account of my youngest son's *Voyage Round the World*, which I edited. He had been sent out to Australia a few years before, in search of health, which had been restored; and I thought that *The Boy's Voyage* might be useful as well as interesting to other young people. The sheets of both books were ready for correction on my return home.

Both books were very well received on their publication in the following November (1871). With respect to the last-mentioned volume, the *Saturday Review* observed: "We should be curious to learn how Mr Smiles has taught his son to write his own language. He cannot, we are sure, have sent him to school, for that is the last place where a boy learns English. If, however, any school can claim the author of *A Boy's Voyage Round the World*, it has at least as good reason for pride as if it had gained the Balliol scholarship."

There was, doubtless, some mixture of joke in this praise. But the fact is, that the boy first learnt his English at a girls' school. He was then sent to St Paul's School, London; but he made so little progress there, that he was removed to La Châtelaine, near Geneva, and placed under the charge of Misses Thudicum and Lotheissen, where he learnt French and German, and acquired a considerable amount of scholastic knowledge. But he was never "taught" to write English. He must have acquired the practice by reading, writing, and possibly by his acquaintance with other languages besides his own.

Both these volumes were re-published in the United States, where they had as large a circulation as in Britain. Both were translated into French and German. *Character* was perhaps more appreciated on the Continent than at home. It was translated into the Italian by Rotondi, and had a great sale in Italy. M. de Gubernatis did me the honour to say that "thanks to Mr Smiles, our people now read something else than bad novels; and this seems to me an immense improvement." Shortly after the publication of the Italian translation, I was appointed an "Honorary President" of the Alessandro Manzoni Literary Institution in Monteleone, Calabria—a place that I have not yet seen. *Character* also gave its name to a new journal published at Mantua, entitled *Il Carattere*, of which the proprietors sent me the early numbers, requesting a communication, to which I acceded; and a society for Mutual Help sprang out of the existence of this new publication.

Of course the Dutch had their translations; they were generally the first to introduce my works to foreign readers. M. Buys translated the title of *Character* into *Ken u Zelven*, as he had translated *Self-Help* into *Help u Zelven*. Professor Mourek translated it in Czech, for the use of the inhabitants of Bohemia. The Prague reviewer, in the *Komensky*, spoke of it as "a golden book—a sort of practical bible." M. Mirko Turic, of Zengg, was very enthusiastic. He said *Character* was still more valuable than *Self-Help*, and was a real treasure for anyone, but particularly for the young. "These great and beautiful truths," he said, "these sublime and noble thoughts, which I find on every page of your *Character*, have so transported me, that I cannot refrain from asking the privilege of translating your beautiful work into my mother tongue, the Croatian language." Of course, I at once gave my assent.

Translations were also made into the Magyar language at Pesth, for the Hungarians; into the Danish and the Russian; and into the Gujarati for the people of Bombay. My friend, Mr Henty, banker of Chichester, told me that he had seen a translation of my book in a shop window at Stockholm, and went in and purchased a copy. Translations may have been made in other languages, of which I knew nothing. I need not recite the encouragements I have received from young men at Moscow, Boston (U.S.), Belfast, India, and elsewhere—setting forth what good my books have done, and requesting me to continue my instruction.

One young lady, who has done excellent work as

a nurse, and as an organiser of nursing establishments, said, "Perhaps, without offence, I may say that
Character has been of more good to me than any
sermon I have heard for a long day." And a young
man at Belfast, whom I do not know otherwise than
by his letter, has said that "this little book has done
me more good, morally and intellectually, than all the
books I have read, and all the sermons I have heard,
for many years." Indeed, I was pleased to learn that
a rector at Malden had read a passage from the work
to his congregation on the third Sunday in Lent,
being appropriate to the subject of his sermon. " I
go heart and soul with you," he wrote to me, "in
what you say about a woman's influence over her
children; for I daily feel that, under God, my wife
has been the maker of all her children's character,
and it is such a comfort to myself to see how they all
look up to her."

I will only quote one letter from my excellent
friend, Sir Arthur Helps, to whom I sent an early
copy:—

"*30th November* 1871.

"MY DEAR SMILES,—
            "Your book, Sir, upon *Character* is a
pestilently dangerous work to send to an official man.
What happens? He takes it up, just to look at it,
and (confound the book!) he cannot help going on
reading it, to the detriment of his official work. No
works, except those which are very dull, ought to be
sent to official people.
        "But, seriously speaking, the book is a most
interesting one; and I congratulate you upon having
done your work so well.—Yours very sincerely,
                            "ARTHUR HELPS."

And now I have to relate how it was that my
work was brought, for a time, suddenly to an end.
I was habitually careless of my health. I did not

take my meals regularly. I had not much of an
appetite, and often went without a dinner. I was
satisfied with a lunch in the middle of the day; and
then, when I should have gone home, and had a
dinner and rest, I had a few cups of tea before sitting
down to work for the evening, and I often continued
until late at night.

The consequence of this style of living was, that
my physical power was getting wasted faster than
my enfeebled digestion could repair it. I wanted the
refreshment of regular food, and the still greater
refreshment of regular rest. The brain weakens
under protracted labour, especially at night. After
writing for some hours, my brain got excited, and
refused to lay aside its capacity for thinking. I
ceased to sleep, and in sleep only does the brain get
perfect rest. I knew that something must be going
wrong; for I was subject to palpitations, and had
frequent flushings of the face, showing a determination of blood to the head.

I was again burning the candle at both ends, and
trying to get more than sixteen ounces out of the
pound. Why did not I stop? Poor, weak, unre-
flecting human nature. "We know the right, and
yet the wrong pursue." I was old enough—for I was
approaching sixty—and ought to have been wise
enough, to know better; and yet I went on with my
evening's literary labour. Montaigne says, in his
Essays, that "pleasure, to deceive us, marches before
and conceals her train. Books are pleasant, but if
by being over-studious we impair our health, and
spoil our good humour, two of the best pieces we
have, let us give it over; for I, for my part, am one of
those who think that no fruit derived from them can
recompense so great a loss."

Nature, or rather the laws of health, came to my aid; though not without subjecting me to a great peril. One evening, after Mr Murray's annual sale, when the whole of the first edition of *Character* had been subscribed for, I proceeded to make the necessary corrections for another edition. Correcting printed sheets is always more fatiguing than writing them in manuscript. It requires closer attention to minute points, such as commas, semicolons, and full stops; while there is not the interest of writing out fresh thoughts. To alleviate the fatigue, I occasionally took a turn at writing out a brief account of my recent visit to the Frisian Islands. I intended this most probably for *Good Words*, but I never had the courage to read over the paper, after the summary manner in which it was interrupted.

I felt a curious humming in my head, and a tingling at the points of my fingers. I stopped work, walked about the room, felt better, and then sat down again. I was proceeding with the corrections, when again the curious sensations returned. I turned down the gas, resolved to cease working for the night. On trying to turn the handle of the door with my right hand, I found that it was powerless. I felt it with the left hand: it was like ice, and hung down like a lump of lead. I turned the handle with my left hand, and went downstairs. It was the same below: my right hand continued powerless.

I entered the room, where only my mother-in-law was present—for the rest of the family had gone to a Penny Reading at the schools connected with St Stephen's Church. I must have made some ejaculation, for the old lady looked round, and saw that something was the matter with me. She rang for the servants, and sent for the doctor. Everything passed away from my recollection; and the next sensation I had was that of being carried from the chair which I had occupied, towards the sofa. In short, I had experienced a sharp attack of paralysis.

Now I had the rest which I needed. Indeed, I was perfectly helpless. I could scarcely move. I could not speak. My muscular power gradually returned, but it was days before I recovered my speech, and still longer before I could write my name. I found that I had lost the recollection of all proper names, and in a great measure lost the recollection of words. When I began to speak, I often used the wrong word. I had to recommence my knowledge of the English language. In fact, I suffered from aphasia.

My judgment, so far as it went, was not impaired, but my power of expressing it in words had left me. I could not read, but my wife read to me. I remember that some articles, then appearing in *Blackwood*, were read, respecting the education of French boys and girls. The boys were said to be prigs, and the girls to be almost perfect. My judgment said to me that this could not be possible—both being children of the same parents. But as the article set me a-thinking, and excited a pain in my head, I had to request a cessation of the reading for that day.

I meditated in my bed, and now determined to "pull up." If I recovered, I might yet spend a few more years on earth, though I feared that my working faculties were gone. But I knew that my only chance was long and perfect rest. I was urged by Mr Gilpin to continue in my employment, which secured a handsome income; but I knew that I could not be satisfied without doing some work for it, and that this might bring back a return of the

disease. This consideration determined me, and I
sent in my resignation. I was now free, and an idle
man!

What was I to do? I had been always accustomed to industrious habits, and could not be
entirely idle. I took exercise, and began to use my
limbs briskly. I read a little, gradually recovered
my use of the language, and endeavoured to spend
most of my time in the open air. When I was
able to travel, I went over to Dublin, to see my
youngest son, who was in business there. Then I
went to see my eldest son, who was established in
Belfast. From Ireland, I went to Dunoon on the
Clyde, where I remained a few months. I gradually
recovered my strength; gained several stone in
weight; and attended to my digestion. I left my
brain to lie fallow.

In 1873, I took a student's ticket at the South
Kensington Museum, and attended at Bethnal Green
for the purpose of copying in water-colours many of
Sir Richard Wallace's paintings in oil. I refurbished
up an old art, and derived a great deal of pleasure
as well as much rest, from copying the works of
Guardi, Bonnington, Descamps, Rousseau, and
others. These bits of my leisure handiwork now
ornament the walls of my sons and daughters. They
are not of much importance, but the execution of
them was a great relief to me. They saved me from
thinking or worrying; and in that way helped the
restoration of my health.

I went on cultivating idleness, and spent a considerable portion of the autumn of this year on the
wild western coast of South Donegal, in Ireland.
There I saw magnificent scenery, and imbibed abundant ozone. Every day saw me stronger and better

able for work.   But I had not yet made up my mind again to follow any settled occupation.   Indeed, Sir Edward Watkin made me a handsome proposal; but I did not see my way to accept it; and, on the whole, I think I was wise eventually to refuse it.

At the end of 1874 (10th November), I experienced a severe sorrow in the death of my dear daughter Edith.   She was a good, affectionate daughter, and a favourite with everybody.

CHAPTER XX

THRIFT—THE SCOTCH NATURALIST—GEORGE MOORE, ETC.

IN consequence of this sad breach in our family, my wife and I resolved to leave Blackheath. She could not bear to remain in a place associated with so much sorrow. There was nothing to attach me to Blackheath, more than to any other place. So we gave up our house, and warehoused our furniture. At first we thought of removing to Belfast, where three of our children were then settled. But after consideration we resolved to refurnish in Kensington, at the west end of London. On the whole it was more convenient, both for ourselves and our family. Our children were now all married, and they could see us there occasionally on their visits to town.

In the meantime my writing faculty had returned, and I was contemplating the preparation of a new book. In 1860, I had written an article in the *Quarterly Review* (No. 215), on the subject of "Workmen's Earnings and Savings."* This was

---

* The articles I published in the *Quarterly*—all written before my illness—were these : " Difficulties of Railway Engineering " (No. 205); "Iron Bridges" (207); "James Watt" (208); "Strikes" (212); "Cotton-spinning Machines and their Inventors" (213); "Workmen's Earnings and Savings" (215); "The Brunels" (223); "Workmen's Benefit Societies" (232); "Iron and Steel" (239); "The Great

afterwards published in a cheap form, and was out of print. An unknown correspondent at Malvern brought the subject under my notice, by informing me that it had been through the recommendations contained in the above article that he had been enabled to initiate many working people in the practice of "Thrift." I will venture to quote part of the gentleman's letter :—

"Many years since, when recovering from a protracted illness, I incurred a debt of gratitude to you for the pleasure and instruction I had derived from your writings, and only the other day I had to feel additionally grateful towards you, for one of the little *exquisite* enjoyments of life. A burly, hairy-faced workman stopped me in the street to thank me 'for making a man of him'! With great gusto he told me that he could never in his life keep a sovereign in his pocket, until he was induced by me to open a banking account with Her Majesty at the Post Office Savings Bank. He had now saved £37, and had just sent his mother 'a fat goose and giblets,' with a grand wool shawl for a New Year gift! 'If it hadn't been for you, Sir,' he said, 'I would never have saved a sovereign.' It may, perhaps, be a source of pleasure and satisfaction to yourself to know that it was entirely owing to your admirable article on 'Workmen's Earnings and Savings' that I took an interest in opening banking

Railway Monopoly" (250); "Life Assurance Companies" (255); "The Police of London" (257).—I ceased writing for the *Quarterly* and other periodical publications for several reasons. First, they were always worked off at high pressure. Second, because the articles cannot be reprinted without the consent of the publisher. When I suggested the republication of my articles in the *Quarterly*, my proposal was declined. Perhaps the proprietor was right, because the articles, being about events of the day, and based perhaps on illustrations of only temporary importance, might have lost their interest by the time of the republication. Besides, in writing articles for a Review, you hand over the fruit of your brain and diligence to another, and cannot afterwards reclaim them. I afterwards preferred writing for myself, at my leisure ; and found it more satisfactory.

accounts for working-people. I started some scores by giving them the *first* shilling, and requiring that they should produce to me *their Bank Book*, with the magical letters on the envelope, ' O. H. M. S.' Since then the Post Office Savings Banks have effected a wonderful advancement in Thrifty Habits. In fact, they have educated the people in thrift."

After a good deal of praise from my unknown friend, of my own small efforts to help the upward-striving army of industry—and turning over in my mind the worth of good words thrown into fruitful ground, where they spring up apace into good works and individual progress—I bethought me whether I might not enlarge the above article, and devote a special treatise to the subject of Thrift. I consulted with my friend, Mr (afterwards Sir) Charles W. Sikes, Banker, Huddersfield, the initiator or inventor of the Post Office Savings Banks system ; and he urged me to proceed with my proposed treatise.* I accordingly sought out all possible information on the subject—Blue Books, Post Office Reports,

---

* In answering my letter, Mr Sikes said : " Excuse my mentioning a very pleasing incident that occurred the other day. A Japanese gentleman visiting Huddersfield came to this Bank, and after being introduced—he talked English fairly—I, amongst other inquiries, asked what English books were translated into Japanese. He said, amongst others, Milton and Shakespeare, which were greatly admired. I asked whether they had not any translations of Mr Smiles' works *Self-Help* and *Character.* His countenance suddenly became lighted up with animation and pleasure. "Oh yes !" he said, "they are my favourites. They are admirable books, and read by nearly everybody." I was much gratified in hearing that the Institution in Japan answering to our House of Commons, has had a copy of *Self-Help* superbly bound in six handsome volumes, and formally presented to the Emperor of Japan, recommending it for His Majesty's studious perusal. I could not imagine a higher honour being paid to the writings of any English author." I hope the reader will excuse the vanity of making this extract from my esteemed friend's letter.

Co-operative Societies' Returns, and the raw material
for a complete book.

As I was then upon the move, and my household
furniture was warehoused, I went down with my
family to St Leonard's, and there I began my treatise.
It occupied me some time there. Then I went down
to Haddington, and proceeded with it; and lastly, I
went to Banff, in the north of Scotland, where I took
lodgings for a few weeks; and there ended my little
work.

The reason of my proceeding to Banff was, to
have some conversation with Tom Edward, the
Scottish shoemaker. I had written about him in *Self-
Help* many years before as a hard-working naturalist,
who, while maintaining himself by his ill-paid trade,
had devoted himself, in the midst of great difficulties,
to the study of natural science. While at St
Leonard's, I had some correspondence with him, but
as he was not very expert at writing out his thoughts,
I thought that it would be better to cross-examine
him on the spot. I did not think of writing a book
about him; but wishing for a change of scene and
change of air, and having little else to do, I went
down to Aberdeen by steamer, and from there
proceeded to Banff by railway.

I found it was as I had suspected. Thomas
Edward had not told me the most interesting facts
in his life. It required some art and a good deal of
literary experience to do that. When I asked him
how it was that he had told me nothing of the results
of his exhibition of natural history at Aberdeen, he
said he did not like to say anything about it. "How
was that?" "I thought of making away with myself," he answered. And then I succeeded in extracting
from him the whole of his interesting story.

U

I went along the coast, east and west of Banff, to see the scenes of Edward's exploits. I went along the sands to the kitchen-midden at Boyndie, and to Boyndie churchyard, where Edward had spent such a terrible night among the tombs; and then eastward, through Macduff, to the rocky coast near Tarlair, where Edward had nearly lost his life in falling from the rocks in pursuit of a wounded bird. I picked up a great many anecdotes in the course of these bits of journeys.

The herring season was on. The piers at Banff and Macduff were covered with herring-gutters; and the fishing-boats were going out in the evening, and coming in in the morning full of glittering fry. Everybody was active. There were numbers of foreign ships waiting for their loads, destined for Hamburg, Stettin, and other ports on the Baltic, for the herring is not caught merely for home use. The bulk of the annual catch is exported for foreign consumption.

Another question suggested itself—that of Race. Where had these fishing people come from, who take to the sea as naturally as the ducks take to water? It was the same question that had stirred me in making my journey through the North Frisian Islands. Take a map, and look at the proximity of Norway to Scotland. Right opposite to the Moray Firth, across the North Sea, lies Norway, containing the keenest sea-going population in the world. The country was too rocky and barren to support a large number of persons. As families increased, the younger people took to their boats—for they were all sailors—and made for new and unoccupied countries. The nearest land, on the western side, was Scotland; and there the immigrants landed in boat loads, increasing from year to year; and eventually peopled the whole of the eastern parts of Scotland. That seems to me a perfectly clear origin of the lowland population of the north-eastern countries.

They settled also in the islands north of Scotland, in the Orkneys, the Shetlands, the Faroes, and Iceland; where they are still as Norwegian as they were a thousand years ago. Indeed, until within the last four hundred years, not only Orkney and Shetland, but the Hebrides, were governed by the king of Denmark and Norway. In 1469, the former islands were pledged for the dowry of Margaret, "Maiden of Norway," daughter of the Danish monarch, who became the queen of James III. of Scotland; but as the dowry was never paid, the islands thenceforward belonged to the latter country, though the race has continued the same. All round the northern part of the island, the people are still purely Scandinavian. Their features and configuration, the names of the towns and farms where they live, and of the headlands and firths or fiords of the sea, are, for the most part, Norse. Dr Jamieson also has shown, in his *Dictionary of the Scottish Language*, that the speech of the people of the lowlands of Scotland has been in a great measure founded on that of their Norwegian ancestors.

The new people brought with them their sea-going habits. The Celts will not go to sea, if they can avoid it. The Highlander is a capable soldier, but a bad sailor. He will fish in fresh water, but not in salt. There are many great Highland military leaders, but no great Highland admirals. Nearly all our leading naval men, discoverers, and arctic voyagers, have been of Scandinavian derivation.

I returned to London with my health recruited and my mind full of new information. The first thing I did was to finish *Thrift*, and put it in the hands of the printers. It was successful when published; and I believe it induced many hard working people to think of "the rainy day," and to lay by something as a store, not only for independence, but for help in the future. It was translated into many languages. The first translation was the Dutch. I bought a copy of the work in a bookshop in Amsterdam, and found that the translator had illustrated it with many notes. Besides being translated into French, German, and Italian, it was also given in Magyar for the Hungarians, and in Serbo-Croatian for the Serbs and Croats.

Of course it was reprinted in America. The Canadians tried to smuggle a low-priced edition into the States, but the London Copyright Association interfered, and in 1875 an action was commenced in the Canadian law courts in my name; and the illegitimate Canadian publishers were required to stop their further interference.* I may mention that the house of Harper Brothers, of New York, were disposed to pay me very fairly for advance sheets; but that, on the attempted smuggling of the Canadian publishers, and the piracy of my books by a big publishing house of New York (Monro), they stopped the practice; and I took my chance of what copies were sold of a book-printed edition, after they had passed the work through their "Franklin Library" series, at from 7d. to 10d. a number.

I then proceeded with my *Life of Thomas Edward, the Scotch Naturalist.* I thought that the

* This was the important case of Smiles *v.* Belford, a leading case on the subject of Canadian copyright.—ED.

volume might be made interesting enough; because
the life of Edward was so full of human nature and
love of science; besides setting forth a fine example
of how difficulties, even the most harassing, might
be faced, battled with, and overcome. But I wished
to see my shoemaker again; and in the summer of
1876, I again proceeded to Aberdeen. Mr George
Reid,* my friend, the artist, agreed to accompany me
for the purpose of illustrating the book. We went
by Fraserburgh round the north coast of Aberdeen,
through Aberdour, Pennan, Troup, and Gamrie, to
Macduff and Banff; and there Mr Reid finished his
fine drawing of the old shoemaker at his last,
with "Here I am Still" underneath, at the end of
the volume. I was much indebted to Mr Reid for
all that he had done; and the success of the volume
was greatly owing to him. I need say nothing
further here; for I have, in the last edition of the
book, said all that has to be said about the subject
of its publication.

In the following year, April 1877, I paid another
visit to Holland. I found the country a good deal
altered since I had first visited it some forty years
before. Travelling by trickschuyt and diligence had
been superseded by travelling by railway. It was now
easy to travel through the entire kingdom, from one
side to another, in less than a day. I still found
the same indications of industry and cleanliness.
But the old dresses were being superseded by those
of French fashion. The ships were still sailing inland
among the fields and trees; sometimes a little above
them. Nearly every bit of land in Holland has been
won from the sea, and it is still kept together by

* Now Sir George Reid, and some-time President of the Royal
Scottish Academy.—ED.

immense dykes and embankments. Everything is
utilised by this industrious people. Even the shells
cast upon the seashore at Katwyk are made into
lime. The wind is not allowed to pass without
paying a heavy toll of labour. It drives the windmills, pumps the water from the polders, grinds
flour and mustard, and is used for all the purposes
for which steam is used in England.

I landed at Flushing, visited some friends at
Middelburg, and then went on to Utrecht and
Amsterdam. One of my objects was to inspect the
new canal cut across North Holland from the river
Y to the North Sea west of Velsen, and then to
visit our ancestors in the province of Friesland. A
letter of introduction from Sir John Hawkshaw (the
engineer of the above canal) provided me with every
facility for my visit of inspection. When the canal
is finished, it will be 23 feet deep, and in the harbour
on the North Sea, the depth will be 28 feet at high
water.

I stayed for a few days in Amsterdam. It is a
remarkable city. It has been made by persecution,
which drove into it first the Dutch and Belgian and
French Protestants, and then the Jews, who abound
there, to the number of 30,000, and are very industrious and wealthy. The Dutch would bear anything
rather than the Inquisition. They sank piles into
the sand—of from 30 to 50 feet in length—and built
upon them houses, and fortifications, and windmills,
which work when the wind blows.

M. Havard has written an interesting volume in
which he compares Amsterdam to Venice. But they
might better be contrasted. There is a constant
busy hum at Amsterdam, while there is a perfect
silence at Venice. At Amsterdam everybody is busy,

and all are on the move. New docks are under construction, and old docks are being repaired. New
houses, warehouses, and places of business are
rebuilding; while at Venice everything is sad and
silent, and brawny fellows are lying asleep about the
doorsteps of palaces, or on the canal stairs. At
Amsterdam, you observe barges filled with goods
poled along, while at Venice you meet gondolas filled
with pleasure-seekers. At Amsterdam everything
looks new; the oldest houses have their colour
constantly renewed; the doors and window frames
are always kept bright; but at Venice the finest
buildings seem going to decay. The cleanliness
of the two cities is not to be compared. The cold
of Amsterdam makes men hardy, and incites
them to work: in Venice the idea is, *dolce far
niente.*

I went to Harlem to see the wonderful portraiture
of Frans Hals in the museum there. The men are
splendid. They are mostly men with fair hair and
blue eyes, with muscular faces and large fleshy noses
—men capable of taking hard knocks and giving
them too. The portraits of the women are also
superb. Jan de Bray also is very good, especially
in his portraits of old men and women. In colour
he is equal to Rubens. P. Soutman, though he is
less known, is admirable. I fancy that from their
colour, the old Dutch must have been considerable
beer drinkers. In this respect they very much
resemble the people of England, where beer is king.
Teniers and Ostade make beer and human nature
the subject of their pictures. One of Wouverman's
works in the Riks Museum at Amsterdam (No.
461) represents a regular shillelagh fight of drunken
men.

I went to the Hague, to take another view of the fine selection of pictures in the National Gallery there. The day was very cold (20th April), for the east wind was blowing bitterly. To show the care which the people take of their cattle, I found that the cows had still *their shawls on!* At the Hague Gallery, I was attracted by the fine portrait of William, Prince of Orange, who was murdered by the Jesuit Gérard in the Church at Delft, in the year 1584. It is a severe, sad portrait, surmounted with his last words: "Mon Dieu, ayes pitié de mon âme: mon Dieu, ayes pitié de ce pauvre peuple!" He died in the arms of his wife, the daughter of Admiral Coligny. Her portrait is also sad and solemn; and she must long have remembered her husband's violent death. I was again reminded of the likenesses of well-known Dutchmen to well-known Englishmen. For instance, Ferdinand Bol's portrait of Admiral de Ruyter at the Hague is very like Cooper's portrait of Oliver Cromwell.

Holland is so small, that by taking up one's quarters at Amsterdam, and using the railway, it is easy to see the whole country within a short time. Among my various journeys, I made one through North Holland to the Helder, to see the immense bulwarks thrown up to preserve the enclosed lands from inundations by the sea. It is curious, as we pass along the Grand Canal which unites Helder with Amsterdam, to see the sails of the vessels occasionally overtopping the roofs of the houses. And yet vessels of the largest kind pass from the North Sea to the capital of Holland in this way; for the Zuider Zee is too shallow to give access to larger ships.

The whole of North Holland, though won from

the sea, is covered with the richest verdure; and the numbers of cattle, the comfortable-looking houses, and the well-clad people, show that the inhabitants are enjoying the fruits of their industry. When I reached Helder, I was told that the bulk of the men were out herring-fishing. The same might have been said of the people at Yarmouth, right opposite Helder, on the further side of the North Sea. The men and women of North Holland and Norfolk and Suffolk are very like each other — not only in their sea pursuits, but in their farming operations.

As in the North Friesland islands, the house, barn, and byre are usually under one roof. Until the thirteenth century, North Holland was united with Friesland, on the other side of the Zuider Zee. A fresh-water lake, which the Romans called Lake Flevo, occupied part of the inland country, until a terrible storm from the north washed away the intervening land, and drove the sea inland as far as Naarden and Harderwijk; when Lake Flevo disappeared. But the race peopling both regions still continued to be the same.

One sometimes wonders where the Suffolk and east of England country people got their half sing-song, nasal twang, which the early Puritans carried with them to the New England colonies of North America, and which is now known as the Yankee dialect or twang. They got it, of course, from Friesland, where it still exists; and where the race is the same, the habits of the people are the same, and the language is in a great measure the same. Yankee is only another word for English; for the Indians could not compass the pronunciation of the latter word, but transformed it into "Yankee." The

Puritans long preserved the nasal twang. I knew it
when a boy; and the last time I heard it was from
the famous Mr Gurney, in the Quaker meeting-house
at Leeds.

The works along the sea-face at the Helder (Hel-
deur, or Hell's door) are of a gigantic character. The
extremity of the tongue of land which forms North
Holland, is exposed to the fury of the North Sea in
storms, and is accordingly defended on all sides by a
rampart of the very largest dimensions. It consists
of gigantic blocks of granite, brought principally
from Norway; and descends into the sea by a slope
of about 200 feet. The dyke is nearly 2 leagues
long, and is 40 feet broad at the summit, over which
there is a very good road. The labour, and industry,
and skill necessary to construct this magnificent
bulwark, and to keep it in repair from day to day,
must have been enormous.

From Amsterdam, on another day, I made a
voyage northward by a *stoom-boot* to Harlingen, on
the Zuider Zee. We were literally *let down* from the
great canal, for the tide was low. Our vessel was let
through three great sluices, capable of accommodating
large ships—for the great dyke, through which we
passed, is the key of the works of the great canal.
The water was so shallow, that our steamer had to
make long detours to keep off the sandbanks. At
one place the water was only 6 feet deep; and we had
occasionally to slacken speed until we reached deeper
water.

We passed the island of Marken, and the decayed
cities of Hoorn and Enkhuizen, so well described by
Havard. An engineer who was on board described
to me the storm which had taken place only three
months before, on the 30th and 31st of January

1877. The waves had then flowed nearly all over the island of Marken; and the inhabitants were only saved by taking refuge in the church, which is situated on the highest point of the island. All their furniture and provisions were swept away by the waves. The people were mostly fishermen, and a subscription was then being made for their relief.

This storm was about the worst which had been experienced for thirty years. It continued for nearly two days. The wind blew strong from the north-west, and sent the waves flying right over the sea walls. A breach was actually made near Hinde-loopen, on the eastern shores of the Zuider Zee, and, had the storm continued for a few hours longer, the whole of Friesland would have been under water. But fortunately the wind abated, and the province was saved. The fact shows, that from day to day the principal part of Holland is preserved by careful industry and self-help—Providence being there, too, helping people to help themselves.

The engineer further told me of the project that was on foot for reclaiming the whole of the land on the Zuider Zee, south of the island of Urk. The Schellingwonde Dyk had already been constructed opposite Nieuerdamer. Ten thousand piles of from 50 to 60 feet in length had already been driven into the mud or clay; and the rows of piles had been filled with various materials. It was believed that the land under the Zuider Zee, when reclaimed, would prove most excellent; and that about 400,000 additional acres — or equal to the extent of our county of Surrey—would be added to the cultivated land of the country.

I landed at Harlingen, one of the principal seaports of Friesland, on the Zuider Zee, from which England receives a considerable proportion of its butter, cheese, and eggs. The Frieslanders are intensely industrious, and not only produce enough food for themselves, but are able to spare a surplus for us. Harlingen stands on the site of a town swallowed up by the sea more than seven hundred years ago. It looks secure enough now; but when the islands of Texel and Vlieland are swallowed up (which now protect it against the stormy west), no one can tell what may again become of Harlingen. The country inland is splendidly cultivated; and the fields are full of well-fed cattle.

Here the people are mostly bright and ruddy, of good stature, fair-haired, and light-blue eyed. The women wear gold and silver plates over their temples; some of them have quite a family fortune round their heads. French fashions are, however, beginning to supersede the ancient Friesland dresses.

As we approached Leeuwarden, the capital of Friesland, I observed the Terpen, or built-up mounds, on which the old churches and farm-buildings stand. These resemble the same erections on the Halligs of the North Frisian islands. These high grounds afforded refuge to the inhabitants from inundation, before the country was properly dyked. They for the most part consist of earth; but as in Holland earth is too valuable to be raised in mounds, when the land became properly protected by embankments, the greater number of the terpen were levelled, and the earth used for raising the low-lying lands. Again here, as in North Friesland, the farmhouses are long and thatched, and house, barn, and byre, are all under one roof.

At Leeuwarden, I went to see the collection of Frisian antiquities. Mr J. Dirks, the director, permitted me to see it, although it was not yet opened to the public. I was helped by a letter from Mr Alma Tadema, a native of the town, some of whose pictures are in the collection of works of native artists. The carvings in wood, gold, silver, and ivory, are very fine. All the old houses of the Frisians, with their ancient furniture, were exhibited. The antiquities of Friesland — with their stone hammers, celts, and arrow-heads—were also there; with the succeeding works in bronze, iron, and gold. Specimens of Frisian dresses were also exhibited from various parts of the province.

After a journey eastward to Groningen—during which I observed that most of the engines on the Staats Spoorweg were constructed by Peacock & Co. of Manchester—a very different state of affairs from the time when we owed nearly all our English engineering to Holland—I returned to Amsterdam; then went on to Rotterdam; then to Middelburg in the island of Walcheren. I here paid a visit in passing to my friend, The Honourable M. Picke, formerly a judge and member of the Dutch Government. Like many of the best families in Holland, M. Picke is descended from a Huguenot, who left France for conscience' sake.

My visit to Middelburg was very pleasant. I was warmly received and hospitably entertained. I went to see the Museum and the new Church (St Peter's). In the latter, I found the monuments of the brothers Evertsen—Ian and Cornelius. They were natives of the town, and were both killed in 1666, in the same naval battle of Zeeland, while fighting for their fatherland. The shirt and coat worn by the leading

Admiral in this engagement, are still preserved under glass in the Museum of the town. There is also a picture of the Evertsen family in the Stadhuis, or Townhall; a fine building erected by Charles the Bold in 1468. Though Admiral de Ruyter was not a native of this place, but of Flushing, the wheel, on which he made ropes when a boy, is preserved in the Middelburg Museum.

M. Picke took me round the island of Walcheren to see the farming, the schools, and the great embankment at West Cappel. At one of the schools, the boys and girls—to whom my name seemed to be known, when it was mentioned to them—sang to me their national song, "Wien Neêrlansch bloed," in splendid style. They sang another popular ballad, which well embodies the national sentiments :—

> "Wij leven vrij, wij leven blij
>   Op Neêrlands dierbren grond,
> Ontworsteld aan de slavernij,
> Zijn wij door eendragt groot en vrij
> Hier duldt de grond geen dwinglandij
>   Waar vrijheid eeuwen stond." *

All over this little island, won from the sea by indefatigable labour, you see the fruits of Dutch thrift, industry, and love of freedom. The meadows, carefully manured, bear excellent grass. Fields of colza, in yellow bloom, are seen far and near. Everything is made to yield its tribute to industry. Even the rushes and reeds on the canal banks, when boiled and sprinkled with salt, are much relished by

* The following is a literal translation :—"We live free, we live blithe, on Netherland's dear ground ; delivered from slavery, we are through concord great and free ; here the land suffers no tyranny, where freedom has subsisted for ages."

the cattle, which thrive upon the food ; and the cows yield abundance of excellent milk.

The fields, the gardens, and the plantations which we passed on our journey, imparted a picturesque and prosperous appearance to the country. There were numerous villas and country seats for the wealthy; the farmers and country people lived in clean, roomy, and comfortable houses; and everything showed that the people were fairly enjoying the fruits of their labour.

Even the storks seemed to be as busy as the people. We observed them at every bit of canal, standing with their long legs in the water, and scooping up with their long bills the abundant frogs or frog spawn for their breakfast or dinner. As the sound of our carriage reached their ears, they gathered themselves together, drew in their neck, shot out their wings, and went off in a long, straddling, unwieldy swing. These storks are, however, the "sacred bird" of Holland. They are not only protected by opinion, but protected by law. The man who killed a stork would almost be regarded as a public enemy.

We approached the great dyke or embankment of West Cappel. It is really an immense work. The island at this point is exposed to the full fury of the North Sea when raging in storms; and the inland country is only preserved from inundation by the tremendous strength and thickness of the embankment. Indeed, the entire region of Zeeland maintains a constant struggle for existence; and its motto is thoroughly appropriate — "Luctor, et emergo" — "I strive, and keep my head above water." Some seventy years ago (in 1808) the dyke burst, and in came the sea water over the whole of Walcheren.

The sea actually stood as high as the roofs of the houses in the streets of Middelburg, and only the strength of the walls saved the place from destruction.

When we saw the place, a large body of men were engaged in repairing the injury done to the embankments in January last; when Friesland so narrowly escaped submergence. About five hundred men were at work, inserting new blocks of masonry on the sea face of the sloping wall, and repairing the *paalhoofd* or groynes at the bottom of the embankment. The ravages of the paalworm (*Teredo navalis*) are prevented by the use of thick iron nails. M. Picke said that, costly though it was, the embankment was worth its weight in silver. And yet it is many miles long, is from 120 to 150 feet in width at the foundation, and has a splendid carriage road along the top. The annual expense of keeping this special embankment in repair amounts to about £700! Of course, the most skilled engineers are constantly at work to preserve the embankments in complete and perfect condition. All this furnishes a further illustration of the energetic vigour of the people of this sea-encompassed nation.

In conclusion, let me say that the following things strike me as marking the characteristics of the Teutonic race, of whom the Dutch form a prominent example: 1. Their individuality, out of which comes their independence. 2. Their respect for the rights of property. 3. Their respect for women, children, home (heim),* and family. 4. Their persistent industry. 5. Their love of the sea; which becomes developed in 6. Their commercial spirit. There may

* *Tuin* (equivalent to the English *ton*) in Dutch, means "garden" or "enclosure."

be other features; but these are enough for the present.

I returned to London from Flushing, on the 3rd day of May 1877. I required some little occupation. For the present I kept all my observations on Race in the form of notes. But I had already another work pretty far advanced, to which I again directed my attention. This was a Memoir of Robert Dick, a hard-working baker at Thurso, who, by dint of close observation, had made some considerable additions to science before his death in 1866.

After my last visit to Thomas Edward at Banff in 1876, I went northward to Thurso, and saw the various scenes of Dick's labours. I also succeeded in obtaining many of Dick's letters to his friends and intimate associates; from which I proceeded to elaborate a sketch of his interesting career. But I had not seen enough of the country itself, and in 1877, shortly after my return from Holland, I proceeded to Aberdeen by sea, then on to Wick, also by steamer; and thence I proceeded all round the northern coast to Thurso and Strath Halladale. I stayed for a few days at John o' Groats, and thence visited the wild coast by Duncansbay Head and Freswick. The late Earl of Caithness had seen an announcement of my visit to the north in an Aberdeen paper, and sent a messenger to John o' Groat's Hotel, asking me to come over and see him at Barrogill Castle. I went accordingly, and enjoyed the hospitality of his lordship. Barrogill Castle is a curious old building, consisting of a square tower with heavy battlemented turrets at each angle; and in the wild old times it may have been capable of making a considerable defence. From the summit of the tower, a fine view is obtained of the Pentland

Firth, with Dunnet Head to the westward, and the
rocky coast of Hoy on the north-west. The
neighbourhood of the castle is bare; for the winds
are so powerful, and the site is so exposed, that trees
will not grow there. An attempt has been made to
enclose the castle with a plantation; but where the
wall ceases, the tops of the trees are sharply cut
away by the sea-drift, as if they had been shorn by a
scythe. I went to see the remnants of " Pict's
Houses" on the estate, and the little haven of Mey,
which the earl had constructed for the accommodation
of the people in the neighbourhood.

Returning to John o' Groats, I afterwards drove
round the coast, by Canisbay and Dunnet, and across
the sands to Thurso, or Thor's town, a regular
Scandinavian settlement. Here I took up my
quarters for several weeks, and visited the entire
neighbourhood, making sketches of the principal
coast scenery. I now found my taste for drawing
useful. I had cultivated it by copying from Sir
Richard Wallace's pictures at Bethnal Green; and
I was now able to make pretty fair sketches in water-
colour, which were afterwards used in illustrating the
Life of Robert Dick. Mr Traill, of Castlehill, took
me round Dunnet Head in his yacht; when I had
the opportunity of making some sketches of that
grand old cliff, round to the entrance of the Pentland
Firth.

After picking up all necessary information, and
making many drawings, I went southward, and after
spending some pleasant days with Mr Fowler at
Loch Broom, we went to Loch Maree and Gair-
loch, and returned by Inverness to the Bridge
of Allan, near Stirling. From this place I made
excursions to Tullibody, Menstrie, Alloa, and the

neighbourhood of the Ochils, to visit the scenes and make drawings of the places connected with Robert Dick's early life. After some time in Edinburgh, during which I visited Mr Peach, the old friend of Dick, I returned home, with my note-book and sketch-book full of memoranda for future use.

I had not yet begun my work for the press. But before I could proceed, I was requested to take up an entirely different subject. My practice up to this time, had invariably been to select my own topics. I might have become a biographer general, and adopted the practice of Dumas, who employed other people to work for him in a sort of novel manufactory. But I refused all invitations to write biographies ; and I only selected those subjects towards which I felt specially attracted. Besides, I worked for amuse-ment, as well as to fill up my unemployed time pleasantly. The only exception I made was in the case to which I am about to refer.

I received a letter from Mr Murray, enclosing one from the late Mr Thomas Longman, urging me to undertake the Life of the late George Moore. I did not know anything of Mr Moore. I had heard of his deeds of philanthropy, and seen an account of the accident in the streets of Carlisle, from the effects of which he died. But that was all. I did not take part in public meetings, and the state of my health required me to avoid them. So that I had never heard Mr Moore speak at Exeter Hall, or at the meetings of the Young Men's Christian Associa-tion, where he was so great a light.

I also received a letter from Mrs Moore urging me to undertake the work. After some consideration, I declined to undertake it. My reasons, I thought, were sufficient. I did not know enough of Mr Moore to undertake his history; besides, my time was already occupied. This, however, was not enough. More pressure was put upon me. Then I began to make inquiries of London warehousemen as to the character and history of George Moore. One said that nothing could be made out of his Life, for that he was "only a warehouseman." Another, who did not agree with his religious views, said he was "a humbug"! A third, a dignified gentleman, who had been Lord Mayor, and had doubtless been "deaved" by George Moore for contributions towards his charities, said "he was a most obtrusive and effusive person"; while a fourth, who, however, was a Cumberland man, said "he was the noblest man he knew"! Here was an extraordinary difference of opinion about a person who had died little more than a year before.

Other views were pressed upon me. Dr Percival, then headmaster of Clifton College, and afterwards President of Trinity College, Oxford, gave me a very strong impression of the life and character of George Moore. Dr Bell, headmaster of Marlborough College, also spoke of him in glowing terms. The late Archbishop of Canterbury, one of the truest and noblest Christian gentlemen who ever lived, had almost a reverence for George Moore. Although warehousemen, even to each other, may not be perfect, there seemed to have been some sterling human merit about this merchant of Bow Church-yard, which seemed to be worthy of commemoration in a biography.

Still, I could not quite make up my mind. There was the poor baker of Thurso waiting. Was he to be abandoned in favour of the warehouseman, about whom there were so many differences of opinion? I

consented, however, to go down to Whitehall to look
over the papers and correspondence. After that, it
might be thought, I was committed. Still I hesitated.
I thought that George Moore had behaved shabbily
to his wife, by leaving her too little out of his large
fortune—less favourably, in fact, than he had left
his first wife by his will. Mrs Moore was, however,
most loyal to her departed husband. She said that
he had never read his will—that his solicitor had
misconceived his instructions—and that, whatever
the result might be, all his intentions were for the
best. There must have been a really fine character
in the man, for whom his wife—though wronged as
I thought—could speak so feelingly and so nobly.

I found that a gentleman who knew George
Moore, and had attended his prayer meetings, had
written a memoir of him. But he spoke of the
deceased merchant as of "a brand plucked from the
burning." Mrs Moore did not like the memoir, and
this is the reason why she was so anxious that I
should take up the subject. Eventually I consented
to go on with the work. I put a good deal of local
colour into it, and made it illustrative of Cumberland
as well as of London life. It must speak for itself.
It was, of course, republished in America, though
without my knowledge or consent. But when foreign
publishers in France, Germany, and even Italy,
think an English book worthy of translation into
their tongue, I think it is, on the whole, a compliment
to the author.

With this exception, I have always selected my
own subjects. It has been said that I wrote the
lives only of successful men. This is, of course, a
mistake. Robert Dick was not a successful man,
for he died not worth a farthing—the victim of

disease and hard work. Thomas Edward was not
a successful man, for he rarely made ten shillings a
week by his cobbling. The engineers whose lives
I wrote, were by no means successful men, so far
as accumulations of money were concerned. Many
brewers, spirit dealers, and grocers die far richer.
Brindley, Smeaton, Metcalfe, Telford, Rennie, Watt,
and Stephenson, were men of moderate means, who
lived in a very quiet fashion; but, as Mr Gladstone
truly says, they were the pioneers of British civilisation.

I have indeed written more about the history of
failure than of success. The *Huguenots in England
and Ireland*, to whose history I devoted a good deal
of time, were a beaten party. They sacrificed everything—property, money, and titles; though they
triumphed in character and principle. The Camisards and Vaudois, to whom I devoted another book,
The Huguenots in France, were thoroughly beaten by
the tyrants who governed them. One of my early
books related to the government of Ireland—one of
the saddest periods in history. It was a record of utter
failure. I hope there is nothing improper in wishing
for the Irish, as a people, a larger measure of success
than they have ever yet achieved.

What I have always endeavoured to do, was to
show that perseverance and courage would, in the
end, lead to success of the best sort. I may here
mention a little incident in the life of George Moore.
At one of the school examinations in Cumberland, as
was his wont, he gave a number of prizes. On this
occasion, Lord Brougham, who was present, presented
Self-Help to a Wigton boy, named Carruthers. The
boy was stimulated to exertion by what he read in
his prize book; and "the circumstance exercised an

important and abiding influence on his whole life."
He was "encouraged to look forward to a sphere of
greater usefulness than the circumscribed limits of
Wigton could afford." This is the description given
in the *Life of Carruthers*, by Dr Whitehead, of Manchester. The boy served an apprenticeship in a
chemist shop; he plodded on, until he became a
surgeon, and settled at Manchester. After thirteen
years of successful practice, he was called in to visit
a family which had been seriously injured by the
December gale of 1883. While attending to their
wounds, a further portion of the building fell in, and
broke the young surgeon's legs. He was fatally
injured; and while lying on his deathbed, he was
troubled principally by the thought that his wife and
children would be left without provision. It was to
appeal for help that Dr Whitehead published the
brief memoir of his life.

The *Life of George Moore* appeared in May
1878; that of Robert Dick, with its many illustrations, six months later. As with the men, so with
their lives. The one succeeded, the other did not.
George Moore went through many editions; *Robert
Dick* did not go through one. The multitude evidently like successful men. What is the use of
reading about men who have failed? Perhaps if I
had written about millionaires, I might have been
more successful myself. Books, however, are always
a lottery; and no one is better aware of this
than I am. The best course is, to write full-hearted,
and make the most you can out of your subject; and
this is the method I always adopted, whether the
result was likely to be successful or not.

CHAPTER XXI

VISIT TO ITALY [*]

I HAD twice before visited Italy; once, while I was
with the South-Eastern Railway, and took a longer
holiday than usual. I went then, with my wife, my
eldest daughter, and a friend, through Switzerland,
over the Splügen Pass, to Milan, then on through
Lombardy to Venice; and home by the Brenner Pass,
Innsbruck, Munich, and down the Rhine. The tour
occupied only three weeks in all. The other visit I
paid, and it was only through a corner of Italy, was
when I accompanied my friend Mr Milsom in his
visits to the Vaudois pastors in the remote parts of
Dauphiny. This journey was made mostly on foot.
We walked (for there was no carriage road) from
Abries on the verge of France, over the Cottian Alps
to the Bergerie of Pra, then down the valley of the
Pellice as far as La Tour, a journey of some 26 miles.
From La Tour, we visited the scenes in the valley of
Angrogna, made memorable by the hard struggle of
the Vaudois in ancient times for life and liberty.

[*] It has not been thought necessary to print in full Dr Smiles'
account of his journey through a country well known to the British
tourist. Descriptions, often interesting and vivid, of places have been
omitted. It seemed sufficient to chronicle one or two slight incidents
of travel, as characteristic of the man and his way of looking at
life.—ED.

This I have elsewhere fully described.* I then proceeded to Turin, and went up the valley of Aosta,
and over the Great St Bernard to Martigny; from
whence I proceeded rapidly homeward, by way of
Lucerne, Neufchatel, Dijon, and Paris. Now, however, as I was free from all office duties, I could
take my own time, and proceed leisurely to Florence,
Rome, and Naples, which I had an anxious desire to
see. In the Preface to the translation of *Character*
into Italian, which I wrote at the instance of my
friend M. Barbera, the Florence publisher, I stated
that I hoped to be able to visit these great cities
before the termination of my brief pilgrimage on
earth.

I set out, with my wife, for Paris, on the 20th
February 1879. Two days later, we reached Nice,
then in the throes of its Carnival. People had
assembled from all quarters to see the show—the
mummeries, the processions, the cavalcades—as well
as each other. It was not possible to pass along the
streets without being pelted with confetti—which did
not consist of confetti, but of hard lime pills. There
was not much fun in this, but the people seemed to
expect it; and young people were arranged on
platforms or at windows along the streets to pelt the
passers-by. The prettiest day was the day of
flowers, when carriages drove through the streets, and
especially along the Promenade des Anglais, covered
with the most exquisite produce of the garden. The
carriage people pelted each other with flowers, and
this was by no means disagreeable.

More pleasant, however, was the visit which I
paid to Mrs Evans (wife of Colonel Evans) at

* *The Huguenots in France, after the Revocation of the Edict of
Nantes.*

Cimiez, near Nice. This good, benevolent lady, had been greatly pleased with the *Life of the Scotch Naturalist*, and was kind enough to send a remittance of ten pounds yearly to Thomas Edward.

.   .   .   .

There happened to be with us in the railway carriage as we went to Naples, a gentleman, who, if he had his way, would make quiet living in Italy as impossible as ever. He was one of the Italia Irredenta Party, and had been at Milan, taking part in a public demonstration. He had a number of flags with him, which he unrolled, and exhibited the vehement sentiments inscribed upon them in glaring colours. He claimed for Italy, not only Nice and the Italian possessions of France, but the Valais, Ticino, and Valtellina, the Italian-speaking republican cantons of Switzerland, and all the shore part of Austria as far as Pola, Fiume, and even Ragusa. In fact, there was no limit to his demands. It was of no use saying to him, that in carrying out his theory, he would set all Europe by the ears. Why not develop, by industry, the country that Victor Emmanuel, Cavour, and Garibaldi had already won? "No! no!" he said, "we must have our own—all that speak our noble language." One of the effects of the Italia Irredenta scheme of governing people according to the language they speak, would be to divide Switzerland into three divisions—and hand over one part to France, another part to Germany, and the rest to Italy. The Swiss are certainly much safer remaining as they are, and governing themselves in their own manner by their perfectly free institutions.

.   .   .   .

In Rome, among my various visits, I went to see that excellent artist and sculptor, Mr Warrington Wood. He has a beautiful residence and studio at the Villa Campagna, close to the church of St John, Lateran. It happened to be his afternoon for receiving company. There were many ladies and gentlemen present. Among others was Mr Adolphus Trollope. Mr Wood received me with great effusion. After some conversation, he turned to Mr Trollope and said, "Ought I to tell Mr Smiles of how I happen to be here?" "Oh, by all means," said Mr Trollope, "he says it is all through you." "How is that?" I asked. "Well," said Mr Wood, "I will tell you. When I was a very young man—it must be now some eighteen or twenty years ago—I read your *Self-Help*. I sat up nearly all night to read it. I was inspired by the example of Flaxman, who, notwithstanding every difficulty, *would* go to Rome. When I went to bed, the thought of his determination pursued me: if he could do it, why should not I? Unlike him, I was comparatively free and unfettered. It is true, I was poor; for I was only a working mason. Before moving, I had made up my mind to go to Rome too. I wished to be a sculptor. I had done a few little things, tried to do more, and struggled hard for improvement. At length I saved about a hundred pounds. When I told my friends of my intentions, they opposed me all that they could. I was getting on: I would yet succeed as an architect. It was of no use. I pursued my determination. I came to Rome, and now (pointing to his works round the studio) you see what I am." Among other things, which he mentioned with gratitude, was the kindness of Gibson, the sculptor. "When I first came to Rome," he said, "I went to Gibson, and asked him to recommend me to some working sculptor. He asked for my drawings and works, to see what I could do. "No! no!" he said, when he had seen them, "do not go into any one's service. Take a place for yourself, no matter how humble; work for yourself, and cultivate originality." I took his kindly advice; and went on from one thing to another; and now, he concluded, "here I am, with my works around me. Such as they are, they are my own." It was exceedingly pleasant to myself to listen to those delightful recollections.

Another visit that I paid was to Rossetti's studio. Signor Rossetti had executed a statue of *Self-Help*— a girl—seated, with a book upon her knee, diligently perusing it. The work was considered very successful, and Rossetti had executed three replicas of it for England. The sculptor was very much moved and excited when I visited him; although I am ashamed to say that I could not exchange an intelligible word with him. His assistant Ceccarini, however, who had lived for a time in Belfast, acted as our interpreter. On parting, Rossetti pressed my hand with emotion to his beard, and asked me to do him the honour of sitting to him for my bust. I accordingly returned more than once, and Rossetti executed an admirable model of me in clay, and afterwards one in marble, very much to his own delight, and to my satisfaction.

During my visits to Rossetti's studio, I had the pleasure of making the acquaintance of Signor Cairoli, then the Italian Prime Minister. Rossetti was executing a little memorial in marble, to be placed over the tomb of his infant daughter who had lately died. Signor Cairoli kindly invited me to visit him at his house, and to see the Signora, who

was a great admirer of my works. She had even
translated one of them. I found the Signora a most
estimable and intelligent lady; and as she spoke
English admirably, I felt at once quite at home.
I may mention that Signor Cairoli still had his
arm in a sling—the one that had been wounded
while defending the king from the attack of an
assassin in the streets of Naples.

It happened that, during my visit to Rome,
General Garibaldi paid one of his last visits to the
city, for the purpose of having an interview with the
young king. The general, though not very old,
was so crippled with rheumatism that he could not
stand, and his right hand, which had so often wielded
the sword, was shrunk up almost into a knot, and
could not be opened out. On hearing of my being
in Rome, he sent a message to me through Signor
Rossetti, informing me that he would be glad to
receive me at the house of his son Menotti, who
lived, with his wife and family, at No. 6 Via
Vittoria. I accordingly proceeded thither about
mid-day, on the 10th of April, 1879. The house
was on the second floor, and it was a very humble
dwelling. There were present, Colonel Canzio, the
general's son-in-law, Colonel Forbes, and Signor
Rossetti.

The old man was still dressed in his red shirt, and
lay on his bed almost helpless. He could barely
shake hands with me—his arm was so shrunk and
weak. But his eyes lightened up when he began to
speak of the goodness of the English people to him.
"The English," he said, "have helped me in every
way. They have been so good to me that I can
never forget them. But they shake one's hands very
much. They shake hands from the heart. What

a day that was at Trafalgar Square, when I passed
through the tens of thousands of your people. And
then I went to the Duke of Sutherland, who is such
a humane man."

He went on to speak to his friends by the bedside
of his escape from Rome in 1849: how, after hard
fighting with the French under Oudinot, Rome was
forced to surrender, and he made for the coast of the
Adriatic with his followers, his dear wife Anita
accompanying them. "We put to sea," he said, "in
thirteen fishing-boats; it was a dark stormy night
when we started. But the clouds at length dispersed,
and the moon shone forth. An Austrian corvette
hovering about was directly upon us; and as our
little squadron of boats scattered and took to flight,
the Austrians fired in all directions; backed, and
fired again and again. They captured nine of the
boats with their crews; but the boat in which I was,
with Anita, and the three other boats, escaped. We
landed on the Italian coast, near Ravenna, and fled
into the country. But the Austrians were at our
heels. We scattered and hid ourselves as we could.
Anita and I took refuge among some standing corn
by the roadside. The Austrians, however, took some
of my friends prisoners. They shot nine of them at
Ca Tiepolo, and buried them where they fell.
Among these was the gallant Ciceruacchio — the
dear fellow!"

The general shed tears, and pointed to the photograph of Ciceruacchio's statue hung up against the
wall. Angelo Brunetti was his real name. He was
only a woodcutter, and dealt in wine and forage, but
he was a true patriot and lover of the people. Not
only so; he was a man gifted with extraordinary
powers of eloquence; and when Garibaldi appeared

in Rome, he donned the red shirt, and became one of his most enthusiastic followers. He was with him all through the siege of Rome by the French, and conducted himself with great bravery. Years after the violent death of Ciceruacchio at Ca Tiepolo, with his son, who was only thirteen years old—and after Italy had become free, the Italians had the ashes dug up, with some medals and fragments of red shirts and handkerchiefs, and removed them to Rome for interment. It was proposed to erect a statue of the People's Tribune, and Rossetti had executed a spirited model; and it was to the photograph of this design that Garibaldi pointed with tears. But whether anything has yet been done to erect the statue, I do not know.

The visit which I paid to Garibaldi was made the subject of reports in the newspapers; for the press in Italy is becoming as ubiquitous as it is in England. I quote from one of the reports, in which I am described as an "old man." I had never before thought of myself as "old," though, taking my years into account, it must be true. The reporter must have been present at the interview, but I do not know who he was.

"I think I told you," says the writer, "that Samuel Smiles was here. The papers are busy with him as they were with Garibaldi during the first days of his visit. He is here with his wife, and is profiting by his visit, taking notes for his new work, which is to be called *Duty*. He has paid a visit to the Queen, who has quite fascinated him, as she indeed fascinates all who approach her. He has been to see Garibaldi, and is having a bust made by Rossetti. He is very much pleased, it seems, to find that he has inspired more than one sculptor with models taken from his works. He is a fine-looking old man, with silvery whiskers encircling a kind and genial face.

His interview with Garibaldi was particularly impressive. You will read a full account of it one day, for he intends to write it himself, and in his own particularly happy style. Garibaldi, as a witness of the interview told me, was quite expansive, and seemed quite electrified when he heard Smiles's name. He spoke of his past, and described in powerful tones the terrible days of his early life. He spoke of his never-forgotten Anita; and he depicted vividly the scenes of his pursuit by the Austrians. Those who heard him felt the blood freeze in their veins. Even those who did not understand English, caught the impression from others, and saw from the listeners that an extraordinary conversation was being carried on by these two men. Smiles will never forget Garibaldi."

I suppose it was from the reports which appeared in the Roman newspapers of my presence in Rome, or perhaps from some conversation with Signor Cairoli, the Prime Minister, that I received a communication from the Palace of the Quirinale, intimating that Her Majesty Queen Margherita was desirous of an interview with me, being an admirer of my works. I felt this to be a great honour, and paid my visit accordingly. It was quite private, and I saw only the Queen herself. As the reporter has stated, I was quite fascinated by Her Majesty. I admired her grace, her manner, and her intellect. I need not speak of her beauty. But she is a true Queen, if it be one of the functions of a Queen to excite admiration and enthusiasm, and make her subjects in love with the institution of monarchy, of which she is the fairest outcome.

I had seen Her Majesty before in the streets of Rome, where she was followed by admiring eyes. For the Queen rides about a great deal, takes part in the philanthropic work of the city, and is never wanting when Royal help is necessary. She visits the poor schools and hospitals, attends public lectures, and is often seen with her young prince, on the Pincio or at the Villa Borghese.

Queen Margherita is charming not only as a queen, but as a woman. She embodies Wordsworth's description of—

"The perfect woman, nobly planned."

I found her simple, gracious, dignified, and yet thoroughly *simpatica*. She conversed with me freely, without the slightest assumption of patronage—spoke about English Literature, and told me of her favourite authors. I may mention that Her Majesty speaks English perfectly, as well as most other European languages. I saw the *Nineteenth Century* on her table. She liked the tolerant Catholicity of England, where Cardinal Manning and Positivist Harrison can meet in the same columns—state their thoughts, and argue out their views without let or hindrance.

She turned the conversation to literature generally. German novels she thought "flat"; French were naughty; and English novels were, of all others, her favourites. Of past writers, Scott was the greatest: then Thackeray. And of the living, she preferred the works of Hardy, Blackmore, and Black. She spoke with emotion of the *Princess of Thule*. Although she greatly admired Tennyson, her most favourite poet was the late Mrs Barrett Browning. She was an immense admirer of the historical works of Lecky.

As I conversed with the Queen, who sat close to me, and before me, my eyes commanded a view of the spires, and towers, and domes of Rome, with St Peter's in the distance. Her sitting-room is beautifully situated in an angle of the palace, and the windows look down upon the ancient parts of Rome, over to the Palace of the Cæsars. But the interest of the conversation prevented my taking note of what was to be seen outside. After about an hour, I kissed Her Majesty's hand, and left the palace delighted with my interview, not less pleased with the Queen's high-bred tact and graciousness of manner, than with her goodness, sweetness, and intelligent conversation. And thus ended my first and last interview with Royalty.

I had now many callers, letters, and invitations. I was desired to visit the schools and public buildings of Rome by persons of distinction. But I had no wish to become a "lion"; and I thought it better to avoid further excitement, and leave Rome as soon as possible. I give only one of the letters which I received, from a very humble person; and I select it as being one of the shortest.

"PREGIATISSIMO SIGNORE,—

"Un povero giovane di Corinaldo (Provincia d'Ancona) orfano sin dall' infanzia, di professione domestico, deve alla lettura dei di Lei scritti se ha potesto realizzare qualche risparmio, per il quale spera meno incerto il suo avvenire. Memore del suo benefattore, verso cui nutre sensi di profonda venerazione, gli invia un osseguioso saluto che ha feducia non verra disdegnato.—Mi creda, devotissimo servo,

"VALERIO VALERI."

Before leaving Rome, however, I had the honour and pleasure of calling upon Augusto Castellani, the distinguished antiquarian and goldsmith. I found him in his place of business, close by the Fountain of Trevi. He received us most kindly, and opened up to us his immense stores of antiquarian art and knowledge. We were careful not to enter upon matters of business. If we had asked the price of an article, he would have shut up at once; it was art, and art only, that took us there; and our conversation was entirely confined to that subject.

Signor Castellani took us upstairs and showed us all over his treasures. He entered with enthusiasm into a description of the most precious. This Etruscan jewel had been dug up in the Campagna, that in a village among the Apennines, and that Greek bronze near the villa of Hadrian. He told us how he had transported to Rome some local goldsmiths from a remote part of Italy, who had preserved, in what seemed to be an unbroken tradition, the art of fabricating granulated gold jewellery after the manner of the Etruscans. In the course of conversation he gave us his ideas as to the races of men who had from time to time imported their art into Italy—the Greeks, the Romans, and the Etruscans, who were the oldest and best of all.

Signor Castellani was anything but a tradesman. He was a historian, an antiquarian, and a philosopher, though with these accomplishments he combined the shrewdness of a business man. But his talk was never of orders, never of trade. Like many of his spirited countrymen, he was an ardent politician; and took pride in the renewed freedom of Italy. His conversation was immensely fascinating, and he kept us until long after the time when he should have left his place of business. At parting, he presented me with his "Della Orificeria Italiana, Discorso di Augusto Castellani," which I greatly treasure.

At last, with many regrets, I left Rome. The evening before, I went down to the Fountain of

Trevi by moonlight, and drank of the waters; as they say one who does that is sure to return. But I have never returned, and there is no probability, at my time of life, that I will ever do so. We left the station, laden with flowers, presented to us by many of our kind Roman friends.

.   .   .   .

I spent some time in Florence, inspecting the pictures and the churches, but to my mind, the most interesting of all the buildings connected with the Church, is the Convent of San Marco; for there the great patriot and martyr Savonarola nursed his heart and mind, and prepared to give up his life for his country and his religion. It is not to be compared in magnitude or splendour with the great ecclesiastical buildings of Florence. But it will be remembered when they are forgotten. You see there the cells of Fra Angelico and Fra Bartolomeo, who were disciples of Savonarola; and pass on to the cell of the patriot martyr himself. There is the little Bible from which he read and preached in the pulpit of the Duomo, his portrait and bust, his manuscripts and devotional emblems, and other interesting memorials. You are taken to the Hall, where Savonarola was engaged in prayer and exhortation when the people broke in, thirsting for his blood. He was taken away, and you may follow his march, amidst a shouting crowd, down the Via Ricasoli, past the Duomo—where he had so often bravely struggled for religion and liberty—and down the Via Calzauoli, where he was eventually strangled and burnt. But I have already described his life and fate, and need not repeat my description here.[*]

* In *Duty*, pp. 132-154.

The neighbourhood of Florence is also full of interest—the summit of the Piazza of Michael Angelo, from which you see the whole of the city lying sleeping at your feet—Fiesole, still further away, on the north side of the Arno, where (besides the lovely drive) one may see the prodigious remnants of the Etruscan architects; but my favourite visit was to the Villa Coreggi, where Lorenzo the Magnificent breathed his last, shortly after his memorable interview with Savonarola. The place lies in the wide valley of the Arno, about three miles to the north-east of Florence. Spring was at its height, and in the gardens the nightingale was singing loudly, even at midday. We were taken to the room where Lorenzo died. From the windows we saw the top of the Duomo and the Campanile, and the spires of the many churches in Florence, rising above the trees; while towards the north were the heights of Fiesole and the soft outlines of the Tuscan hills in the distance. The room contains a picture of Savonarola exhorting the sovereign. Lorenzo is represented as in the agonies of death—his hand clutching his bed-sheet. The picture is perhaps too terrible for the place; but it is very characteristic.

Before concluding this short account of my visit to Florence, let me add a short statement of personal interest to myself; illustrating also the peculiar kindness of my Italian friends and well-wishers. Signora Giglioli, a lady of literary eminence in Florence, called upon me shortly after my arrival. I was not at the hotel when she called, but she left her card, on which was written—" I do not think you can realise with what feeling of deep gratitude every Italian who has read *Self-Help* and *Character* thinks of you. Books like these were so much wanted among us."

I had the pleasure afterwards of seeing the lady, and making her friendship. I was introduced to her husband, a professor in the School of Medicine, who, by the way, was a pupil of our own Dr Huxley of London. They furnished me with an introduction to Professor Mantegazza, the author of some works of great popular interest. He showed me over the fine collection of skulls in his museum — among others, the skulls of the Etruscans — which were beautifully formed, though small and round (*Brachy-cephali*, or broad skulls), evidently showing a connection with the Greeks.

The professor, like myself, was interested in the subject of race, and was about to make a journey into Finland, for the purpose of seeing the Finns, and making photographs of the people. He was trying his hand with the apparatus, and made a photograph of me, which, as some of my friends tell me, is "villainously like." The professor, like most of his fellow-countrymen, was pleasant, agreeable, and full of intelligent conversation.

I had afterwards the pleasure of being introduced to Pasquale Villari, the author of the well-known *Life of Savonarola* and *Niccolo Machiavelli and his Times*, as well as to his charming wife, Linda Villari, daughter of an old friend of mine, Mr White, formerly Member for Brighton—showing again how small the world really is. At Baron French's, I met some peculiarly interesting people—the great Greek scholar, Marchese Ricci, Gaetano Camerota of the Educational Department, Professor Eccher; and last, not least, the Misses Horner, daughters of the late Leonard Horner of Edinburgh.

On the 27th of April, the Rev. Mr Macdougall, who knows everything that is going on about Florence, sent me a note intimating that he had a very gratifying piece of news to communicate to me, namely, that a presentation was to be offered to me by a number of Italian friends who greatly appreciated my works. This was a thing altogether unexpected ; for the kindness I had already received was ample enough reward.

But the presentation was made. It consisted of a handsome album, its cover inlaid with beautiful Florentine work, and on its front were these words :—

"Al Dottore Samuele Smiles.
"Alcuni tra i molti che in Italia sentono la gratitudine pel bene fatto dai suoi libri.

"FIRENZE, 28 *Aprile* 1879."

To this interesting inscription were affixed the signatures of Villari, Mantegazza, Giglioli, Barbera, Baron F. Reichlin, De Gubernatis, and fifteen more notable Italians. It seemed as if I must cross the Alps and come a long way from home, to have my small services in literature recognised. It was indeed a most kindly and generous act, for which I shall never cease to be grateful.

I placed in my album photographs of the King and Queen of Italy, of Garibaldi (which he signed with his crumpled hand and presented to me), of Signora Giglioli and her husband, of Cairoli, and my other honoured friends and well-wishers ; and the book shall go down to my descendants as an heirloom.

I left Florence, and went on to Bologna by the route along which Savonarola came on his first journey southward. The country was little

changed. The houses were all old, and the
Apennines were the same as ever. I took sketches
as I went along, though we were annoyed by some
English "vampires," who got into our carriage.
But that need not be dwelt upon.

.   .   .   .

One of the most interesting things in Bologna was
the University, where we found that female professors
had been ornaments of learning, almost from time
immemorial. For instance, there was Signora
Calderini, Professor of Jurisprudence in 1360, more
than five hundred years ago; and at a later date,
there was Laura Passi, whose brows are represented
surmounted with laurel, Professor of Philosophy;
Tambroni, Professor of Greek, and Manzolini, Professor of Anatomy—all learned and celebrated women.
I brought away a collection of the photographs of
these illustrious celebrities. So that what we are
now working for—the emancipation and intellectual
improvement of women—was effected by the Bolog-
nese in the days of their greatest liberty. Their
ancient motto still continues to be "Libertas."

After a visit to Padua—where women were also
celebrated for their learning in olden times; and a
second visit to Venice—always full of interest; we
went on to Verona, Milan, Bellaggio on Lake Como;
then across the country to Stresa on Lago Maggiore:
and after a few days there, home to London by Turin
and Paris. Our entire journey occupied a little over
three months.

I cannot, however, refrain from mentioning the
honour which I received a year later from His
Majesty the King of Italy, who conferred upon
me the rank of Chevalier of the Order of SS.

Maurice and Lazare. This was done in the kindest and most complimentary manner through his Minister in this country, His Excellency Count Menabrea, a gentleman of great distinction, well worthy to represent his nation. I was informed that the King had conferred upon me the honour, "as a token of His Majesty's appreciation of my very valuable works."

I may mention that, while Count Menabrea was Prime Minister, he had issued a letter to the Consuls of Italy in all countries, pointing out the valuable examples of encounter with difficulties, finally overcome by courage and perseverance, published in *Self-Help*, and requested them to furnish accounts of the lives of Italians, from the countries to which they had emigrated, in order that a similar book should be published at home, for the encouragement and benefit of Italian citizens.

In my communications with Count Menabrea relative to the above matter, I desired to be informed whether any satisfactory information had been received from the Italian Consuls, and whether anything had been done towards publishing the work which he had proposed when issuing his circular. His Excellency was pleased to say that my work, and another of merit by M. Sessona, "Volere è Potere," were still the books principally read; and that no work, such as he had proposed, had yet been published. He concluded as follows:—

"Du reste, Monsieur, vos ouvrages sont bien avenus dans mon pays où ils ont excité et excitent encore un vif intérêt. Ils appartiennent à cette saine littérature qui a pour bût le bien et l'amélioration des conditions de l'humanité, et ils sont dignes de votre belle devise: *Industria, virtus, et fortitudo.*

Moi aussi j'ai une devise anologue : *Virtus in arduis*, qui m'a servi de guide dans ma carrière, car je prétends être le fils de mes œuvres."

I hope I may be forgiven the little vanity of quoting this flattering passage.   And with this I leave my ever-memorable visit to Italy.

CHAPTER XXII

GROWING OLD

I THINK I have now nearly written out my little autobiography. After all, as I said to my friend Mr Haigh, there is not much in it. The life of a business man, or of a literary man, is not of much interest. There is no romance—no adventures—nothing of stirring moment. It is only a little bit of human life, working on from day to day, and striving to make the best of the little circle in which providence has placed it. And the time speedily arrives, when all this must come to an end; for "the night cometh when no man can work."

Still, the nature of man is to do something. My habits were always industrious, and I could never be idle. Accordingly, after our autumn tour in Scotland in 1879, during which I visited Mr Purdie at St Andrews, Dr Farquharson at Finzean in Aberdeenshire, and my dear friend Mrs Priestly at the Laggan on Speyside—I settled down for the winter; and proceeded with my little book about "Duty."

I had been so pleased with my first visit to St Andrews, that in 1880 I took a furnished house at Kinnessburn, overlooking the links, for several months; and there I invited my children and grandchildren to join me. It was a pleasant time; and with the company of neighbours, and friends, and family, the months passed healthfully and delightfully. We had many a gay time on the links, following the red-coated golf players, or by the sands on the seaside, or driving about the country. And there I finished my book, and sent the MS. to the printer. I need not say anything about its reception: *Duty* must speak for itself.

Next year (1881) I went to Homburg; for rheumatism, in this damp climate, makes sad inroads upon old joints and muscles. I took with me the notes of Mr Nasmyth's autobiography, to rewrite them and work them up into a consecutive narrative during my leisure hours. Some months before, I had received a visit from Mr and Mrs Nasmyth, when they desired me to write the biography of the inventor of the steam-hammer. I had asked for the necessary information many years before, when engaged in composing *Industrial Biography.* Mr Nasmyth had furnished me with all that he thought necessary at the time, and it was very interesting; but now that he had thought over the matter—and being an idle and yet an active man, like myself—he was of opinion that some further account of himself and his contrivances might be useful, as a guide and incentive to others. I was accordingly quite willing to help him in his project.

I desired him to write down everything that he recollected, anyhow, and then I would put it into shape. It was a matter, however, of greater labour than I had expected; far greater than this little memoir of my own life. For here, I knew all the little recollections of my own small career; but there, I had to get into the heart of the life and recollections of another and far greater man. I got the first volume of Mr Nasmyth's recollections, and took it to Homburg with me. A good deal of it was written out in almost microscopic handwriting. If anyone were to see the original book, they would recognise the labour I had in bringing the recollections and the narrative into shape. I had to give it a beginning, a middle, and an end; for it had no end. In fact, I wrote it all out, from the first page to the last.

After proceeding with the memoir to a certain extent, I went into Switzerland, to Pontresina; and after some residence there (during which, owing to the high altitude, I could not sleep), I went over the Stelvio Pass, to Innsbruck, Salzburg, Munich, and down the Rhine, homewards to London. Then I again proceeded with the book. After considering the matter, I thought that the best form in which to place it before the public was as an Autobiography. To this Mr Nasmyth eventually consented; and it so appeared.

No book could have been better received. The two leading *Quarterlies*, the *Times*, the *Athenæum*, and all the leading papers, were full of its praises. And yet, according to my ideas, the work did not succeed so well as it should have done. A previous book of mine—the *Life of George Moore*—had been reviewed in none of these important publications, and indeed it had received some rather carping and adverse notices. Yet it had been far more successful, so far as circulation went. *George Moore*, with no illustrations, went off like "hot rolls," while *James Nasmyth*, with abundant illustrations, "hung fire." The *Life of George Moore* was translated into French, German, and Italian; whereas *Nasmyth's Autobiography* was translated into none of these languages. Of course, both were republished in America.

It was only another illustration of the lottery of book publishing. One never can tell what will be the success of a book. It may be in its title, or in its matter, or in the way in which it is presented to the public. George Moore was a merchant and philanthropist; James Nasmyth was a manufacturer and inventor. Their lives were written equally well. Why did the one book succeed more than the other? I cannot tell.

But a rather knowing bookseller hinted the possible secret. He said, "If it had been published as a life *by you*, it would have been a great success; but it is by an unknown author, and you are merely its 'editor.' You see what the *Times* says—that 'Dr Smiles's work has been a light one, and that the volume is very much as it left the hands of its author.' Of course that is the opinion of the public, and that is why the book has not succeeded so well as it should have done." There may be something in this; but I still think that, notwithstanding the fact that I was the shaper and author of the book, as much as of the life of Edward, the book was properly cast in the form of an Autobiography.

I remember sending the manuscript of an article to the *Quarterly*. Mr Elwin was then editor—a most able one. He took my material, and without using anything else, he rewrote and reshaped it into an admirable contribution. I learned a great deal from Mr Elwin's treatment of my subject. I was not offended; on the contrary, I rejoiced at his throwing his own mind and heart into the theme. The article I refer to was entitled "James Watt."

I did the same with the *Scotch Naturalist*. I took up his tale, and made his case my own. I gathered together his random articles, and retold his stories afresh, and, I think, with increased interest. I imparted to them that which Edward did not possess, and which I did—some literary art; and I did the same with the *Autobiography of Nasmyth.* Soon after the appearance of the *Scotch Naturalist,* the *Scotsman* announced that Thomas Edward had prepared a supplement to his life, which would shortly be published. I heard from several publishers that they had been applied to about this continuation, but that they had not accepted it. They wished me to revise and rewrite it. But I could not undertake to do so. Indeed, I doubted the wisdom of publishing it. I thought it better, after Edward had obtained his pension, to "let well alone."

After I had got *Nasmyth's Autobiography* out of hand—finally corrected and published—I went over to France, with my wife—always a faithful companion—in order to avoid the east winds of February and March. Since my attack of brain disease some years ago, I have always spent a considerable portion of my time in travelling. Change of scene, and change of diet, with complete rest, set me up again for a new spell of work. Not that work for gain was necessary, but work for some special purpose. Besides, I had always some hobby to exercise my mind upon, even while travelling. Varieties of work recruit the springs of pleasure, and give a new zest to holiday-making. Though I was growing old, I did not feel my sense of enjoyment to diminish. "It is a poor wine," said Jeffrey, "that grows sour with age." I combined exercise with mental recreation—walked as much as I could—and reflected upon many things which presented themselves in the course of my observation.

One thing especially struck me, as it had often

done before in the course of my continental journeys
—the large number of armed men, drilled and ready
to kill with the most death-dealing instruments. At
every frontier, between one country and another,
there was a huge army watching another huge army
over the boundary line—doing nothing but drilling
and marching—eating off the head of industry, and
very likely to bring political perdition on Europe;
perhaps breeding future revolutions and national convulsions. If all this was for the protection of trade, it
was like setting so many bull-dogs to watch the door,
and to worry alike friends and customers. All these
men, in the prime of life, had been withdrawn from
the pursuits of agriculture or industry—and were waiting, armed to the teeth, for what was to happen next.
We are not much better ourselves, though our army
is recruited by volunteers, and not by forced conscrip-
tion, which tells so fearfully upon the condition of
France, Germany, and other continental nations. I
remember a story told me by Sir John Lefroy, while
Colonel at Woolwich. An Egyptian Pasha had
come to England, and made an inspection of the
Manufactory of Arms at the Arsenal. An observation was made to him respecting the beauties of the
Nile, and the extraordinary construction of the
Pyramids.

"Ah!" said the Pasha, "I wonder at you Englishmen thinking of the Pyramids. They are all humboogs! What I like in England are your Big Guns:
they are not humboogs!"

But the hobby that most influenced me during
this little excursion to France, was the subject of
Race. I had always endeavoured to detect the differences which existed between one people and another
—in their shape, figure, complexion, habits, and

customs. For instance, it was curious to see the
contrast between the population spread over the face
of England and that over the face of France. In the
one case, the residences and farm-houses are all apart,
separate from each other; while in France, the farming population are assembled in clusters of villages,
many of their dwellings being far from the fields
which they have to till and cultivate. In England,
this arose from the Anglo-Saxon's comparative indifference to society, to his self-dependence, and his
love of home-comfort; whilst in France, the cluster-
ing of the population in villages arises from their love
of society, their love of talk or converse, and the
pleasures which come from assembling together. This
has been observed by many travellers; and it all
arises from the difference of race between the one
country and the other.

But my principal object was to see something of
the Basques—perhaps the oldest people in Europe,
living upon the soil which they occupied, some say
twenty centuries before the Celts made their appearance in France. I found them at Pau, where they
are recognised by their *berret* or cap, not unlike the
lowland Scotch bonnet, while the women cover their
heads with the red hood or capulet. But these
ancient costumes are much better seen further south.

Pau contains a large colony of English. The
Hotel de France was full of them. They had an
English club; an English drag, with a post-horn; an
English fox-hunt, where the fox was let out of a bag
and hunted; English races, English polo matches,
Scotch golf, English cricket, and three English
churches. A number of the English were very
"horsey." Those who did not talk about horses,
talked about shares—Brighton and Egyptian Unified.

It seemed difficult to get rid of the London Stock Exchange. Yet Pau is a very pleasant place. The view of the Pyrenees, covered with snow, towards the south, extending all along the sky line, is very grand; some say it is unsurpassed, though it is not equal to the view of the Oberland Alps from the Münster Platz at Berne.

On the same plateau on which the Hotel de France stands, and overlooking the river Gave, is one of the most remarkable buildings in France—the historic castle in which Henry of Navarre, the Bon Roi, was born. Here is the cradle in which he was rocked, and the playthings of his youth. The castle has been subject to many changes. At one time it furnished an asylum to Calvin, Theodore Beza, and the early reformers; then it was assaulted by the Biscayans during the civil wars in Béarn, the marks of the shot fired by them being still seen on the walls of the Tour de la Monnaye; it was eventually sacked and despoiled by the Revolutionists of 1793, though the cradle of Henry IV. was preserved, another being substituted in its place. Abd-el-Kader was a prisoner in the castle in 1848; and Queen Isabella occupied it in 1869. Westward of the castle lies the park, beautifully laid out, and abounding with noble trees. It stands high above the Gave, and affords a splendid view of the peaks of the Pyrenees, which bound the distant horizon.

The weather became cold, and snow began to fall. We had left London when the birds were singing in Kensington Gardens, for the sunny south, and the further south we went, the colder it grew. We left Pau and went by rail along the line of country so much celebrated in Napier's *History of the Peninsular War*—by Orthez, so well known for its fierce fight; to the Bidassoa, which Wellington crossed in spite of the heavy forces arrayed against him, and then to Bayonne, below which he crossed the Adour—a memorable instance of his intrepidity and force of character. At Bayonne, we landed amidst a fierce snowstorm. In spite of it, we made our way at once to Biarritz, where we found peace and quiet at the Hotel d'Angleterre.

When the weather had subsided, we found Biarritz a charming seaside place. Wonderful walks by the shore, north and south; the long Atlantic waves coming in, even in the quietest weather, ten or twelve feet high, and dashing themselves as spray on the sands. The south coast, by the Chemin de la Côte Basque, was the favourite walk. The hills of Spain were seen, beyond the bay, covered with snow, and the rocky clefts, over which the waves dashed, were full of brightness. Summer seemed to have come while we remained here—from the 10th to the 24th of March.

The pleasantest excursion we made while at Biarritz, was to St Jean de Luz, a Basque town about ten miles to the south. It lies at the mouth of the Nivelle, where it falls into a beautiful bay. Here we saw the Basque race in perfection—Basque men, women, and children. They are a fine-looking people—though rather small; but they are sturdy, agile, and vigorous—dark-haired and dark-eyed— very like the remnants of the same race still found in Wales. In Spain, where they are very numerous, they were known as the Iberians; in Wales, as the Silurians. They are supposed to number about 840,000 people, north and south of the Pyrenees.

There is a wonderful old Basque church at St Jean de Luz—a large hall-like apartment, without aisles, and having wooden galleries running round three sides. The sanctuary is up a steep flight of steps, and occupied by three altars. Notwithstanding the devotion of the Basques, they are still believers in witchcraft and the evil eye. The Basque "brownie" is equivalent to the Devonshire "werewoman." Christianity has not yet been able to uproot the old pagan superstitions. But I cannot here enter into the subject of the special race to which the Basque people belong. We left Biarritz for Paris, crossed the Channel, and reached home by the beginning of April.

Three months later, on the 4th of July, I started for a short tour in Ireland, accompanied by my young friend, Count Giuseppe Zoppola. My friend was amazed at the wreckage of the empty houses in Dublin. Wherever a house was empty, every window was smashed — a curious indication of the mischievousness of Dublin boys. We put up at the Shelburne—the cleanest hotel in the city. We went round and saw the renovations made in the Cathedrals of St Patrick and Christ Church—the one made by the greatest brewer in Ireland, the other by the greatest manufacturer of ardent spirits. Wonderful, what porter and whisky have done for Dublin! We saw the splendid buildings by the Liffey—the Bank of Ireland, once the Irish Parliament House, the Custom House, now almost disused, the Exchange, and the Four Courts—all splendid buildings. Then we went to Phœnix Park, and passed the spot, marked with a cross, where Lord Frederick Cavendish and Mr Burke had been so foully murdered. A sad sight! the driver of our car passed it with a groan.

I observe a great difference amongst the people

generally, since my first visit to the south of Ireland some forty years ago. There were then a great many more beggars about the cities, towns, and villages than now. The people seemed to be very poor. And yet they were apparently much gayer. The cardrivers, ragged though they might be, were full of wit and humour. Now, though well dressed, and much better off, they were only surly. At the Phœnix Park, the Dublin garrison were under review. It was a fine sight, the united bands playing the forces past the Irish Commander-in-chief, the picturesque city lying beyond the green sward along the Liffey, and the Wicklow Mountains in the distance. The cardrivers stood apart and whispered together. There seemed to be no rejoicing in their hearts at the sight. After seeing all that was to be seen in Dublin—the museums, which are very fine, and the Picture Gallery, which contains some excellent specimens of ancient and modern art—we set out for Galway and Connemara.

The country looked very smiling and prosperous as we went along—past Maynooth and through the southern parts of the counties of Meath and West-meath, where the pasture land is the richest in Great Britain. We crossed the Shannon at Athlone, the sight of which brought to mind the contest at that place between the French and Irish forces under the command of St Ruth, and the English and Dutch under the command of General Ginckel, less than two hundred years ago. The place was carried after a furious assault, and the French and Irish retreated to Aughrim, where they were defeated principally by the French Huguenots, and driven southward towards Limerick. There were kings on both sides—James II. and the Catholics on the one, and William III.

and the Protestants on the other. Will these days
ever return?

At Athlone, three dark-coated gentlemen got into
our carriage. There seemed to have been a function
or conference going on at the place, as many of the
same cloth were seen along the platform. Our
neighbours brought an ill odour with them. One
of them had been imbibing liberally of the "wine of
the country," and was disposed to speak loudly to
his friends. The others were very quiet and
peaceable.

The soil became poorer and thinner, large stones
and rocks appearing at intervals; then the sea came
in sight, and at length we reached Galway amidst a
torrent of rain. Rain is no doubt the cause of the
greenness of Ireland—Green Erin—always open to
the rain clouds of the Atlantic. I need not say much
of Galway. It is a decaying town. It is too far
out of the reach of traffic and commerce. Its flour
mills are silent, for the corn comes ready ground from
America; its fisheries are neglected; and nothing is
done to encourage new industries. While at Galway
I read a speech of Mr Parnell, delivered after the
opening of the Exhibition at Cork. He urged the
investment of capital for the employment of native
labour—a most excellent subject truly.* But who
will invest capital in a country where property, the
result of industry, is not secure?

There is plenty of capital in Ireland as well as
England; and wherever there is a likelihood of a
remunerative return, it is readily invested. Mr
Fawcett, in his *Political Economy*, points out that

* I have dwelt upon this subject in *Men of Invention and Industry*,
pp. 256-323. The book was written, in some measure, from the result
of this visit to Ireland.

nowhere can capital be had if it cannot be had from England. But see what is done for the investment of English capital in Ireland. An English company proposed to take some old deserted buildings on the river Corrib, for the purpose of establishing a woollen manufactory. The splendid supply of water power was their first consideration, and the cheap supply of labour was the second. The projectors were of opinion that what the Scotch do at Hawick and Galashiels—working up their own wool on the spot, into trouserings and blanketings—might be equally done in the West of Ireland. But on inquiry of the proprietors of the disused buildings, they were informed that the sum required for ground rent was £500 per annum. Of course, the idea was preposterous; the projectors went elsewhere with their capital, and the buildings continue tumbling to ruin.

A little further up the river is a large space enclosed by a square stone wall. The space was enclosed for the purpose of burning seaweed in order to make iodine; but why erected so far away from the sea, no one knew. The seaweed had to be carried up there through the canal, as well as the coal. At all events, the speculation stopped with the building of the wall, and no seaweed has ever been burnt there.

I went to the Court-House at Galway, where the Commissioners were then sitting for the purpose of reducing the landlords' rents under the recent Land Act. The farmers seemed very poor people, and were, for the most part, cultivators of small holdings at moderate rents. Will the reduction do them any good? We must hope so. Even if the land were their own, without capital it is probable that they could not make more than a slender living out of it.

Rent has not much to do with alleged distress. The
Irish people pay more for whisky than for rent. The
rental of agricultural land in Ireland, in 1881, was
estimated at £11,518,392; whereas the amount
spent in intoxicating liquors was £13,823,102; or
£2,304,710 more in drink than in rent.* The
amount paid to tenants for tenant right has much
more influence upon the farmers' condition than the
amount paid to the landlords for rent. Sometimes
the amount of tenant right is enormous; but no one
proposes to alter it.

And yet the labourers' condition in Ireland must
be improving. When Inglis visited the country in
1834, he said that the labourer considered himself
fortunate in having employment at sixpence per day
throughout the year. But this wage must be now
more than quadrupled. You cannot get labourers to
work in the country for twelve shillings a week. In
Dublin they won't work for less than five shillings a
day. If they can get it, so much the better. It
would be a great thing to be accomplished, if the
Irish people could be induced to rely more upon
their own efforts, rather than on money raised
from the taxpayers, or on reductions of rent
squeezed, no matter by what means, from the
landlords.

No doubt there are many excuses for the poor
people of Ireland. They have been too much accustomed to rely upon other people's help, and too little
upon their own industry. Their clergy, who have so
great an influence over them, ought to enjoin upon
them the virtues of self-reliance, prudence, and fore-
sight; because, after all, the prosperity of a people
must depend eventually upon individual exertion.

* *Times*, 29th March 1881.

No idle people were ever prosperous, and no
industrious people were ever poor. As Bishop
Berkeley said long ago, "The wealth of a country
bears proportion to the skill and industry of its
inhabitants."

While at Galway, I had frequent interviews with
the last remnant of one of the Thirteen Tribes who
settled there in the thirteenth century. He was a
baronet, and his father had formerly represented the
county. His patrimony had been squandered, and
he was now as poor as his tenantry. Still he was
"hail fellow, well met," with everybody; and to us, as
strangers, he was very kind. He took us to his
Castle on the river Corrib; and a fine old ivy-covered
place it is—venerable, picturesque, and admirably
situated. There are some splendid old trees about
the grounds; yet everything has the look of neglect.
The house inside has been for the most part stripped
of its finest furniture. The arras, which used to
decorate the staircase, has been removed and sold.
It is an unhappy position for the inheritor of this
beautiful place—his capital has been squandered by
his predecessors, and he can do but little to improve
the condition of his tenantry. There is some fine
marble on the estate, but for lack of capital it cannot
be properly worked and brought to market. We
were taken to see the village connected with the
estate. But it was a sad sight. Most of the houses
were in ruins; some had been demolished; for a large
number of the tenantry had emigrated.

We intended to proceed to the island of Aran at
the entrance of Galway Bay, to see the wonderful
remains of the ancient building there, most probably
the work of some extinct race; but a tremendous
storm set in from the south-west, and the little

pleasure-steamer did not start. We took the opportunity, however, of going up Lough Corrib, to see the remains of the once famous Abbey of Cong; the sail up the lough is very pleasant; the islands and foreground varying from time to time, while the lofty hills of Connaught bound the distance. Numerous castles, or ruins of castles, are seen on either side; but there is a great want of wood. The numerous islands which we pass are woodless; the Irish proprietors forgetting that trees grow while we sleep, and that a not unimportant revenue can be obtained from the growth of wood. At the top of the lough we reached the landing-place at Ashford, near the fine country seat of Lord Ardilaun, sur-rounded by woods. We were told on board the boat, that the owner had been giving employment to several thousand workmen in the improvements of his estate; but when his agent was murdered a few years ago, and his body thrown into Lough Mask, he paid off the workmen, and left the place: very much to the dismay of the poor working people of the neighbourhood.

The principal object at Cong, about a mile from the landing-place, is the old Norman Abbey, now in ruins. The last native king of Ireland, Roderick O'Conor, is said to have died here in the twelfth century. The Abbey of Cong was formerly noted for its great riches; and the remaining buildings, though in ruin, furnish evidence of the artistic beauty with which it was decorated. What remains, however, is now merely a shell—the best view of the ornate windows being obtained from the gardens, which are beautifully laid out. The river which joins Lough Mask to Lough Corrib runs close behind; and the monks had a method of making the salmon catch themselves in the traps which they set under the bridge—all for the good of the monastery.

In the evening, we took a long walk towards Lough Mask. The face of the country was very singular. It was covered for miles with dense blocks of carboniferous limestone, apparently serrated together, without a scrap of vegetation. Under these blocks, the river between the two Loughs runs underground; only emerging at intervals. An attempt was made during the Starvation Crisis in Ireland to make a canal between Lough Corrib and Lough Mask: but though much employment was given to the poor people, the canal—the marks of which still stand—could never hold water, and it was eventually abandoned. The constructors probably did not know the use of puddling. What Brindley said would have been applicable—"Puddle it, again and again."

From the high ground on Blake Hill, we enjoyed the beautiful view of Lough Corrib and Lough Mask —the latter of hateful memory. The mountainous group round the western shores of Lough Mask looked very grand in the evening twilight. It was sad to think of the murderous scenes which had recently taken place in so quiet and apparently peaceful a place. Not far off was the site of a great battle— that of Southern Moytura, or Matura Cong—where the ancient Firbolgs met the Tuatha de Dananns, and after four days' fierce fighting, achieved a victory. Fighting seems to have been the constant occupation of the ancient Irish, long before the invasion of Strongbow.

We might have stayed longer at Cong, but for the inn, which was a hideous place. It was like all the other inns in the Connemara district—thoroughly incomplete — bad food, bad beds, bad everything. Moths, and the wings of moths, abounded everywhere. We found the same evidences of inaccuracy, inattention, and incompleteness, in the course of our entire journey. Little is done to attract and retain visitors. Hence visitors do not come to enjoy the beautiful scenery of Connemara ; and if they do come, they go away as speedily as possible.

I need not cite my further experiences in the West. We went from Galway to Recess on Lough Glendalough — then by the Twelve Pins, past Mr Mitchell Henry's new Castle of Kylemore, to Letterfrack—where we found letters from home. We next travelled along Killary Harbour—which very much resembles a Norwegian fiord, running far inland—to Leenane ; then through the inland country, by the banks of the river Erriff—where the salmon fishers were busily at work—to Westport on Clew Bay with its thousand islands. From Westport to Ballina by railway, and from Ballina to Sligo by an outside car. At Sligo we found some pleasant friends, with whom we spent a happy time, then across Ulster to Belfast, where we found comfort and hospitality. We were now amongst a new race—where industry, self-reliance, and energy, are regarded as among the essential elements of manhood. But I have already given a full enough account of the self-help of the people of Belfast in my little book on *Men of Invention and Industry.*

From Belfast I proceeded, with my friend Zoppola, by Larne and Stranraer, to the northern part of Cumberland, for the purpose of visiting my dear friend Mrs Moore at Whitehall. We were accompanied from Carlisle by my wife, who enjoyed the visit as much as we all did. Mrs Moore had been pleasantly associated with me in the preparation of the life of her revered husband; and I think the volume in which that life has been embodied is likely to do some little amount of good in this world, by showing that sympathy and kindness are of far greater importance than money-making and selfish accumulations. After a few days at Whitehall, during which we saw the Border towers and scenery of the neighbourhood, we proceeded to Melrose, Edinburgh, and Loch Awe; then we returned to Dunkeld, from which I made my visit to the porter-astronomer of Coupar-Angus. My tour was not yet ended, for at York my wife went on to London, while I journeyed back to Saltburn-on-the-sea, for the purpose of visiting Mrs Cooke, the widow of the famous astronomical instrument maker of Buckingham Street, York. After I had accomplished that object, I proceeded across the country to Bangor, North Wales, where I had the pleasure of several interviews with another self-taught astronomer, John Jones, the slate-counter at Penrhyn Quay. But all that history I have recounted elsewhere, and need not dwell upon it here.

When I reached home, I proceeded with the collecting, revising, and writing out of my history of a few men of invention and industry; as a sort of supplemental volume to the accounts I had already published in *Industrial Biography* and *Lives of the Engineers*. I had proceeded pretty far by the beginning of 1884, when, one morning, on lifting up a picture to hang upon the wall, I felt my mouth full of blood. What? was this the foreshadowing of the end? I sent for my friend Dr Parr, and he examined me. My lungs were sound. There were no tubercles or signs of them there. But my pulse was bounding, and it seemed that I was too full of blood. I was put upon low diet, and I gradually recovered my strength. I laid my books and writing to one side, and took another little holiday. I went over to Belfast again, and obtained from my friend Mr Harland the history of his important and significant life for my forthcoming book; and after I had accomplished this purpose, I proceeded to Edinburgh to take part in the Tercentenary Festival of the University, which was celebrated in April of that year. I was kindly invited by Sir George Harrison, the Lord Provost, to reside with him and partake of his hospitality during my stay in the city. But I desired to be as free from excitement as possible, and preferred to live in a hotel where I was free to come and go, or to rest according to inclination.

Everything went off in the most perfect manner during the celebration of the Tercentenary. The reception of guests at the museum, followed by the students' torchlight march; the procession of the professors, graduates, and distinguished guests to St Giles' Cathedral, and the sermon there, followed by the lunch at the University new buildings; the assemblage of distinguished foreigners, and the granting of degrees to them, followed by the grand banquet at the Drill Hall; the numerous receptions by the advocates, the Royal Scottish Academy, and the students; winding up on the fourth day of the celebration with a splendid exhibition of fireworks—during the whole course of which the conduct of the assembled multitude was most admirable—all went off in perfect order.

On returning home, I finished my book, and sent the manuscript to the printers. Being still full of

my old fad about Race, I desired to pay a visit to
the western coast of Norway, to see the country from
which the piratical Vikings came in ancient times
—men who had crossed the sea in open boats and
made raids upon all parts of the coast of Great
Britain and Ireland. I had visited Christiania and
the Miösen Lake in the south many years before,
after my excursion to the North Frisian Islands;
but now I wished to visit the western coast of
Norway, and observe some of the extensive fiords
which penetrate inland from the sea, sometimes for
a hundred miles or more.

I had the pleasure of being accompanied by my
friends, Dr and Mrs Parr—both delightful companions, full of conversation and of anecdotal recollections, the result of close and intelligent observation
of character. We left Hull late on the night of the
31st of July 1884 by the *Hero*, and, after a pleasant
voyage, reached the islands off the coast of Norway
early on the morning of the 3rd of August. We
first touched at Alesund, and then steamed northward
between the islands and the mainland. Out at sea,
we had met some rough weather, but inland we were
protected from the ocean and steamed quietly along.
On the land side we observed the serrated hills crested
with snow. Little bits of land, covered with soil
washed down from the mountains, afforded but little
space for cultivation; but wherever there was a patch
of land, there was a cottage upon it, and the space
was turned to use. Fishermen's boats and little
vessels were seen lying in the creeks; for the people
are fishermen as well as farmers—the women mostly
staying at home, while the men live by the sea. The
mountains, as they came in sight as we steamed
further along, looked peaked, and jagged, and

ragged. I do not wonder that the old Norsemen, when they found themselves possessors of a rock-bound country incapable of cultivation or extension, should have desired to leave it for a land more responsive to their industry.

Our steamer stopped at the little town of Molde, opposite the entrance to the Romsdal Fjord. We saw the furrowed snow-covered peaks of the mountains in the distance; but we were not allowed to land. A telegram had been received from England, to the effect that cholera had broken out; it proved to be a mere scare, though some bad cases of British cholera had occurred at a town in Lancashire. The harbour master at Molde prohibited anyone leaving the vessel; so that we were perforce under the necessity of going forward to Trondhjem, and leaving our trip up the Romsdal Fjord to some future period. The voyage to Trondhjem was nevertheless full of interest. We steamed back through the Molde Fjord, and northward through the Jul Sound—*sound* or *sund* being one of the numerous names which we have derived from the Scandinavian. The mist hung low upon the mountains, under the snow. We passed light-houses, and bits of farms, washed at foot by the sea. The country looked wild, bleak, and in-hospitable. The jagged rocks stood up in some places in long ridges—washed bare by the constantly falling rains from the west. Sometimes scarcely a house was to be seen. In other places, if there was a bit of land washed down from the adjoining hills, there was a dwelling or two, but they seemed only temporary, built of wood, and not unlike an enlarged cigar-box. In one place, we observed three cows on a height, but no sheep were to be seen. There was

no corn in the fields. In fact, there were no fields—
only rock, with occasional patches of scrub and bits
of grass. No wonder the old Norsemen left this
sterile country.

The next town we reached was Christiansand, a
very busy fishing place, situated on four promontories
of rocky islands. Little steamers were flying between
the different islands. Immense quantities of fish
were laid drying upon the rocks. When the split
fish, or klipfish, had been dried, they were built up
into stacks. These are taken, for the most part, to
Spain and other Catholic countries. Men and women
were equally at work; but it was pleasant to see
that home was not neglected, for, as we passed the
windows, we observed that they were crowded with
flowers in bloom.

We went on again, past islands and rocky cliffs
swept by the waves—past Smölen and Hitteren—
and then we entered the Trondhjem Fjord. The
scenery about here is not very interesting. But one
of the curious things to be seen, is the boats scudding
across the fiord, sometimes impelled by sail, sometimes by oars, and sometimes by both. Many of the
boats were *manned* by women only. They seemed
as deft with the oar as the sail. And the curious
thing was, that these boats were built in the style of
the old Viking war-boat. The tradition of boat
building had lasted for more than eight hundred
years. When the boat was enlarged to the size of
a ship, it was impelled by a large square sail amid-
ships. But the oar was still used, especially in
steering—on the steerboard or starboard side.

On reaching Trondhjem, we were not allowed to
land until we had been examined and passed by the
sanitary doctor of the port. We had to remain on

board all night; and next morning, a dapper little
man, the Trondhjem surgeon, mounted the ship's
side, and had us all mustered and examined. There
was nothing wrong; we were all well, with no sick on
board; so at last we were permitted to land on the
shores of Gamle Norge.

Trondhjem is a very quiet little town or city.
And yet it is the capital of Mid-Norway. At one
time it must have been a place of great importance,
for it was from this place that some of the most
formidable piratical expeditions sailed for the shores
of great Britain and Normandy. It was here that
the *Long Serpent* was launched on the Nidd, and set
sail for England, with other war-galleys, full of
Bareserks. Trondhjem was the principal station of
King Olaf Trygvesson, the famous sea-warrior, who
built and launched his ships here, and set forth on
his famous expeditions.

But there is nothing of the piratical character
about the Norwegians of the present day. They are
quiet, peaceful, and honest. As we landed, we
observed the tallness and fine figures of the men—
generally much better-looking than the women. They
were, for the most part, fair-haired, with blue or light
grey eyes; though the Professor of Antiquities at
Christiania informed me that two-thirds of the
Norwegians were fair, and one-third dark. The
darker people, however, must inhabit the inland
parts of the country, as nearly all we saw were fair-
haired and blue-eyed.

We went to see the cathedral, which is in course
of restoration. It seems to have fallen for the most
part to ruins; but now there is every probability of
its being restored to its original splendid condition—
the work being liberally helped by the State. The

structure seems to be a combination of Norman and
early English. More than half of the whole building
has already been restored. More than half the
houses in the city are built of wood, so that every
precaution is taken to keep the fire brigade in a state
of perfect efficiency. Great fires are, however, still
common in the place—the great fire of 1858 having
destroyed 60 houses, and rendered about 1000 people
homeless.

After seeing all that was to be seen at Trondhjem, we took a passage by the steamboat for
Bergen, and set out the same night at twelve o'clock.
We passed the same line of coast that we had already
seen, and remained two nights on board. At Alesund,
we passed the place from which Rolf the Ganger
had set out for the conquest of Normandy, where
his castle is now in ruins. We went sometimes
inside the islands which surround the west coast of
Norway, and sometimes through the open sea,
though there were usually long crests of rocks far
out, over which the waves were wildly beating themselves into spray.

We stopped at Floro to take in some cargo of fish,
where we were reminded of the likeness of the men
to our people at home. The fishermen very much
resembled those at Peterhead, Fraserburgh, and
Gamrie, in Aberdeenshire and Banffshire. The
young women were the same, only in the one case
they were Pigs (or pigge) and in the other Lassies.
It seems to me that the English are more like the
Frisians and Danes; and that the Lowland Scotch,
the Cumbrians, and Northumbrians, are more like
the Norwegians. At the table d'hôte on the steamer,
I sat opposite a gentleman who was the very picture
of the late George Stephenson, the engineer.

At breakfast, in the cabin, as well as elsewhere, we had *flad-brod*, similar to the oatmeal cakes introduced into Yorkshire and other counties in England by the old Northmen. In short, there are numerous resemblances between the Norwegians and Eastern English and Scots—their manners and customs—their maritime instincts and love of the sea—their steadiness, orderliness, and courage—all of which I cannot particularise here, though I hope to do so in my long-contemplated work on Race. But will that ever be written? At present it seems to me to resemble that of the hero of Bulwer's Caxtons, who contemplated a Great Work, "The History of Human Error," which was never written, or at least never finished.

We landed in Bergen, a fishing town, very picturesquely situated. The principal street along the harbour is called the Strand, just as our street along the shore of the Thames in London is called by the same name; and the Danes or Northmen had their principal church on the north side of the Thames in the Strand (St Clement Danes), and on the south their principal church was St Olave's, in Tooley Street—or St Olave's Street. The population here is very mixed, not so pure as at Trondhjem. These are both fair and dark, and not so tall and well-formed; but this is the case in most commercial towns.

After staying a night at Bergen, at a not very agreeable hotel—though it was said to be the best in the place—we started by steamer for the Hardanger Fjord. The morning was very fine. The sun was out; the view of the boats and ships, with their background of mountains, looked large and grand. We were preceded down the Byfjord by a great steamer bound for England. Though Bergen is surrounded by greenery—being originally called Björgvin, from "the pasture between the mountains"—the vegetation rapidly disappeared as we emerged from the land-locked bay. Then we came to bare, striated rocks, with not a vestige of vegetation. Passing islands without number, we reached the Björne Fjord, and passed through a magnificent panorama. Here trees and vegetation were abundant. Indeed, this fiord seemed to me, under the morning sun, to present a combination of the beauties of Loch Lomond and the Lake of Como. As we passed along, the names of places reminded us of those at home. The lighthouses on the points of land were Fyrness (Furness). There was Lunden; not far off was Selby; and Lerwick, near the entrance to the Hardanger Fjord. This inlet of the sea, which runs more than 100 miles inland, consists of many fiords, each called by its special name. But I need not commemorate them here. The nautical instincts seem to have accompanied the Norwegian people everywhere. At the little hamlet of Rosendal, the inhabitants, though they were but peasants, had five beautifully modelled yachts and schooners on the stocks, of from 80 to 150 tons burthen—some of them nearly ready for launching. In the distance, amongst the trees, was the seat of Baron Rosenkrantz, one of the two last remaining barons in Norway; for titles of nobility were abolished in 1821.

The further we went, the loftier the mountains became. We went in and out, sometimes under precipices, at other times along the fertile undulating sward, shut in by some lowering mountain near at hand. We saw the water shooting from the hill-tops in falls, some of them very fine. For the Folgefond is always covered with its snow-mantle; this great mass of snow, and ice, and glaciers, covering about 150 square English miles; during the summer it is constantly sending down its melted waters to the valleys below. We passed on—the scenery constantly varying—until we at length reached the little hamlet of Utne, situated near the confluence of four fiords, radiating to the four points of the compass, and surrounded by the most beautiful mountain scenery.

We were fortunate in getting accommodation at the little inn, and there we remained for about a week. The landlady could not speak English, and we could not speak Norwegian; but we very soon succeeded in finding an interpreter; for most of the Norwegian visitors at the little inn could speak English; some of them perfectly. The landlady was a widow; and though old, she managed her house perfectly. Her name was Thorburn—spelt Thorbjorn—a well-known Border Scottish name.* She was, indeed, very like some of my own immediate relations. She was not, however, called by her own name, but was known in the neighbourhood as Mother Utne; and a fine old mother she was.

The house was of a rather primitive character. It was built of wood, like most of the Norwegian houses. The outer lobby, or hall, was pretty wide and spacious; its windows overlooked the fiord and the mountains on the further side; while it was set round about with forms for the visitors. Doors opened from the hall into the dining or eating-room on the right hand, into the kitchen in the back centre, and into the drawing-room on the left. In the middle of the

* There are also Thorburns in Banffshire and Wigtonshire—places where the Northmen settled.

hall was a winding wooden staircase leading to the
bedrooms above. Everything was primitive, clean,
neat, and comfortable. There was plenty of light,
and plenty of air. The food was good, though not
luxurious. Everything was simple and unpretending.
Old Mother Utne was dressed in the costume of the
Hardanger Fjord—a red bodice round her waist, and
a large winged white cap on her head—which, by
the way, the Norse people imported into Normandy,
where the like head-gear still exists. The price
charged for our accommodation was unusually
moderate.

It happened that most of the visitors staying at
the little inn were from Bergen. They were mostly
professors, teachers in the higher schools, and therefore educated people. The daughter of the Burgo-
master of Bergen was there, as well as the President
or Speaker of the Municipal Council. They could,
nearly all of them, speak English; and some of the
ladies sang and played admirably. We had therefore
fallen by accident into a very pleasant place; and
soon felt ourselves quite at home. There was plenty
of pleasant walking in the neighbourhood; the walk to
the summit of the lofty hill behind Utne commanding splendid views of the surrounding waters and
mountains. There was also boating on the fiord close
at hand; and an occasional excursion up the Sor
Fjord, with its surrounding majestic scenery. We
had then distant views of the Folgefond and its vast
snow-covered crest. The visit we paid to Ullensvang,
and the Protestant pastor there, was very pleasant.

As we passed Kinservik, on our way to Ullensvang,
the place was pointed out where the Scotch ships used
to come for timber—Scotland, in past times, being
very bare of wood. The sailors emptied out their

ballast before taking in their return cargo; and the ballast now forms a ridge of stone which passing ships have to avoid. The place is called Skotto-fluen, or Scottish shoal. The fare paid to our boatmen on these occasions was very moderate; and when a little present was made over the fare, the boatmen shook hands with us all round.

Politics exist in Norway as well as England. We found there were democrats as well as conservatives in Mother Utne's party. The democrats have now the control, and are alleged by the conservatives to be merely a mob government. One conservative lady, with whom we got into conversation, told us that the democrats were only the Torske, or Codfish people. Having made some inquiry about the Torskes from a supposed neutral person, he told me that the democrats repudiated the name; and they were, he believed—though occasionally mistaken —working for the good of the people.

There was one circumstance related to me by the Librarian of the Bergen Free Library, which I thought of much interest. She told me that the Municipal Government of Bergen — following the example of Gottenburg and Christiania—had resolved to give no further licenses to drinking shops, because of the increasing vice of drunkenness; but that they had permitted a company of known and respectable men to take possession of the public houses, and keep them under strict control. This number was limited, and strict regulations were laid down for their guidance. The sale of spirits was to be entirely prohibited on Sundays and Saints' days, and also on Saturdays and the eves of festivals, after 5 P.M. The laws relating to the sale of wine and beer were much less stringent.

The company was formed; the capital necessary to purchase the public houses was subscribed; and operations began a few years ago. It was arranged between the company and the municipality that whatever profit was made, over and above the 5 per cent. on their capital, should be handed over to the town for the purpose of promoting public improvements. The results have been perfectly satisfactory. Not only have the profits been such as to pay the 5 per cent. interest on the capital, but a large surplus has been annually handed over to the municipality. This has been expended in maintaining the Free Library and the Museum, and Musical Bands which play at certain hours, and in laying out public grounds and parks for the recreation of the public. Why should not this admirable example be followed elsewhere?

We left this pleasant place with regret, after many hand-shakings, congratulations, and good wishes. We went down the Hardanger Fjord, and passed the villages, and falls, and rocks, and mountains, which we had seen on our way up. After a few days in Bergen, we started for Hull, and steamed south, partly amongst the islands, to Stavanger. Here a number of emigrants came on board. They were mostly young persons, and their mothers and sisters stood along the shore, weeping and sobbing. But it was as it had been for a thousand years: the youth must go to some more productive regions—for the world was still but half peopled. Before, young men from Norway had gone as pirates; now they went as honest emigrants—willing to work their way with energy and industry. As the ship left the shore, there was a "hip! hip! hurrah" from those on board —but what of those poor mothers and sisters left on shore? During the evening, after we were well out to sea, the young Norwegians sang Folk-songs and danced national dances until a comparatively late hour. After a pleasant voyage, we reached Hull, in the midst of a yacht-race; and could scarcely land because of the crowd which lined the pier and the shores of the Humber.

In the following November, my little book entitled *Men of Invention and Industry* was published. It had a large sale, and was well received by the press. So far as I am concerned, reviews of my books have been generally fair. Reviewers have praised my efforts to entertain and instruct the public, quite as much as they deserve. This I can say with justness and fairness; because the reviewers know as little of me personally as I know of them. They say their say about my works, and I am perfectly content. The book was translated into Italian and Dutch; perhaps into other languages, but of these I cannot tell. Of course it was republished in the United States. I sent over advance sheets to Harper & Co., New York, as a "protection," they told me, against a piratical publisher. The Harpers used to give me a sum for my advance sheets, but they do this no longer. They publish my books in their Franklin Square Library, and sell them for some 6d. or 7d. Of course they can give me no allowance out of this; but when the book is published at a dollar, they send me a trifle of the profit.*

The reason of this is, that a man with a Highland name—doubtless descended from some old Highland Cateran—has set up an enormous piratical establish-

* In justice to Messrs Harpers, a statement of their payments to Dr Smiles is given at the end of this chapter, on page 382.

ment in New York. He pounces upon all the best books that issue from the English press, and publishes them without any communication with the authors, and, of course, without any remuneration for their labours. The freebooter in question has, in this way, established one of the largest publishing houses in America, and is said to be making an immense fortune out of the brains of English authors. The Harpers had treated me very fairly, considering the law of their country, which protects book piracy as well as other industries. I have no doubt that the best of the American publishers are willing to secure an alteration in the law, and to give some fair consideration for the brain work of English authors; as the legislatures of France, Italy, and Germany already do. The fault is not so much in the American publishers, as in the American people and their representatives in the legislature.* Charles Dickens suffered far more than I have done. In one of his letters he said, " I have no hope of the States doing justice in this dishonest respect, and therefore do not expect to overtake these fellows, but we may cry 'Stop, thief!' nevertheless, especially as they wince and smart under it." I believe, however, that the American people will yet wipe out this blot from their flag; and follow the example of England and the principal continental governments, in securing a limited copyright to foreign authors.

But authors and publishers are treated almost as badly at home. In 1844, Mr Murray brought under my notice the large borrowings made from my works by a Christian Society, supported by public donations and subscriptions. The Church Catechism enjoins us "to keep our hands from picking and stealing . . .

* The law of 1891, such as it is, had not then been passed.—ED.

not to covet nor desire another man's goods, but to learn and labour truly to get our own living." But what can be said of a society which seizes the books belonging to other people, boils them down, and undersells the original owners. Mr Murray showed me a volume entitled *The Prayer Book and Commentary*, taken largely from the Bishop of Derry's *Bampton Lectures* (1876), on "The Witness of the Psalms to Christ and Christianity." This book had been boiled down by the Society in question, and sold at a very low price. Whole pages had been taken verbatim, in most places, without acknowledgement; in fact, the materials and body of the cheap book had been provided by the brain work of the original author. This cannot be Christian, for it is not honest. It may be well to give "pure literature" to the people, but is it necessary that they should steal it? Nor is this the way to teach "the people" honesty; but, on the contrary, dishonesty, even though the literature be "pure." The practice reminds one of the broom-seller who sold his brooms for next to nothing, because he stole them "ready-made."

As regards myself, Mr Murray showed me two volumes issued by the same society, which contained large extracts from my works, without which, indeed, these volumes could not have been published. One of these contained the lives of James Watt and George Stephenson, from my *Lives of the Engineers*; Henry Maudslay and Joseph Clement, from my *Industrial Biography*; and James Nasmyth, from the *Autobiography*, which I recently edited and published. It is true that this volume of boiled-down biographies is very badly done, and contains too much high-flown language. But the other volume, published by the same society, is very ably done, by a thoroughly practised writer. It contained George Stephenson *again* (twice boiled down by the same society in one year), Thomas Telford, from my *Lives of the Engineers*, and Thomas Edward, from my *Life of the Scotch Naturalist.*

In the first book, the author or editor only incidentally refers to me as "almost the only astronomer who has examined a zone of these heavens"— why this ridiculous statement when it refers merely to engineering and invention?—and further on, he adds of his own work, "He has been obliged to use the material that lay readiest to his hand." Of course! my books were the readiest, and with this help and a little elbow-grease, he could readily boil them down, to enable the society to undersell me. In the case of the second volume, the author cites me often by name, and pays me many compliments, for which I thank him; but I am sorry that a writer of his powers should condescend to help a society which "steals its brooms ready-made."

Mr Murray desired me to insert a protest against this method of dealing with other people's property, in the *Times* and the *Athenæum;* but I had no wish to enter into a controversy on the subject. I must have travelled several thousands of miles—from Leeds to Newcastle, again and again—from London to North Wales—to Eskdale in Scotland—to Birmingham, Cornwall, Banff, and many other places, to collect the materials for my works; and I spent many years in searching numerous documents, and writing them out for publication; and now this society takes possession of the whole, "uses the material that lies readiest to its hand," boils it down,

and undersells me by means of public subscriptions!
I do not know what other people may think about
this practice, but honest authors and honest
publishers cannot fail to regard this system of
purloining and underselling as a public nuisance,
which ought to be abated.

*Sums paid by Messrs Harpers to Dr Smiles for their
editions of his books.*

1867. *The Huguenots*		£100
1868. *Lives of the Stephensons*		100
1871. *Character*		100
1871. *Boy's Travel round the World* . . .		30
1873. *Huguenots after the Revocation* . . .		25
1873. *Self-Help.* New edition . . .		15
1875. *Thrift*		100
1876-7. *Scotch Naturalist*		100
1879. *Robert Dick*		200
1887. *Life and Labour*		50

Royalties.

1880. *Duty*, 10 per cent.
1882. *James Nasmyth*, 10 per cent.
1884. *Men of Invention and Industry*, 10 per cent.
1894. *Josiah Wedgwood*, 10 per cent.
1891. *Jasmin*, 10 per cent., later 12½ per cent.

CHAPTER XXIII

APPRECIATION FROM FOREIGNERS

23rd December 1885. — This day I enter my seventy-fourth birthday. I was reminded of this at last Sunday's service — the 20th morning of the month. "The days of man are but as grass: for he flourisheth as a flower of the field. For as soon as the wind goeth over it, it is gone: and the place thereof shall know it no more." Alas! I am growing old, and the time is rapidly coming when I too must depart and join the majority. And yet how many things have I yet to do, or at least designed to do. Many of these I must leave to others. I have generally had work enough mapped out to fill at least ten years of life. This, I suppose, has arisen from my habits of forethought and industry.

How different is my feeling of a birthday now, from what it was when I was a boy. Then the days dragged along slowly: they seemed to tarry; and I longed to be a man, and doing man's work. Now the years seem to fleet like the wind, and succeed each other far too rapidly. Does this mean that I lead a happy life? Even as a man, I felt it like a pastime to grow old; but now it is different. How many things to do; how many things left undone. Fontenelle said, "Si je recommençais ma carrière, je ferais tout ce que j'ai fait." I cannot agree with this view of life. I have spent much of my time carelessly and foolishly; missed many opportunities for improvement; wasted powers, indulged in false hopes, and wandered after meteoric follies. I wish I had the power to retouch my life, as the artist retouches his picture. But I cannot do so. My life must stand or fall by what I have done, not by what I have dreamt. I have been getting together, page by page, that which is good or bad. It has become stereotyped in me, and must remain there so long as I live. My past deeds often come before me, like a succession of pictures. Things long forgotten come up again one by one; and often those which occurred in the early portion of my life, come back the clearest and most distinct. In the course of a few more birthdays, the whole story will be told, and the book will be finally closed, so far as this life is concerned.

I have indeed many things to be thankful for. A good constitution, which has enabled me to stand a considerable amount of brain work—and even to recover from my attack of paralysis fourteen years ago, and since then to do a little more work for the benefit of others; a fair amount of intellect, which, however, could only be brought into action by much perseverance, as will be seen from the preceding pages—"perseverance" which, as Carlyle says, "is the hinge of all the virtues." I have also been blessed in my home life—first in my bringing-up by my devoted mother, and next by the affection and prudence of an excellent wife. I could reveal much about this; but it will be enough to say that the results—in the growth, and culture, and moral development of our children—with whom she had much more to do than myself—have proved everything that I could have wished; for they have been our joy and comfort from childhood to manhood and womanhood; and now my grandchildren gather about me in clusters.

Another thing has given me pleasure. I have made friends, through my occasional works, in many foreign countries—though my correspondents have never seen me, nor I them. They have judged me merely by my writings. My pen has been a sort of electric wire that has bound us together. Some of my foreign correspondents asked for my photograph, and I sent it—in one case to a medical gentleman in practice at Nagy-Károly, in Hungary. Its arrival seemed to cause a sort of enthusiasm in his family. In answering my letter, he asked to be excused for his delay.

"The physician in practice," he said, "is perhaps less master of his time than any one. It is all the more necessary that I should ask your pardon for my offence against duty and good manners, because I fear that you will find it difficult to believe what great joy your kind present has created for me and my little family. The arrival of your letter was a fête-day for us. Even my little eight-year-old boy jumped round with joy, and could not look at the picture enough. Accept our heartfelt thanks, and be assured that both letter and portrait will be preserved by us as a precious memento. I can say with a certain amount of satisfaction, that I have never thought of you as otherwise than your portrait shows you. True genius and mind are pictured as clearly in your works as in your features. Darwin is right once more. . . . When you wrote your books with the wish that you might spread the good and the true in the world, bringing help and energy to others, I can assure you that you have reached your aim, and may think of the future with calm. I know of no single book in literature, out of which so much good may be drawn as out of yours, and I have never found in your works a single sentence that, even in error, could be taken as anything leading towards immorality. How few authors could pride themselves on this!"

The book which he particularly mentioned was *Self-Help*, and although a translation had been published in the Magyar language five years before, containing illustrations from Hungarian history, he thought that a better translation might be made, which he proposed to publish in the periodical of a committee to which he belonged (Szatmármegyei Közlöng) under the title of "Smiles's Pearls." This he afterwards did, and sent me the numbers of the periodical in which the translations appeared, though to me they were in an unknown tongue. In sending them, Dr Franz Takecbouzts said, "It will be a child of your own, and will perhaps be gladly received in its Hungarian dress."

Another enthusiastic Croat, in words of praise which I cannot repeat, desired to have my sanction for his translation of *Character*. I may, however, quote the following: "Your *Character*," he said, "is a real treasure for anyone, but particularly for the young. Each boy, each girl, should read this book, to find in it great men and women as examples for guidance in their own journey through life." I had much pleasure in giving my sanction to his translation. He had read the work in the Italian, but in order to do his work from the quick, he set to work and learnt English, and afterwards addressed to me his first letter written in the English language. The young man, Mirko Turic, was then living at Agram, a student of philosophy; and he afterwards sent me a copy of the translated work.

Another gentleman, V. E. Mourek, a professor at the Royal Imperial College at Budweis, in Bohemia, addressed me as to the proposed translation of *Character* into Czech. I agreed, and the work was published in parts, and afterwards in a completed

book. He told me that the work had been very
favourably received. He quoted, from the many
reviews, an extract from the *Komensky*, a paper
devoted to educational interests. "This excellent,
golden book is indeed worth a whole library. And
if it is, as it deserves to be, for every individual a sort
of practical Bible, which ought to be read again and
again, it is above all important for the educators of
youth, for, as it says, 'Nations are gathered out of
nurseries, and they who hold the leading strings of
children may even exercise a greater power than
those who hold the reins of government.' . . . Smiles's
book is written in such a flowing, easy, and agreeable
style, that whoever reads it, finds not only instruction
and elevation of thought, but also the most agreeable
mental repose and pleasure. His theoretical explana-
tions are full of flashing thoughts and grains of gold,
which by their proverb-like character will be easily
and for ever impressed upon the memory. . . . We
wish that everybody who knows how to read might
own this golden book, that it might help to educate
indefatigable workers, upright, unselfish, and energetic
characters for our own nation, which more than any
other stands in need of them." Professor Mourek
also translated *Self-Help* and *Thrift* for Bohemian
readers, I understand, with equally happy results.

I had another application of a similar character
from Sarazios in Bosnia. The writer seemed to be
an Englishwoman—Adeline Paulina Irby. She said
in her letter :—

"SIR,—
      "An able and hard-working Dalmatian
Slav, the son of a peasant, who by his merit and
industry has attained the position of a local official,
has sent me two MS. chapters of his translation into
the Serbo-Croat language of your valuable work

Thrift. He says the translation is nearly finished, and he wishes to publish it as soon as possible in the Cyrillic and Latin characters, that it may be read both by Serbs and Croats. He has translated from the English original with the help of the German and Italian translations. The style is excellent. This Dalmatian, Nicola Vackovic, an Austrian official at Zara, writes to ask me if I could obtain for him the permission of the author to translate the book. I venture to forward his request, being very anxious that this book should be made accessible to Serbs and Croats, for whom such works are very desirable."

I granted the necessary permission, but what became of the translation I do not know, as I do not think I was favoured with a copy of it.

Although I derived no benefit from these various translations, yet I was satisfied that these little books —the results of the occupation of my leisure hours— must have been of some value to others, otherwise they would never have been thought worthy of being published in other languages. My reputation with foreign translators and foreign readers—who knew nothing of me, nor I of them—might in some measure be regarded as a sort of reputation with contemporary posterity. The supposed value of the thoughts in the books were the only ties between myself and my translators.

A generation must have passed since I wrote the first of them—that is, the first of my books that anyone would read—and they cannot fail to have made a considerable impression on the rising generation. *Self-Help* was published in 1859, and a generation has grown up since then. Boys who read the book then—and 20,000 copies of it were disposed of in the first year—are men now. I have met some of them, and they have thanked me heartily for my words of encouragement. One, whom I met at dinner with my friend Mrs Songton, took me to one side, and said, "I have often wished to meet you, and to thank you for the good your books have done me. When a young man, I was on the slide downward. I was careless, thoughtless, and a searcher after pleasure. Some one made me a present of your *Self-Help*, and it saved me from the downward course. It became my manual: I read it constantly, in the morning and at night. I read it during a long railway journey. And then I endeavoured to put its lessons into practice. It gave me courage; it gave me strength. I became sober, punctual, attentive, and trustworthy. I worked perseveringly; at length I was taken as a partner into the firm with which I am connected, and now I am a prosperous man." I have seen the gentleman since, and he is still profuse in his congratulations.

Only a year ago an Indian, of Bombay, Dhanjibhái Dorábji Gilder, writing to me requesting permission to translate *Self-Help, Character, Thrift*, and *Duty*, into Gujerati, said, "I have read your invaluable work *Self-Help* at least half a dozen times, and am greatly charmed with it." Another correspondent, a medical man near London, says he writes to me out of sheer gratitude, thanking me for the help and cheerfulness which my books have infused into his life. "I wish," he says, "that every young man might read them, and be stimulated to further endeavours to do his duty to God and man." Another, a curate in a country church, says, "I should like to say what an immense help your books *Self-Help* and *Character* have been to myself, from the age of eighteen. I think I may say, next to the Bible, I have read them more than any other works, and am always indebted to them for the stimulus which I obtain from them. I find them invaluable for illustrations in my addresses and sermons." Another young fellow, whom I greatly esteem, has sentences from my books stuck up in ornamental characters on the wall of his bedroom, which he studies every day, and endeavours to carry into practice. There is a fine memorial to a good man, which I saw in the Church of St Maria degli Angeli (which opens from the Diocletian Baths) at Rome, which I hope might be mine. I think the words run as follows :—

> " Virtute vixit,
> Memoria vivit,
> Gloria vivet."

Notwithstanding such words of praise, I have, as already stated, been taken pretty sharply to task for not having said anything about those who failed. One writer said that the greatest of men as well as the Son of God failed and was crucified. Another writer—a poet—has recently repeated the same idea, in some fine verses : *—

> " Behold the leader of a vanquished cause,
> His arms extended on the bitter Cross !"

I think this scarcely fair. A great deed of sacrifice, destined from all eternity, should not be put in comparison with the little deeds of man on this transitory earth. But was the sacrifice of Christ really a failure, and was Christianity a vanquished cause? I have no wish to discuss the question. The virtues of constancy, energy, perseverance, industry, patience, accuracy, cheerfulness, hope, self-denial, self-culture, self-respect, power of good example, nobility of

* *Spectator*, 19th December 1885—" On last looking into Smiles's *Self-Help*."

character, which form the subjects and illustrations
of my book, are not only compatible with Christianity,
but, in my opinion, form the essential characteristics
of it. I did not pretend to teach divinity, but to lay
down a few of the more important lessons, as guides
to this daily work-a-day life; so very important while
it lasts, though so soon to come to an end.

One of the above writers asked, "Why should
not Failure have its Plutarch as well as Success?"
The poet asked, "Is there no Homer for the beaten
side?" There is no reason whatever why those who
fail should not have their Plutarch and their Homer.
The world of letters is wide, and the task is there
for those who choose to take it up. But I have
already given a sufficient answer to this charge in
the preface to the last edition of *Self-Help*, and there
is no need to pursue it.

I might, however, illustrate the subject by a little
anecdote. Two ministers of the Church of Scotland
were deputed to visit some congregations in the
Highlands. In the course of their tour, they had to
cross a ferry. They entered the boat, which was
rowed by a single oarsman. The ferry was wide: in
fact, it was a loch or fiord running up among the
mountains. The winds are very treacherous in those
parts. When the boat had got half-way across a
heavy storm arose, the waves dashed over the
passengers, and they thought they might be lost.
One of the ministers proposed to offer up a prayer.
The Highland boatman overheard him, and said,
"The wee ane may pray, but the big ane maun tak
an oar." The ministers prayed and worked together.
The strong arms of the "big ane," with the help of
the Highlandman, sent the boat rapidly through the
water, and they reached the opposite shore in safety.

"Weel done, the big ane," said the boatman. The "big ane" was the late Dr Norman Macleod.

One of those who failed, wrote to me, a few years ago, the following very touching letter :—

"DEAR SIR,—

"A modern Quixote (who has, however, more serious foes than windmills to contend with) humbly asks for a few words of friendly advice and encouragement from a true friend : for such have you been to me (without your knowledge, it is true), but not unintentionally, for I am one of the monster generation now struggling into manhood, and to that you have been talking for years, by means of your delightful books. I have this minute laid aside your *Self-Help*—a faithful, though, I fear, a much neglected companion for years, and I was much struck by a passage referring to *mutual support*, combined with which you quote those words of Wordsworth, where he says that manly dependence and manly independence go hand in hand to form true manhood.

"It immediately occurred to me how much a few lines of advice might help me on my way, and in the face of the tenets of this 'age of stone'—where the spirits of the departed must materialise ere we believe in them—I dare to write to one *personally* a perfect stranger, but *intellectually* one of my greatest friends. I am 'a miserable idler'; over twenty years of age; and my ignorance is lamentable. With fairly average abilities, I see others passing me daily in the race. I *cannot* work, and yet I am *miserable* in consequence. I am not, I trust, as yet enslaved in vice, but the agony and despair my idleness entails upon me, must soon guide me to the bourne from whence it is hard to return.

"The only happy time I know is when I have some *compulsory* employment. I see others equally idle with myself, but they are happy in some mysterious manner; their consciences do not seem to annoy them; and I, I fear, losing all ambition, will soon become the same—like the fabled Lotus eaters —without hope and without care. A pleasant life,

forsooth, for a *man*—a creature endowed with so
many wonderful ideas.

"Sometimes I sit down for a short time, perhaps
to write, perhaps to some sterner and more clearly-
defined duty; but soon my foe seeks me out, and
suggests that I defer the duty (perchance a congenial
one) to some other day, which, of course, means
indefinitely.

"To think, with all my opportunities, how much I
might know, how high up I might stand in my
profession, how my wages might be doubled, if I had
only chosen to work—instead of frittering away my
time upon some trivial objects, or succumbing to a
horrible oblivion, a death in life, total paralysis of the
mind, a body without a soul, a life all the more
terrible from momentary glimpses of a better life.
And now, Sir, it is to you that I now take the great
liberty of writing and further requesting a few lines
of advice and encouragement to one who is almost
without hope.

"It cannot be entirely from physical causes, as I
live quietly enough. I take it, that it is from early
novel reading, and a too warm imagination, with a
strong mixture of vanity, etc. Pardon my writing,
dear Sir, and if ever I become known to you, I trust
that your advice has not been thrown to the wind, but
has taken root in ground not wholly bad, and has
blossomed in eternity. Faithfully yours, in *secrecy*,
—— ——."

I do not give the name and address, as I do not
know whether the poor fellow who wrote the above
letter is alive. I answered it, but what could I say?
I could only urge him to persevere, to get into the
right path and keep there, for he had evidently
plenty of ability, and should have had enough of self-
respect and self-control to back it. I filled up my
letter with thoughts like these; but it never reached
him. In a few days it was returned through the
Dead Letter Office, with the words written on it,
"not known." Yet I addressed my letter according
to the exact address he had given me.

I have often been amazed and distressed to find what a number of helpless and idle creatures exist in this busy world. Some of them think that it is want of "luck" that attends them; but when I make inquiry, I find that it is oftener careless-ness and indifference, idleness and a tendency to viciousness; and very often the break-down of character of these unhappy people comes from their devotion to drink and its sordid accompaniments. It is not so much the want of mental powers as the lack of will and self-help. They will do nothing for them-selves, but expect other people to help them; and when they have been put in a position to make an honest living, they suddenly break down, and then they have to begin again at the beginning. Not exactly at the beginning, for they have put them-selves back in the world, and (their character being deteriorated by their previous failure) they have to start again from a lower level than before. Sometimes they send round begging letters; their story is miserable—a wife, children, and no money; the rent to pay, and nothing to pay it with; otherwise the furniture will be seized, and they will be left destitute. It is difficult to refuse such applications, and when once you have yielded, you are thought cruel if you afterwards refuse. I have known many men who might have made themselves independent through the exercise of moderate frugality and self-control, yet who have been under the necessity of descending to these degrading conditions. I am disposed to agree with Conversation Sharpe, a man of large experience, who said :—

"Untoward actions will sometimes happen; but after many years of thoughtful experience, I can truly say, that nearly all those who began life with me have succeeded as they deserved to succeed, or they have failed as they deserved to fail."

Carlyle, too, has said a great word for Perseverance.

"Perseverance," he says, "I particularly respect : it is the hinge of all the virtues.   On looking over the world, the cause of nine-tenths in ten of the lamentable failures which occur in men's undertakings, and darken and degrade so much of their history, lies not in the want of talents or the will to use them, but in the vacillating and desultory mode of using them ; in flying from object to object, in starting away at each little disgust, and thus applying the force which might conquer any difficulty to a series of difficulties that no human force can conquer. . . . Commend me, therefore, to the Dutch virtue of perseverance. Without it, all the rest are little better than fairy gold, which glitters in your purse, but when taken to market proves to be only slate or cinders."

February 1887.—I little thought when I last left Rome, that I should ever again visit the eternal city. There is a tradition that if you drink the waters of the fountain of Trevi, and hide some money there before departing, you are sure to return. The tradition has, at all events, proved true in my case, for on a fine moonlight evening I drank the waters, hid some coin, and after eight years' absence, I am in Rome again.*

.   .   .   .

We returned to London on the 5th of May.

Everything was then far advanced towards the celebration of the Queen's Jubilee. I was born in the reign of George III. I remember that king's

---

* There follows in the MS. a long account of Dr Smiles's second visit to Italy, and of the hospitality and attention with which he was received. It is, however, only a note of travels, which it has been thought better to omit.—ED.

death, and the accession of his son George IV. I saw that monarch during his visit to Edinburgh in 1822. William IV. followed, and reigned for several years; and then came the accession of the noble, virtuous, and ever to be esteemed Victoria—the mother of her people.

I did not intend to take any part in the celebration of the Jubilee, except lighting up my windows on the 21st of June. But the Lord Mayor sent me an invitation to the "Banquet to Representatives of Literature, Science, and Art," held on the Saturday preceding the commemoration, and I had the pleasure of attending that specially interesting meeting. Still more agreeable was the invitation which I received from Lord Lathom, the Lord Chamberlain, to attend Her Majesty's Jubilee Thanksgiving Service in Westminster Abbey on Tuesday the 21st of June. The procession from Buckingham Palace to Westminster Abbey was distinguished principally for the admirable behaviour of the immense crowd which assembled along the streets to witness the procession. The procession was too much divided to be imposing: it was not to compare with that of the King of Italy's birthday. But it made up in spirit and cheers what it wanted in music and military effect.

The commemoration in Westminster Abbey was much more important. But I need not describe that memorable event. The concourse of people was remarkable, including as it did, princes and royalties; men and women of mark from all parts of the world; the Queen and her illustrious Royal Family, not the least of whom were her eldest daughter the Crown Princess of Prussia, and her noble husband the Crown Prince, who looked every inch a king. Pens better than mine have described that great event. The ceremony, especially the last part of it, when the Queen called her sons and daughters to her side, and gave them severally her kiss and her blessing, was of the most touching description.   All honour to that thoroughly good, humane, and noble woman, the best of wives and the best of mothers.   She has maintained the virtue of her court, ruled her people wisely, and ever constitutionally, during her reign of fifty years, and will always be remembered as the best and wisest Queen that has ever sat upon the British throne.

After the commemoration of the Queen's Jubilee, London rapidly emptied.   At the end of July, my wife and I went over to Belfast to see my son, his wife, and my numerous grandchildren there—eight in one family.   We were most royally entertained, and saw much of that vigorous town, so celebrated for its flax manufactures, its shipbuilding, and its manifold industries.   There we renewed many old friendships, and made many new ones, and thence, we went across the Irish Sea to Barrow—a place that has grown from a village to the dimensions of a city during my lifetime.   Then to Brent How, to see a dear friend, and witness the annual sports at Grasmere.   We had seen them some seventeen years ago.   Then, it was a simple village festival : now, it is like a racecourse with four-in-hands, stage-coaches from Windermere, barouches, waggonettes, gigs of all sorts, and a multitude of people.   What would Wordsworth have thought if he had been alive?

After a visit to Lancashire we journeyed to Harrogate to drink the nectar of that famous watering-place, and returned home after about six weeks' absence.

CHAPTER XXIV

In October 1887, I received a present from General
Edelmiro Mayer, Buenos Ayres, which gave me
much pleasure. It consisted of four octavo volumes,
beautifully bound in Russian morocco, gilt-edged,
printed in fine type, and contained in a case, over
which was inscribed, *El Evangelio Social*, "The
Social Gospel." On examining the books, I found
they consisted of four of my works, translated into
Spanish. One of them was *Character*, which had
gone through five editions; another was *Duty*, four
editions; *Self-Help*, three editions; and *Thrift*,
which had just been published. The first editions of
Character and *Duty* were exhausted on the day that
they appeared.

It seems that General Mayer had been engaged
in the American Civil War, 1861-65, in the course of
which he had learnt English thoroughly, and was
consequently able to translate the works into Spanish,
his native language. The volumes were accompanied
by criticisms from the Buenos Ayres press, in which
General Mayer was complimented for his patriotism,
his literary ability, and the honour he had done to
his country in translating these works for the benefit
of the public. Religion was asleep or dead, but

morality remained; and the translator, it was said, had performed an honest man's work by publishing in the Spanish language the work on *Character*, at a time when a high ideal of personal character is proclaimed in a manner, only feeble and intermittent. The works most read in Buenos Ayres were those of Paul de Kock, Zola, Rousseau, and others, "only fit," it was said, "for the hands of the common hangman."

Faustino Jorge, chief justice of Buenos Ayres, congratulated General Mayer on having translated those works, "which will so greatly benefit our society."

"Nowadays," he said, "when we notice that the principles of morality are almost forgotten, and bad actions generally escape the just punishment of reprobation, now that indifference or selfishness influence the manifestations of our social life, I think that these works have come out at an opportune moment. Untruthfulness, against which the author wages war, the principles of morality which he develops with so much effect, and 'the right road' which he traces with a master hand, are themes requiring the attention of every one of his readers, who can temper his spirit and modify his conduct. Edelmiro, my friend, you cannot imagine the joy I feel in seeing you follow this road, and dedicating the passing hours of your life to an intellectual work which dignifies and gratifies the heart, the mind, and the soul."

The Ex-President of the Argentine Republic informed General Mayer that he had *Character* at his bedside, and that it should be at the bedside of every man. The Minister for Foreign Affairs said that, if laid to heart, it would prove more useful than all the charitable societies put together. But the lady poetess, Josephina Polliza de Sagasta, was even more enthusiastic in her eulogium. "To diffuse the pure doctrines contained in these works," she said, "as you (General Mayer) have done by translating them, is to offer to erring humanity, perhaps doubtful of the old faith, a religion, perhaps the only one free from the influence and modifications of progressive time. The doctrines of these books form a school of true consolation—their holy motto being, 'The Clearness of Conscience.'"

It is not possible to cite the testimonies of the Buenos Ayres press. They would bring a blush to the author's and even the translator's cheeks. The books were recommended to be read by young and old—by youths and maidens, as well as by those of middle and even of advanced age. *L'Amico del Popolo* said of *Duty*, "In the hour of greatest despair, when courage weakens and faith fails, the reading of a few of its pages, and the heroic examples mentioned in the work, will evoke the needed valour, and stimulate the faithful performance of duty, even though it be at the sacrifice of life." The *Standard of Buenos Ayres* said, "Rome gave a crown to him who saved the life of a citizen. How many crowns shall we award to General Mayer for providing healthy reading for his countrymen?" My last quotation must be from the *Deutsche La Plata Zeitung:* "Alexander the Great slept with his Homer, Demosthenes, and Thucydides; and every notable man of the times should have at hand The Social Gospel."

It may not be without interest to mention the various languages and dialects into which *Self-Help*, *Character*, and my other works have been translated. The first translation of *Self-Help* appeared in Dutch; then in German (two translations); Italian; French; Spanish (at Madrid and Buenos Ayres); Portuguese

(at Rio de Janiero); Russian (two translations);
Polish; Danish; Norwegian; Swedish; Czech;
Croatian; Hungarian; Japanese; Chinese; Siamese;
Turkish; Armenian; Pali; Hindustani; Gujerati;
Bengali; besides numerous reprints in the United
States of America.

During the months of February, March, and
April, 1888, I resided with my wife at Torquay, and
thereby avoided the bitter east winds of London.
As we grow old, we are less able to resist the harshness of the wind from that quarter. Charles Kingsley
wrote some verses in praise of the east wind; yet
the east wind helped to kill him.

During my stay at Torquay, I proceeded with a
work on which I had been engaged, at intervals, for
many years—I mean the Life and Correspondence
of the first and second John Murray. It involved a
great deal of labour—reading the correspondence of
that celebrated publishing house for nearly three-
quarters of a century—from the times of Drs
Langhorne and Johnson to Hallam, Borrow, and
Head, who appeared as authors in comparatively
recent years. The earlier letters had been carefully
analysed and docketed by Mr John Murray, junior
—now the fourth of the series of distinguished
publishers. My principal work was in reading the
letters, and abstracting whatever might be useful in
evolving the lives of the first and second John
Murray. It was a sort of drag-horse business; but
I had agreed to undertake it; and I proceeded with it
to the best of my ability. Sometimes, the parcels of
letters had not been examined and docketed; and when
more could not be had, I proceeded with some other
work; for I could never bear to be idle. I did my
literary work in the morning, and sometimes in the

afternoon; devoting the rest of the day to out-of-doors exercise. At length, I desired to have the whole of the remaining correspondence; and I could then proceed without the previous examination and docketing. It was then merely a question of reading and abstracting; and in course of time I saw my way to the end of the work. After I had made my extracts, I then proceeded to weave them into a narrative of the life. Of course, the greater part of the labour was connected with John Murray the second—the great John Murray—publisher of the works of Byron, Milman, Washington Irving, Isaac Disraeli, Barrow, Hallam, Heber, Lockhart, Crabbe, and many other distinguished men. When in the autumn of 1888 I went to Royat for the benefit of my wife, who went through a course of the baths there, I obtained a fresh batch of the correspondence, and proceeded with the work, and as it was somewhat tedious waiting at Royat after the examination of this correspondence had been completed, I resolved to make a short tour round the south of France.

．　　．　　　．　　　．　　　．　　　．　　　．

At Brive, a lady and gentleman got into the carriage in which I was. The gentleman, who had been imbibing something stronger than wine, moved opposite to me and began talking. I answered, and the lady, finding my French was not *comme il faut*, said, looking at me, "You are English." Then *she* began talking. She was a native of Southampton, and had married the Frenchman opposite, who did not know a word of English. She could therefore speak very freely. She had a bad opinion of the French Government, and of the French army. "There's an immense lot of them," she said, "infantry, cavalry, and artillery. But they are of little use.

Of course they must fight. They are raised and paid for that—to the great oppression of the French taxpayers." "And who are they to fight with?" I asked. "Oh, of course, the Germans. But the German army is better disciplined, stronger, and perhaps braver. The French, however, are not to be despised for their bravery. They trust to their *élan*. Yet, in my opinion, they cannot stand against the Germans. And the next time the Germans invade this country, they will take a much larger slice of France than they did after the last war. They want a commercial port, and a war port, near the Atlantic. There is Havre, a commercial port, and Cherbourg, a war port, ready to their hand. See if they do not annex the original country of the Teutonic Franks north of the Seine." "Well," said I, "that is a very poor prospect for France; and it also means a danger for England." "Well," she answered, "I cannot help it. Time will show." The train then stopped, and we got out at Perigueux.

In further illustration of the effect which these great armaments have on the imagination of the inhabitants, I mention some remarks made to me by a waiter at Royat. He was not a Frenchman, but an intelligent Swiss. In answer to my inquiry as to the number of soldiers at Clermont Ferrand — where Boulanger was in command a few years ago—he said, "I do not know; but there is an immense number of them; and you see the new barracks constantly being erected round Clermont." "Yes; that looks like war: it's of little use having masses of troops assembled together unless fighting be meant." "Oh, yes," he said, "they will all go to Germany!" "What? as invaders?" "No; as prisoners; as

Bazaine's and Napoleon's army did." Mr Hammerton, in his work on *French and English*, takes a very different view. The French will not go to war, he says, unless they are cock-sure of victory. We can only wait to see the result; but a sad time seems to be hanging over Europe, with masses of soldiers standing at arms—all withdrawn from labour —in France, Germany, Austro-Hungary, Italy, and Russia!

Perigueux is an interesting town, full of ancient buildings. Many of its old streets are narrow and tortuous. There are several old turrets in the midst of the ancient walls, which at one time surrounded the town. Perigueux belonged to the English in the fourteenth century. The French King John had been taken prisoner by the English army at Poitiers in 1356, and was sent to London. A rearrangement of the French provinces took place, and Aquitaine was ceded to England. During the time of the English occupation, the Montaigne family settled in Perigord. I knew a gentleman in London some years ago who claimed a relationship with the French branch. His name was Michel Montaigne. He said his ancestors had remained in England, while the other branch of the family had gone to Aquitaine during the English occupation. The château in which Michel Montaigne was born, in 1533, is still to be seen near Saint-Michel-Bonneparé on the river Dordogne; with his sleeping chamber and the place of his library covered with inscriptions in Latin and Greek, now partly effaced. His motto was "Que scais-je?"—What do I know? These are said to have been the last words he uttered. Emerson, in his *Representative Men*, describes Montaigne as The Sceptic. Gibbon says that during the bigoted

sixteenth century there were only two men of liberality
in France—Henry IV. and Montaigne.

Having seen as much as I desired to see of
Perigueux, I proceeded by rail, through a pleasant
country, to Agen, the chief town of the department of
Lot-et-Garonne. I was desirous of seeing this place,
because of the interest I felt in the life and works of
Jacques Jasmin, who was not only a poet but a
barber and hairdresser! Everyone knows the fine
translation by Longfellow, of Jasmin's *Blind Girl of
Castel-Cuillé*, included in all the editions of his works.
I had also read the review of Jasmin by that masterly
critic, Sainte-Beuve, in his *Portraits Contemporains*
(vol. ii.), as well as his notice of Jasmin in *Causeries
du Lundi* (vol. iv.). More than thirty years ago,
while Jasmin was still alive, I wrote an account of
him for a London weekly; and some years since,
when asked to contribute an article for an American
paper published at Boston, I supplied a paper on the
same subject.

Jasmin, though of very lowly condition, did much
to beautify his own life, as well as the lives of the
people amongst whom he lived. He has been called
the Saint Vincent de Paul of poetry. Like Burns,
the ploughman of Ayrshire, and Reboul, the baker of
Nismes, Jasmin was a man of true poetic fibre—
happy himself and the cause of happiness in others.
He wrote in Gascon, the *patois* of his district,
like Burns in his Scottish Doric, and touched the
hearts of the people. In the South of France,
no one was so popular as himself. He went from
town to town reciting his poetry, all for the sake of
charity—receiving crowns, and laurels, and medals—
yet he was always happy to return to his home at
Agen, and resume his business of barber. Though

he may have been somewhat vain, he was not spoilt
by his success; but to the end of his life he was
content to remain in his humble position.

Agen has no good hotels; tourists rarely pass
through, or stop in the town. I put up at the Hotel
du Petit St Jean, near the statue erected by public
subscription to the memory of Jasmin, in the Place
Jasmin. The statue, tall and imposing—with his
outstretched hand, as if reciting one of his own poems
—stands nearly opposite the little shop on the
Gravier, in which he carried on his trade. There is
no other statue in the town, except that erected to
the Republic, which is represented by a beautiful
woman. And yet Palissy, the great potter, J. J.
Scaliger, the great scholar, and Lacépède and Bory
de St Vincent, the distinguished naturalists, were
born here or in the neighbourhood; but no statues
have been erected to them. Palissy, however, was
a Huguenot, who narrowly escaping death at the
massacre of Saint Bartholomew, ended his life in
the Bastille.

I first went in search of the birthplace of Jasmin.
It is situated in a poor street, in a poor quarter—No.
15 Rue Fon de Raché. Jasmin called the house a
"palace of rats." In the passage the rafters are still
overhead; and a strong beam of wood supports the
roof of the little room in which the poet was born.
I next went to the Petit Seminaire in the Rue
Montesquieu, where he received his first elements of
education. Then to his shop on the Gravier, behind
the avenue of lime trees, which form a fine promenade.
In front of the door was an extended signboard
marked "Coiffeur," with a barber's basin suspended
at the end. The name of "Jasmin" still stands over
the door. I entered the shop, and found a barber

boy shaving a fat customer. Making an apology for
my intrusion, I was invited to enter the little room at
the back of the shop, where Jasmin used to receive
his deputations, and exhibit his array of golden
laurels, and where his wife used to assist him in the
reception of distinguished visitors.

I went to the Place de Repos of Jasmin in the
cemetery. The grave-digger, even at that early hour
of the day, was a little the worse of liquor; but he
took me to the spot, where Jasmin's son had erected
a monument to his father's memory, "A notre bon
Père," at the highest part of the cemetery. There are
added the words, "Jasmin fils décédé le 27 Janvier,
1885, à l'age de 66 ans." Jasmin's body had at first
been buried among the graves of the common folks;
and his son had removed it to this ornamental
monument. On our return, the grave-digger pointed
out the cross under which was buried a "much better
poet than Jasmin," one Delbes, also a poor man,
whose works are unknown to me.

In the afternoon, I crossed the suspension bridge
over the Garonne. The people seemed to be making
holiday. The river was alive with boats and bathers.
On arriving at the other side, I heard a drum beating,
and went to see what was to do. Not far from the
river, I found a number of men and women, of the
working order, dancing on the grass. The drum
was accompanied by a fife, and the musicians beat
and blew with great energy. It was a sort of country
dance, a mixture of a Scottish reel and a waltz. At a
certain part of the music the dancers clapped their
hands, and the pairs went under the joined hands of
the leading couple; just as in the English Roger de
Coverley. Some of the dancers were very spirited;
the men taking the girls in their arms, and swinging

them round, then saluting them with a kiss. Some of the dances reminded me of the dance in Franzonette, so well described in Jasmin's poem.

I returned to Royat by another route, through Villefranche and Aurillac, reaching home about the beginning of September. In writing the life of John Murray, which I began at the end of 1879, I found it necessary to give an introduction to the history of publishing and bookselling; and for this purpose I read and abstracted from many books. Then there was the life and history of Mr Murray's father, the first publisher of the House of Murray. This involved the examination of many very ancient letters; and next the birth, education, and early life of the main subject of my story. I must say, I sometimes felt very much wearied at the heavy labour involved by the work I had taken in hand; and sometimes weeks passed before I could extract a few grains of wheat from many bushels of chaff. This was, however, unavoidable; for the whole correspondence must be read and sifted. Eventually, after years had passed, I found myself within sight of the close of my undertaking. On the 31st of July 1888, I handed to Mr Murray the Preface, the Introduction, the "Life of John Murray the First," and the first three chapters of the "Life of John Murray the Second" (the Great Murray); and having worked steadily at the correspondence, I was able to hand to Mr Murray Chapter XXXIV., being the end of the work, at the end of January 1889. The whole formed about 2000 pages of manuscript, written on post quarto paper; and calculated to make 2 vols. 8vo, of the size of my original *Lives of the Engineers.*

Having thus finished what I consider to be a very heavy undertaking, I thought myself entitled to a holiday; and where can one turn for shelter from the east winds of England, but to Italy and the South? Hence, on the 13th of February 1889—after I had finished copying some of the interesting letters of Mr Murray to Lord Byron—I set out from London for Paris, on my way towards the south. I was accompanied by my wife and her maid, and by a young lady, the daughter of a dear friend. We left behind us the cold, grey atmosphere of London, and in four days were basking under the sun of the Riviera.

After a few days' stay at Monte Carlo, we set out for Rome; and after a night's journey, arrived there in the morning. It was my third visit to Rome, and it is unnecessary to describe the various sights which we saw there. We visited old friends, and made many new ones. Shortly after my arrival, I was "interviewed" by Professor Paladini, and a notice of my arrival in Rome appeared from his pen in the *Riforma*. The other daily papers followed. I had then no end of visitors, and invitations to evening receptions. Among the first that I attended was one at the house of Mr Morris Moore, Professor of English at the University of Rome. There I met, amongst other illustrious persons, Signor Cesari Donati, the translator of *Self-Help* into Italian several years ago, under the title of *Chi si aiuta Dio l'aiuta*. Signor Donati informed me that the translation had gone through eighteen editions, and over 75,000 copies had been sold—an extraordinary circulation for Italy. He also told me that my works had tended to imbue the rising generation with self-respect as well as self-help, and that those who had read *Thrift* saved their earnings for future needs, instead of throwing them away upon State Lotteries. I came to the conclusion that I am much better known in Italy than at home; indeed, I have received more recognition there from the King and Queen down to the humblest of their subjects than in my own country. On the King's birthday, the 14th of March, I received an invitation from Commendatore Bonghi, a deputy of the Italian Parliament, and President of the Press Association, to attend a special reception in my honour at the rooms of the society. His letter was as follows:—

"My dear Sir,—

"Amongst contemporary English authors there is no one better known, or more heartily admired in Italy, than yourself. The Press Association in Rome, of which I have the honour to be President, desires to express this fact in a concrete form, by asking you to honour with your presence a soirée to be given at the rooms of the Association (Via delle Missione) on the evening of Thursday, the 14th inst., at 9½ o'clock. We hope to gather together a fair number of your compatriots, and of your American cousins, who otherwise might have no opportunity of offering their greetings to the author of *Self-Help*, as well as many Italians to whom your name is already a household word. In their names, and in my own as a brother of the Pen, I ask you and Mrs Smiles to accept the cordial invitation of the Press Association, and beg to subscribe myself, faithfully yours,

"R. Bonghi.

"Camera dei deputati, Rome,
"*13th March* 1889."

I accepted this invitation with pleasure. On our appearance at the rooms of the Association, Signor Bonghi took my wife under his protection; I followed, with Mrs Rowland Taylor; then Professor Paladini, with Miss Nora Hargrove. The room was crowded; we were received with applause as we approached the adis, where the musical performers were assembled. We were informed by Signor Bonghi that telegrams had been received from Venice and Florence. The message from Venice saluted the author "whose story of the triumphs and heroisms of English industry was educating the rising generation of Italians in honesty, courage, and perseverance."

Professor Paladini said, "You will have a real Italian evening"; and it was so. Happily, there were no speeches, but introductions, conversation, and music.

Signor Bonghi said that he had received a letter from Signor Crispi, Prime Minister, "regretting his inability to offer in person his salutation to the illustrious author, because of the diplomatic dinner of the year, held on the King's birthday, at which he was called upon to preside." Notwithstanding this circumstance, many distinguished persons were present. The Minister of Finance, to whom I was introduced, paid me a pleasant compliment: "I have had my children educated," he said, "by reading your books." There were many ladies present, Italian, American, and English; one of the last, who must surely have been a Scotswoman, told me that she had been " brought up on oatmeal and *Character*, and had found the diet most invigorating." A very pretty compliment!

Not long after, I was asked by Guglielmo de Sanctis, President of the Society of International Artists, to sit for my portrait. The request came to me through Mrs Rowland Taylor, who said, "We cannot have you with us always, and we desire to retain a recollection of you in your portrait." I accordingly accompanied Mrs Taylor to my first sitting. The lady kept up a lively conversation, and under these favourable conditions, the artist made considerable progress. Next day, I gave him two sittings, but at the end of the second, De Sanctis said, "I must have you talking cheerfully; I cannot put life into your face unless you converse with spirit and frankness. Bring with you to-morrow some ladies to talk to and amuse you." On the following day, I took with me my wife and Miss Hargrove; and after an hour's sitting and talking, De Sanctis finished a very spirited sketch.

At the middle of March, we visited Naples and Pompeii.

. . . .

After visiting the antiquities at the museum, we proceeded to inspect an institution of a more modern character — the Fröbel Institution established at Naples by Mrs Salis Schwabe a few years ago. It may be mentioned that, before Italy became united under Victor Emmanuel II., the first constitutional king, popular education was very much neglected. In Naples and Sicily, under the reign of King Bomba, next to nothing was done. Naples was the home of the Lazzaroni; willing to beg, but not willing to work; poor, idle, uneducated, yet by no means unhappy. Even the dirty and tattered are merry. The climate is so delicious, that but few clothes are needed; and, as for food, a little maccaroni satisfies the poor man's appetite. Indeed, with such a genial atmosphere, a house is scarcely needed for shelter. Hence begging is a kind of legitimate trade, and not considered a disgrace. The idle man lying on the pedestal of a statue, holds out his hand; the boy lying on a passing waggon does the same. An emblematic statue representing Naples, would be a person holding out an open hand.

Climate has thus a good deal to do with the condition of the humbler classes of Naples, long enslavement and degradation have done the rest. In northern climes, men must work at remunerative wages in order to be sheltered, to dress, and to gain the elements of subsistence; whereas, in Naples, the sun is almost sufficient, with a few soldi for maccaroni. Then political slavery has done much to lower the national character, and efface all desire to rise to a higher moral and intellectual condition.

Garibaldi was aware of these conditions, and desired to remedy them, so far as he could. After his victories over the Neapolitan troops at Reggio and San Giovanni, and the proclamation of Victor Emmanuel as King of Italy, at Naples, Garibaldi issued an address to the women of Italy in 1861, on the subject of public education. Why he especially addressed the women, more than the men, was thus explained by himself:—

"The political liberty," he said, "acquired by the greatest portion of the Peninsula does not suffice for the great mass of the people, who must likewise physically partake of its benefits, and attain that degree of education which alone can emancipate them from the degrading prejudices and ignorance in which the corrupt portion of mankind has tried to keep them. Sufficient food, work, and education: these are the ends which benevolent souls try to obtain for the people. Woman, with her innate tendency to educate a family, is more fit for such a purpose than man; she is more delicate in feeling, more generous. Let the powerful of the earth approach the poor; let them comfort, educate, assist them. Then will disappear from human society that immense gulf which separates the poor from the rich, and in many parts of Europe makes the labouring classes desirous to subvert social order, and to bring about the destruction of the upper classes as the sole

means of mitigating the misery of those below them. I
have that profound faith in the good feeling of Italian
women of all classes, that I venture to address them,
and to invite them to realise this noble end. In the
hundred cities of Italy, let there be formed committees
of ladies, with the object of collecting means of every
kind in Italy and other parts of the world, to assist
the needy, and to establish schools for their education."

Garibaldi's appeal found a warm echo in the
hearts of Italy's noblest women; and committees
were formed with the object of carrying his admirable advice into effect. The Italian ladies first endeavoured to concentrate their activity upon Naples
and Palermo; to imbue the people with religious and
patriotic feelings, respect for the laws, love of labour,
cleanliness, temperance, and education. They invited
the co-operation of the ladies of foreign countries,
especially of England. Among those who received
and read the letter of the Italian ladies, signed
by the Marchesa Pallavicino Trivulzio, was Mrs
Salis Schwabe, of Manchester. Her heart was
deeply moved by the letter; and she collected within
a short time the sum of £2000. She also induced
the late Jenny Lind Goldschmidt to give a concert
in London, the profits of which amounted to above
£1000. With the help of this money, an elementary
school was established at Naples in 1861. The first
superintendent of the school was Miss Reeve, an
English lady, who threw herself into the work with
enthusiasm; but, unhappily, she fell a victim to the
cholera in 1865; and then Mrs Schwabe herself took
up the noble work.

The Italian Government and the municipality of
Naples took an increasing interest in Mrs Schwabe's
educational institution. The Government placed at

her disposal the Ex-Collegio Medico, formerly an
extensive nunnery, with numerous apartments, and a
large garden fitted for a playground, in the centre of
what had been the cloisters; and the municipality
granted her 24,000 francs for the purpose of repairing the buildings, and adapting them for school
purposes. Mrs Schwabe's original intention had
been merely to establish a kindergarten on the
Fröbel system, together with elementary schools
for the poorer classes; but her scheme was shortly
after enlarged, so as to give a good practical education
to the children of the upper classes as well as the lower.
Under the ministry of Signor Bonghi, she obtained a
grant of the building until the year 1906. Mrs
Schwabe also received from the Italian Government
an extra subsidy of 50,000 francs towards the
rebuilding of a wing of the institution; and she
subsequently obtained an annual subsidy of 12,400
francs from the Ministry of Public Instruction. With
this assistance, and other subsidies from several
corporations at Naples, together with the interest on
50,000 francs with which Mrs Schwabe had endowed
the institution, education soon made considerable
progress. In 1887, the Italian Government, by a
Royal Decree, granted a Charter; and it is now
known as *Instituto Fröbeliano Internazionale, Vittorio
Emanuele II.* The building at the same time was
granted to the institution for ever.

When I visited the schools on the 18th of March
1889, there were present 1005 boys and girls; some
of the poorer, and others of the better classes. The
little children were taught on the kindergarten
principle; the elder children were taught in four
elementary classes, and a training college for teachers
was also established on the Fröbel system. The boys

leave the schools in their eleventh or twelfth year; the girls, however, continue their studies in the higher school until their seventeenth or eighteenth year; and, after passing a Government examination, they may enter the Training College for Teachers. The leading idea of the founders and patrons of the institution is, to guide the child from infancy, developing its faculties; enabling the little ones, with the growth of years, to become useful and happy members of society; preparing young girls for their future calling, as good and virtuous wives, as well as proper educators of the rising generation.

Nearly half the number of children attending the institution belong to the poorest class; and at midday they are fed, after having been taught. Industrial schools are to be added, where the boys may learn trades, and the girls cooking, and thus become capable, when they have left school, of earning their livelihood or managing their homes, as useful, intelligent, and independent citizens. It must be added that considerable difficulties had to be encountered and overcome in bringing the institution to its present prosperous condition. Amongst these difficulties was the opposition of the priests. The instruction given at school was confined to the elementary branches, the founders being of opinion that religious instruction should be left to religious teachers. The latter, however, viewed with great jealousy any instruction given to the rising generation except by themselves. Indeed, they threatened some poor mothers who sent their children to the schools, with severest penalties. They would not confess them; they would not grant them, when dying, the last offices of the Church. Though some mothers may have been deterred, yet the greater number continued to send their children to the institution. They could not refuse the advantages of education, which were so freely offered them. In course of time, it is to be hoped that these religious, or rather irreligious, difficulties will disappear.

At the lunch which Mrs Schwabe's niece offered us, we met Signora Zampini Salazaro, who contemplates founding a school for the higher education of ladies in Rome, after the manner of those already founded in England and Scotland. As half the human race consists of women, it is necessary that they should be trained and educated to fulfil their duties in the station of life which they may be called upon to fill. If their state of education be low, and their moral and social condition degraded, the fact must necessarily react upon society at large. Men will always be what women make them; and for the elevation of man himself, it is needful that women should be properly educated. Queen Margaret of Italy is strongly in favour of this view; and it is to be hoped that, before long, an institution for the higher education of women will be established at Rome, and, it may be, at Florence and Naples.

.   .   .   .

After a few more weeks spent at Rome, we proceeded to Florence to visit some old friends. The Florentines were anxious that I should be fêted there, in like manner as at Rome; but I resisted their inducement, and preferred to remain in quiet. It was quite sufficient for us to listen to the serenade to which Colonel Fregerio, commander of the cavalry regiment of Aosta, invited us at his apartments on the Lung' Arno. The band was an excellent one, and played during the evening Neapolitan airs, marches (of which, strange to say, Boulanger's was the best), and many selections from classical music.

We reached London exactly three months after the date of our departure. This, I think, must finish my last visit abroad; or, at least, to Italy. In a few months I shall enter my seventy-eighth year, and when a man arrives at that age, his best refuge for the remainder of his little life is home. And this must end my autobiography.

The unpretentious MS. here comes to a close. Increasing infirmity and the burden of years now put an end to the labours of Dr Smiles' industrious pen. The reader must for himself compose a fit peroration. Appropriate material is to be found in the evidence of failing power which the closing pages of the auto-biography do not conceal. Dramatically enough, they show the author's industry, the ruling passion of a lifetime, battling courageously to the end, happily not without the solace of a deep contentment derived from the consciousness of a day's work done, and of a completed career of honest human endeavour. The rest is silence. It remains only to put on record that Mrs Smiles died on the 14th February 1900, and that her husband, surviving her by a little more than four years, died on the 16th April 1904.—ED.

INDEX

PRINTED BY OLIVER AND BOYD, EDINBURGH

CPSIA information can be obtained at www.ICGtesting.com
Printed in the USA
LVOW131950020713

341224LV00001B/156/A

9 781430 449324